REAL MEN

HAVE FEELINGS TOO

REAL MEN
HAVE
FEELINGS
TOO

GARY J. OLIVER, Ph.D.

MOODY PRESS
CHICAGO

ISBN 0-8024-7125-0

1 3 5 7 9 10 8 6 4 2

Printed in the United States of America

To George Arthur Oliver,
My father and my friend

You helped give me a love for God's Word; you were my first hero, and you are still one of my heroes.

To Jimmie Davis,
Evangelist, musician, teacher
Founder, Boys JIM CLub of America

You were a model of what it meant to be sold out to Christ; you invested your life in building boys rather than mending men. And now you are receiving the joy you taught about as you behold your Savior face to face.

To H. Norman Wright,
Teacher, mentor, friend

For the past twenty-five years you have been a model of honesty, integrity, patience, and humility; your encouragement and faithful friendship have been your greatest gifts.

CONTENTS

ACKNOWLEDGMENTS

In a book about men, I am deeply grateful to three men who have stood by me. These faithful friends have loved, encouraged, and challenged me; and they have helped to keep me faithful. My thanks to Paul Nauman, Chip Carmichael, and Dan Trathen.

In addition, my thanks to the following "real men," whose friendship and encouragement over the years have contributed to my spiritual, intellectual, and professional growth:

Bill Bynum	Bob Saucy
Dave Dixon	Gary Smalley
Dick Kremer	Tom Stipe
Clyde McDowell	John Trent
John MacArthur, Jr.	Warren Wiersbe
John W. Montgomery	Gary Wilburn

A special word of thanks to Jim Bell, editorial director of Moody Press. Jim believed in the need and value of this particular book and of the "Men of Integrity" book series. From the outset he has been a source of wisdom, support, and encouragement.

Finally, Jim Vincent went above and beyond the call of duty as general editor of this project. He challenged ideas, asked wise questions, and helped to clarify, shape, and polish a lot of material. The clarity of this final product is due, in part, to Jim's hard work.

Introduction

A CARDBOARD GOLIATH

Will I dig the same things that turned me on as a kid?
Will I look back and say that I wish I hadn't done what I did?
Will I joke around and still dig both sides?
When I grow up to be a man.

Will I look for the same things in a woman that I dig in a girl?
Will I settle down fast or will I first want to travel the world?
When I'm young and free, oh how will it be?
When I grow up to be a man.

Will my kids be proud or think their old man's really a square?
When they're out having fun will I still wanna have my share?
Will I love my wife, for the rest of my life?
When I grow up to be a man.

What will I be?
When I grow up to be a man.[1]

The Beach Boys' song "When I Grow Up to Be a Man" came out in the fall of 1964. I was starting my senior year in high school, and the Beatles were singing their first hits, "I Want To Hold Your Hand" and "She Loves You." Manfred Mann was singing "Do Wah Diddy Diddy," and

Louis Armstrong had the number one hit with, believe it or not, "Hello, Dolly."

In retrospect those were much simpler times. When the Beach Boys asked the question "What will I be when I grow up to be a man?" the uncertainty centered more around "What would I do?" I wondered, *Would I be drafted? Would I get a good education? Would I have a good job? Would I get married and stay married?*

A generation ago society was clearer on what it meant to be a man. The roles were much more clearly defined. The questions were much simpler. Men did certain things and women did certain things. A man's identity was in what he did. His gender role was the foundation of his identity. I'm not saying that was healthy or right. That's just the way things were.

Today the social climate has changed. The questions have changed, and so have the rules. Men are no longer sure of what it means to be a man. Men are faced with an abundance of contradictory and inconsistent attitudes that supposedly define masculinity. The questions men are facing today are deeper and more complex than they have been before.

"A MAN'S MAN"

Perhaps the most basic question is, "What does it mean to be a man?" Clearly most people have their own idea of what a man is and does. For example, when you hear such expressions as "He took it like a man," "Act like the man of the house," or "Are you a man or a mouse?" certain characteristics probably come to your mind. What are those characteristics? Where did you learn them? What are they based on? They may spring from the standards of our society, the clear teaching of Scripture, or both. Do you consider them as valid today as they were twenty years ago?

If you are a man over age seventeen, you probably grew up in a home with a father who didn't know how to nurture, didn't talk much, and wasn't available for you. Up until twenty-five years ago the primary role of the man was to be the breadwinner. A "man's man" was someone who could cuss, chew, spit, swear, fight, fuss, feud, and fornicate.

Yes, that's a caricature, but the movies portrayed men that way. John Wayne and Clint Eastwood were big box office heroes. In sports the big heroes were the brash and cocky Muhammad Ali and Joe Namath. Many men bought the myth: a successful male was primarily interested in success, money, sports, and sex—and not necessarily in that order.

The caricature of today's male is almost totally different. He is someone who gives more acknowledgment and expresses feelings, except for out-of-control anger. He has a greater investment in his family and home; more than just a "helper" to his wife, he invests greater time and effort than his predecessor in being a husband and a father. This is a myth, too, but increasingly it's a goal. The 1990s male may not always succeed, but he does want this role. Ten years ago only 27 percent of dads were in the delivery room; now the number is more than 80 percent. National magazines show ads with fathers holding babies and playing with children. Many major department stores now include changing tables in the men's room.

A second question men are facing is, "How are men and women different?" A generation ago that question would not have been taken seriously in many circles. But times have changed. On a merely physical level that is an easy question to answer. But once we move beyond physiology it becomes much more difficult.

When I speak on men's issues I often ask the participants to write down their response to the following question: "Apart from obvious physical differences, make a list of what distinguishes men from women. What traits, characteristics, and roles are purely 'male' and what are purely 'female'?" How would you respond? You might be surprised at how difficult that question is to answer.

A third question is, "How and when does a boy become a man?" In many cultures that is an easy question to answer. There are clear and distinct "rites of passage" through which an adolescent goes to become a young man. Many African cultures have a ceremony in which the men of the village, including the boy's father, come to the boy's home and require the mother to give the boy to them; they require the boy to come out to be initiated into manhood. In the Jewish faith, at age thirteen boys have a Bar Mitzvah that signifies their coming of age.

What's the criterion in American culture? Age? Amount of money earned? Graduation from college? Getting married? Becoming a father? Indeed, ask yourself what is the criterion in your own life. When did you know that you had become a man?

A fourth important question many men are being forced to ask is, "What is my role as a man?" Is it being a single and successful businessman? A husband? A father? One man told me that "My head gives me one answer and my heart gives me another." This is an important question to answer. But the answer may not always be clear.

At a recent conference a man in his mid-forties approached me with an expression of both concern and frustration. He had two roles that he enjoyed, husband and father, yet he was unsure about his skills or even his duties in each role. "I love my wife and kids, and I want to be a godly man, but I'm not sure where to start."

"Could you give me an example of one of the problem areas you face?" I asked.

"Well, my wife tells me that she would like me to be the leader, but I'm not sure what that means. When I do something that seems to me as 'leading,' almost always I've guessed wrong. She tells me that I've either done the wrong thing or that I've done the right thing but in the wrong way." Over the years I've heard similar comments from hundreds of men.

Whether you are unsure of your very nature as a man or your specific roles and duties as a single or married man, you probably are like most men you know—searching to be comfortable with who you are, yet for some reason feeling uncomfortable.

As Christian men we want to honor God and obey Jesus Christ in our personal relationships. Many men wonder how their faith should affect their sense of masculinity. By virtue of being a male you are facing a crisis of identity. Every American male is. What do I mean by crisis? *Webster's Eighth New Collegiate Dictionary* has two pertinent definitions: *crisis* is "an emotionally significant event or radical change of status in a person's life . . . an unstable or crucial time whose outcome will make a decisive difference for better or worse."

Men are reeling from the challenges and changes that have taken place in the past twenty years. They have been bombarded on every side by conflicting and contradictory signals from their mothers and fathers, wives, women, children, pastors, friends, and peers. On the one hand they are are told, "Be strong but don't be macho." On the other hand they are told, "Be sensitive but don't be a wimp." It wouldn't be so hard if there were an objective Macho-Wimp scale one could turn to for help in evaluating attitudes and behavior. Unfortunately there isn't. Herb Goldberg has effectively described the crisis facing today's male:

In recent years there has been a dramatic change in the perception and functioning of the male in our culture. It has become increasingly clear that the gender orientation known as masculinity has serious and troubling limitations and, consequently, has put the male clearly in crisis. He is accused of being chauvinistic and oppressive. He is fearful of abandonment by his increasingly autonomous and powerful woman. He is burning himself out physically and emotionally in pursuit of a success trip and other goals whose fruits are all too often questionable and meager. He hears and reads endless discussions about his declining sexual performance and increasing "dysfunction" supposedly caused by women's new assertiveness. He is lacking a support system with other men to help him through these crises, and he possesses little insight into the causes of what is happening to him and has few inner resources to draw on for nourishment during the difficult periods. He is truly a cardboard goliath, unable to flow self-caringly with the changing social scene.[2]

A cardboard Goliath. What an accurate description of today's man. He is accused of having all of the privilege and power. And in some ways he does. Look at the composition of the Congress, the Supreme Court, and the CEOs of the Fortune 500 corporations. Men do typically earn more money then women doing the same job. Yet he has had to pay an enormous price for this privilege and power. Many of today's men have paid with their health, their emotions, and their relationships. Even if you are self-employed or a day laborer, with a tight budget and frustrated, you still have power.

The chapter title for one of Joyce Brothers' recent books is "Man, the Weaker Sex." In this chapter she documents the disturbing physical toll of manhood: men live about eight years less than women, die from almost all major diseases at significantly higher rates, and as young boys suffer from autism, hyperkinesis, schizophrenia, stuttering, and behavior disturbances, leading to hospitalization at vastly higher rates. There are few survival or health statistics that don't show a disproportionately negative rate for men, not to mention the impoverished quality of most men's personal lives. Most men have pursued excellence as breadwinners, work machines, and performers, and everything else in their lives has suffered.[3]

MEN UNDER FIRE

Based on studies reported in the past few years, it's become clear that growing up male can be hazardous to your health! The pressures on men begin in their childhood. Consider the following statistics:

- Infant boys receive fewer demonstrative acts of affection from their mothers and are touched less than infant girls.[4]
- Not only are boys touched less frequently by their mothers than girls, they are talked to less, and for shorter durations.[5]
- Infant boys are more likely to be held facing outward, toward the world and other people. Girls are held inward, toward the security, warmth, and comfort of the parent.[6]
- When a child complains of a minor injury, parents are quicker to comfort girls than boys.[7]
- When boys become teenagers they are told they must be prepared to be mutilated or die in order to protect women and children and the ideologies of their nation.[8]

As adults, men find their health under attack.

- Men have a 600 percent higher incidence of work-related accidents than women, and men die from work-related injuries approximately 20 to 1 over women.[9]
- Suicide rates are about four times higher for men than women.[10]
- Men make up 80 percent of all homicide victims, are victims of about 70 percent of all robberies, and make up 70 percent of all other victims of aggravated assaults.[11]

Not only have men paid with their health and emotions but they have also paid with their relationships. Historically men have been made to focus on individual achievements while women have been encouraged to focus on personal relationships. The primary job of the man was to provide the necessary physical resources, and the primary job of the woman was to provide the necessary relational or nurturing resources. In this arrangement we've been told that women were the losers and men were the winners. That analysis is at best simplistic and at worst not true.

Both men and women were winners and losers. Unfortunately what men lost was a fundamental part of what it means to be human. Today as an adult, you may have been squeezed into that male mold—you are achieving in your job but feel hollow.

Recently I did a psychological evaluation for an executive who was being examined for stress-related health problems. Due to the schedule Jeff allowed himself to keep he was suffering from burnout. He owns several different companies that employ more than two thousand people. He owns homes in three different parts of the country, and he flew into Denver on his own Lear jet. Most people would look at him and say, "There is a successful man."

The clinical interview went as expected until I asked Jeff about his marriage and family. At this point his eyes became moist as he told me that although he was still married he and his wife had become functionally married singles. He started to cry as he told me, "I'm not close to any of my three children. Each one of them has told me that they aren't interested in following my footsteps. They told me, 'Dad, the price is too high.'" The price was his time with his family.

"Dad, if being as successful as you are means my kids not having a father, I can't afford that kind of success," one of his sons said to him.

Toward the end of our time together Jeff said, "Dr. Oliver, I am worth millions of dollars, but I now see that in terms of meaningful relationships I am bankrupt."

The causes of the emotional and health toll on men will be explored in the chapters that follow. They rise from our inability or unwillingness to express emotions to a fundamental fear of failure that could show our weaknesses. Yet weakness is a true part of every person, male or female.

Another factor that has contributed to the crisis is what might be called "The New Sexism." For years we have been made aware of the effects of men's sexist attitudes and practices toward women. Our awareness has been appropriately raised in regard to the disparity in power and privilege between men and women. However, it seems as if the pendulum has swung a bit too far.

In doing research for this book, I performed a thorough literature review. During the review I was amazed at the disparity between books and research on men and women. At the largest bookstore in Denver the women's section had more than thirty shelves; the men's section had seven. In the bookstore of one of our nation's leading universities the "gender issues" section contained more than one hundred titles related to women; seventeen titles related to men. In my review of research done in the last ten years, studies that focused on women's issues outnumbered men's studies by more than ten to one.

Even in our local evangelical churches specific programs and activities for men have been at best minimal and at worst non-existent. Most churches have all kinds of organizations and growth opportunities for women. Many church bulletins have a special section listing a wide variety of women's activities. But for years there has been, apart from the periodic "Work Day," virtually nothing for men.

Why? In part because men haven't been interested. We've been too busy being "men" and doing the things that men are supposed to do. I've talked with countless pastors who have been frustrated by their inability to get men involved in church activities. Oh, there's been the token Father/Son or Father/Daughter banquet that many men have felt obliged to attend. But apart from that the special needs of men have by design or by default been ignored.

THE TIMES ARE CHANGING

However, all of that is changing. The day of the stereotypic, unconcerned and uninvolved male is coming to an end. What makes me say that? First of all, you are reading. Not only are you reading, but you are reading, of all things, a book on men and emotions. Why is that such a big deal?

Publishers estimate that more than 80 percent of books are read by women. When one of my friends asked me the subject of my next book, I told him it would be designed to help men understand, value, and deal with their emotions. "Well, that should be a great seller," he jokingly replied. "Most men I know aren't sure emotions really exist and, if they do, they aren't important to them."

"That used to be true," I responded. "However, today many men are sick and tired of being sick and tired. Men are starting to ask some painful questions and are searching for meaningful answers." If you don't believe me, then ask yourself the following questions:

Why are secular and Christian publishers scrambling for books for and about men?

Why has a book of poetry and myth about men sold more than 500,000 copies and been on the *New York Times* bestseller list for more than forty weeks?

Why in the past few years have millions of men spent millions of dollars on millions of books about masculinity, relationships, fathering, and identity?

Why are men all over the country flocking to support groups and paying between $400 and $800 for weekend seminars and "wild-man" retreats?

Why do hundreds of thousands of men pay big bucks to hear talks on relationships?

Why did more than 20,000 Christian men from all over the United States attend a conference in 1992 on "What Makes A Man?"

In the past couple years I've been asked a lot of questions about the "men's movement." What is it? What's it all about? Why are the men having a movement? Why now?

The men's movement is a grass-roots response to the crisis facing men today. The response takes many shapes and forms, but it is happening all across our country. An increasing number of men refuse to settle for the status quo. Several Christian men have told me, "When Christ said, 'I've come that you might have life and have it more abundantly,' certainly He meant more than I have been experiencing!"

Another question I'm often asked is, "How is the men's movement different from the feminist movement?" The feminist movement was and is primarily a sociopolitical movement. It was in part a healthy and legitimate response to the repression, inequalities, and abuse of women. It sought equality and increased power and political influence. In contrast, the men's movement is not about gaining more power, privilege, and prestige. It is much more personal and relational. It's about how to be human, how to feel, how to love, how to be better husbands, fathers, and friends.

Many men find this a scary proposition. Others are critical because they are afraid it is part of an international plot to feminize men. That may be the agenda of some. However, the majority of the men's movement (and certainly the Christian men's movement) is not about the feminization of men; it's about the humanization of men. You might be asking yourself, "What does he mean by that?"

When I have the privilege of speaking to men's group I often ask them to do a word association. "I'm going to read off a list of words to you. As you hear those words I'd like you to think about which gender you associate those traits with, male or female." Then I slowly go through the list of words: love, kindness, gentleness, patience, thoughtfulness, compassion, tenderness, meekness, sensitivity.

As you read that list of words, what was your association? Do those words tend to best describe a man or a woman? With few exceptions, almost 100 percent of the men associate those words with women. They consider those attributes to be primarily feminine.

Here's what for many is the shocker. All of those words are descriptors of our Lord Jesus Christ. *And that's the problem!* Those words don't describe a woman. They aren't feminine, they're human! They describe emotions and actions of healthy males and females. But sin has so damaged and distorted our culture that what God designed to characterize healthy people now characterizes only women. That's tragic!

The men's movement has tapped into men's hunger for relationships, community, healing, health, hope, and recovery. Man's deepest need is to know that he is accepted, understood, loved, and affirmed. Men all over the United States are looking everywhere they can, trying to find answers to their questions, relief from their pain, and healing for their wounds.

As we will see, real men know and express their feelings. When we do this, we no longer are cardboard Goliaths. We are strong men, assured of a true masculinity—a masculinity that transcends the trends of society and rests on our special creation as men designed to seek after God.

1

THE MYTHS OF MASCULINITY

D o you remember what it was like when you went from elementary school to junior high? Clyde does. He said, "I can remember my first week in junior high as if it was yesterday." The kids were bigger, the ninth grade boys seemed like men, and the ninth grade girls looked a lot different than the girls in sixth grade did.

"I still remember my first day in gym," Clyde said in a reflective tone. "It's almost like it happened yesterday. I wasn't very big for my age. I didn't have any body hair yet. And before that day I had never realized how important the size of my genitals was until a big kid with hair all over his body pointed at me and told his friends to look at the kid with the 'teeny weeny peeny.' I'll never forget the combination of fear, humiliation, and shame that I felt." As he shared his memory with me I could tell that, even twenty-five years later, he still felt some of the humiliation and shame.

Think back to when you were in junior high. What was the name of your school? Who was your best friend? You followed certain rules made up by those you respected, and this helped to define your masculinity. And you had certain heroes. What was it about those heroes that you wanted for yourself?

Each of us has a conscious and unconscious model of masculinity that we measure ourselves by. Hopefully that model has changed since junior high, but we still have one. Every man brings his understanding of the cultural mythology of masculinity wherever he goes. Unfortunately many of the early lessons little boys learn about what it means to be a man often become the sword on which their identity and self-respect will be impaled as an adult.

One of the most effective ways I've found to help men remember the rules that helped to shape their development as males is a little sentence completion exercise. You can do it too: on a sheet of paper, write down the sentence "Real men _____." Now complete the sentence with seven phrases that describe what you thought it meant to be a "real man" as you were growing up.

I'm sure that over the years your ideas of what it means to be a "real man" have changed. Today, what do you think of when you hear the word *masculine*? When you hear someone say, "He's a real man," or, "He's a man's man," what kind of man are they talking about? Does anyone in particular come to mind? What does it mean to be a real man? Do you believe that *you* are a real man?

Our society puts a lot of pressure on men to be "masculine" but men aren't always clear about what that means. That was true when we were kids and its even more true today. Psychiatrist and family therapist Frank Pittman writes:

> As a guy develops and practices his masculinity, he is accompanied and critiqued by an invisible male chorus of all the other guys who hiss or cheer as he attempts to approximate the masculine ideal, who push him to sacrifice more and more of his humanity for the sake of his masculinity, and who ridicule him when he holds back. The chorus is made up of all the guy's comrades and rivals, all his buddies and bosses, his male ancestors and his male cultural heroes, his models of masculinity—and above all, his father, who may have been a real person in the boy's life, or may have existed for him only as the myth of the man who got away.[1]

These social pressures lead to stereotypes or myths of what it means to be a man. If we don't understand these myths they can be dangerous. We can allow them to squeeze us into a developmental mold that restricts our growth. They lead us either to not notice or to ignore individual differences. They lead to a kind of all-or-nothing thinking—either we're a "man" or we're not.

SIX MYTHS ABOUT MEN

During the past several years, I've worked with hundreds of men who have shared their stories with me. In talking with them I collected a list of stereotypes—myths of masculinity—that they felt governed or at least greatly influenced their development. Though the list of myths exceeds fifty, the different myths fit into six main categories. We will look at each of them. As you read the six, ask yourself, "Was my view of masculinity influenced by this myth? If so, how? Is it possible that this myth is still influencing the way I understand what it means to be a man?"

Myth 1: Men Are Big, Brave, and Strong

One of the first myths that most men mention concerns physical size and strength. Most boys associate muscles with masculinity. If you are over forty you probably remember the Charles Atlas advertisements in comic books and magazines. The ad shows a guy and his girlfriend at the beach. A bigger guy comes up and kicks sand in his face. The little guy says "That's the last time that will happen to me." So what's the answer? Enroll in the Charles Atlas body-building program. Then you can be a real man and kick sand in the face of other wimps and not look like a weenie in front of your girlfriend.

This particular myth was encouraged by many of the stories we heard as children. You remember them, don't you? They're the ones in which the man is portrayed as the big, strong, competent, conquering hero. In the classic myth the hero, almost always a big, strong man, ventures forth from everyday life to conquer supernatural and seemingly overwhelming forces in the name of his quest. He returns, weary but victorious, and he is richly rewarded. What effect did these stories have on our view of male and female?

A delightful example of this prototypical male is seen in *Beauty and the Beast*, the Academy Award-winning Walt Disney movie. The beautiful Belle is a smart, sensitive, and verbal woman. In the nearby town lives a vain specimen of masculinity, Gaston, who believes he is God's gift to the world, especially the women of the world. He has the intelligence of a Cro-Magnon man and the sensitivity of a manilla envelope. In the local tavern the village men extol Gaston's strength and athleticism: he fights, bites, wrestles, and has "biceps to spare." Gaston grandly accepts their praises and adds a few more.

I'm not so unrealistic as to say that size and strength isn't important. I was one of those guys who signed up for the Charles Atlas course. Then my friends told me about the Joe Weider course guaranteed to give you a Weider Body. We all signed up for that one too.

There is nothing wrong with wanting to be healthy and strong. But size and strength are not the determining characteristic of masculinity. I've worked with males who were paragons of physical strength but who were relationally and emotionally preadolescent. While they spent hours every week pumping iron their mental and emotional muscles atrophied.

Though physical strength and aggressiveness were the male traits that had traditionally selected men out for two activities, (1) hunting, fishing, and farming, and (2) face-to-face combat, society has experienced major changes in the past one hundred years. Today physical strength is relatively obsolete as an important male role requirement.[2] How many jobs can you think of that you would associate with money, power, and status that require exceptional physical strength?

Men are also expected to be brave. They should be willing to spend their lives for their country, to go down with the ship. To admit insecurity, doubts, or fear is to be other than a real man. So what do we do with the fear that all of us experience? The same thing we learned to do with most of our other emotions: stuff, repress, suppress, deny, or ignore them.

It's this false sense of masculinity that can lead to a sense of invincibility. A great example of this occurred during the 1992 U.S. Olympic trials when one of the premier athletes in the decathlon failed to qualify for the Summer Games in Barcelona, Spain. As a man who felt secure and thought he could never fail, Dan O'Brien lost out in the decathlon because he refused to try lesser heights in the pole vault, and finally failed at the only height he attempted. Had O'Brien accepted a lowly vault of 14-5 instead of gambling all or nothing on 15-9, he would have easily taken at least second place and a trip to Barcelona. Instead, he missed the Olympics, a possible gold medal at the 1992 Summer

Games, and extending a lucrative advertising contract with Reebok shoes.

O'Brien powerfully illustrates another aspect of this myth. Big, strong, and brave men cannot fail; they must be confident, secure, and not vulnerable. As this decathalete explained: "I felt invincible. I felt it was impossible for Dave [Johnson, his closest competitor] to beat me and that I would be on the Olympic team for sure." About his failure, Dan said, "I felt real numb at the time. I wanted to turn to someone and say, 'This shouldn't be happening to me.'"

Of course, the O'Brien story illustrates presumption and pride, but I think it also shows that many men, wanting to appear strong and invincible, seek to be independent and to feel secure, leading to the myth of "I cannot fail," or at least, "A man can succeed on his own, without close friends or the need for help."

Myth 2: Men Aren't Emotional and Don't Express Affection

Until recently men were usually portrayed as calm, cool, and rational, even in the face of great danger. Their emotional displays in the media were limited to righteous anger and "golly, gosh, aw shucks" tongue-tied expressions of love. In contrast, the women would swoon with emotions at the slightest provocation. Emotions, of all qualities and quantities, are her trademark. It doesn't seem to matter that there are numerous exceptions to that stereotype. It is still alive and well.

The myth is false. Men *are* emotional. The problem is that most men don't understand their emotions and they have not learned healthy and appropriate ways to express them (though they do express feelings in various ways). But contrary to the opinions of some women I've worked with, all men haven't had emotional bypass surgery. Their emotions may seem in hiberbation, but they are there.

Numerous exceptions exist to the stereotypical emotionally bound male. These exceptions suggest that, rather than being something inherent in all males, the difficulty in emotional awareness and expressiveness is more a function of social rather than biological influences. After all, women too sometimes find it difficult to reveal their feelings.

In the musical *Fiddler on the Roof,* Tevye struggles with the reality of his daughters' desire to get married because they are in love. This flies in the face of tradition. At one point he considers his love for his wife, Golde, and her love for him. He turns to her and asks "Do you love me?" Golde is obviously caught off guard by his question. After going through a list of all the things she has done for him during their many years of marriage she finally concludes that yes, she must love him—though she would not initially say those three words, "I love you."

In my research for this book I came across another even more interesting exception to this myth that men don't express their feelings—the story of Annie Oakley. The delightful musical *Annie Get Your Gun* describes a young and confident female sharpshooter, Annie Oakley. She doesn't believe that femininity is synonymous with inferiority and incompetence, and says so in the song "Anything You Can Do, I Can Do Better." Frank Butler is a world-class marksman in the Buffalo Bill Wild West Show. He is a bona fide man's man. When Annie meets him in competition she defeats him. But she falls in love with him and soon realizes that "You can't get a man with a gun." She deliberately loses her next competition with him, he realizes he loves her, and they live happily ever after.

That is the musical version. The true story of Annie Oakley and Frank Butler is a bit different. When, in 1875 as a teenager she defeated Frank Butler, he wrote, "It was her first big match—my first defeat. The next day I came back to see the little girl who had beaten me, and it was not long until we were married."[3] For the next fifty years Annie was the featured sharpshooter in the Buffalo Bill Wild West show. Frank worked as her manager. They traveled and worked together throughout the United States and Europe. They remained deeply in love. Frank was a sensitive man who continued to express his love and affection for Annie in love poems and press interviews. They died in 1926, within eighteen days of one another.

When I read the true story of Annie and Frank I was amazed. I found myself asking, "Why did the creators of the musical dramatically change the true love story?" The most obvious conclusion is that the real story didn't fit the current cultural gender stereotypes of romantic love. Men are supposed to be smarter, stronger, and more competent than women. Obviously the real Frank Butler didn't fit the stereotypic insensitive, insecure, and relationally brain-dead mold of masculinity, and so, for the story to be acceptable, what really happened had to be changed. Score one point for the myth.

Men and women do differ in how they verbally express love, anger, and other emotions. Many men do act as if they've graduated from the Marcel Marceau school of verbal expression. However, this difference isn't because women are naturally "emotional" and men are naturally "rational" or, as one woman put it, "because women are naturally open and men are naturally emotionally brain-dead."

Many of the differences in the ways men and women express emotions are the result of cultural traditions and expectations. Women are expected, encouraged, and even required to reveal certain emotions, and men are expected and required to deny or suppress them. Research shows that men generally express their feelings much less that women do. In fact, that's part of the old male caricature. It's partly true. But there's a reason for it. It's called cultural expectations.

Many men have told me that learning their emotional language is like learning a foreign language. When some men do begin to be more open and vulnerable with the women in their lives they may get a mixed message. One is a positive message of affirmation, "I'm glad you are opening up and sharing your concerns with me. Knowing your weaknesses as well as your strengths helps me feel closer to you." The other message can be more negative and come out of fear. "I guess I'm glad he's opening up, but when I see his weaknesses I get concerned that he may not be strong enough to take care of me and the kids."

It doesn't matter if it is verbal or nonverbal. Most men are quick to pick up this second message. If they do, it is highly unlikely that they will interpret it as a legitimate fear that can be understood and talked through. They are much more likely to interpret it as their feared rejection, and it may be a long time before they risk being vulnerable again.

Myth 3: Men Aren't Weak, They Don't Break Down, They Don't Cry

Men don't reach out for help. Men can do it on their own. This third myth is clearly related to the first two, yet it deserves special mention. Tears are a sign of weakness to most men. Perhaps you even completed the sentence "Real men . . ." with the words "don't cry."

I enjoy watching old movies. And I do mean old movies. You know, the ones available only in black and white and that feature more than car chases, infidelity, immorality, fighting, and weirdos torturing and dismembering other people. The ones that were made before Hollywood knew how to spell ninja.

I remember my reaction one Saturday night years ago watching an old movie with my parents. During a particularly sad part of the story I was aware of tears forming in my eyes. On a couple of occasions I remember looking around to make sure no one in my family noticed. I never told my friends that sometimes I would cry during sad movies. It wasn't something you talked about. I thought they might make fun of me.

The issue with this myth isn't that men should cry. I'm not suggesting that the mark of a true man is to weep uncontrollably at television commercials. However, based on what we read in Scripture real men should have the ability to shed tears at appropriate times. It's not a matter of having to cry. It's more a matter of being secure enough and aware of your emotions that when you experience tragic, painful, or devastating situations, you have the ability to shed some tears.

At the end of the 1992 football season, Mike Ditka was fired as head coach of the Chicago Bears. At his press conference he expressed genuine emotion and shed a few tears. No one laughed at him or called him a "girly-man." In fact, most of the men I talked with could relate to his pain and respected his appropriate expression of emotion.

Myth 4: *Men Are Great Lovers and Have an Insatiable Appetite for Sex*

During one adult Sunday school class I divided the students into male and female groups and asked them to come up with a list of three things they could do that they thought would communicate love to their spouse. Although they were intentionally being somewhat humorous, the women's group came up with the following list: #1 Sex, #2 Sex, and #3 Sex.

On one hand, it really is funny, and the entire group had a good laugh. On the other hand, this particular myth has devastating consequences for men. It has placed men under expectations so unrealistic that no one can live up to them. I've talked with countless men in their fifties who were depressed and discouraged because of their decreasing ability to "perform."

This myth has kept men prisoners of internally imposed pressures. The myth is that men of all ages are like they were at age nineteen. The only thing they really want in a relationship with a woman is "it." Take a look at heroes like Magic Johnson whose sexual promiscuity led to AIDS, Warren Beatty who according to the media has slept with most of Hollywood, and the current world record holder, that paragon of virility and masculinity, Wilt Chamberlain, who recently claimed 20,000 scores. Oh, oh, oh, what a guy!

It is true that there are some men whose emotional, mental, and physical development becomes arrested at age nineteen. Certainly men are different from women in the value they place on their perceived need for sex. However, the vast majority of men I have surveyed and worked with don't claim to be great lovers, nor do they have an insatiable appetite for sex. (However, a few of the older ones wish they still did.) For many men this places enormous pressure on them and can create a performance anxiety that can cripple their ability to function sexually.

Not only does this myth cause men to place unrealistic expectations on themselves, it also keeps them from developing healthy attitudes about sex. Sex becomes reduced to performance, and the person is lost. It has led to a lot of misunderstandings about what it means to be a sexual man.

As women buy into this myth it causes them to place unhealthy, unnecessary, and unfair expectations on their husbands. They look at their husbands through the "all men ever want is one thing" grid. I've talked with many men whose sincere attempts at trying to be more "romantic" were misinterpreted by their wives as just another guise to get them in the sack. Because men carry the major responsibility in the role of lover, they also carry a greater burden of failure.

Bob was a successful Christian businessman. He was a very young and healthy fifty-five. But he had been having problems in his sex life, and it had taken him three years to build up the courage to talk with someone about it. "From the time I understood the difference between male and female the challenge was to get some, to make it, to go all the way, to hit a home run, to score."

Bob continued, "No one told me what sex was really all about. Certainly my dad didn't. I guess we were just somehow supposed to magically know. When I think back to high school, sex to me was basically penetrate, ejaculate, and then, well, then evacuate. Get out of there, leave, disappear, find someone else to "prove" yourself with. My motto was slam, bam, thank you, ma'am."

Bob's not that different from many of the men I've worked with. Probably you or a good friend will read Bob's comments and say to yourself, "Yeah, I know exactly what he's talking about."

Myth 5: A Man's Value Is Determined By What He Does and How Much He Earns

Work is necessary for survival. If we're fortunate, it will also give us some pleasure in doing it or at least in a job well done. However, for many men, unlike women, work tends to serve a third purpose. It defines their masculinity. It is the yardstick by which they measure if they are a success or a failure. Many actually believe their worth is measured by their job status.

When I first met Rob and Gail in my waiting room they seemed like a pleasant couple. As soon as Rob sat down in my office he said, "I've got to be honest with you, Dr. Oliver. I'm not sure why we're here." Gail immediately jumped in, "And that's the problem!"

As Rob and Gail began their story, I realized that it was similar to ones I'd heard hundreds of times before. It's a common scenario. The man starts out by being committed to work and then becomes consumed by his job. Since real men work hard, the more he does the more successful he feels.

As far as he is concerned the marriage is great. His wife tries to let him know there are problems, but his denial is so strong that her concerns and complaints may not even register with him. Or he writes it off to "she feels this way every month."

The wife will often ask the husband to go with her to talk with the pastor or a marriage counselor but he reasons, *Why should I? Everything is fine.* So the wife has an affair, leaves, builds her own wall, or looks for her children to give her the validation and affection she needs and deserves. That may work until the last child leaves home. But once the nest is empty, once the kids are gone, there is nothing left to fill the void. The fact of their relational bankruptcy becomes unavoidable.

Although Gail did not go to the extremes of some women, she decided she could not have any kind of an emotional relationship with Rob. *He's functionally incapable of an emotional rela-*

tionship, she told herself. So she poured herself into her children, her music, and her friends; meanwhile she and Rob drifted further apart. When they came to see me they functioned as married singles.

Few things are more important to a man's pride, his identity, his sense of value and worth, and his manhood than work. That's why many men become addicted to their work; they become workaholics. There's a difference between loving what you do and having a passion for your work, and being a workaholic. If you can set your work down, let it go at the end of the day and not ruminate about it throughout the weekend, you aren't addicted to it.

Any addiction, even to work, serves to keep you separate from other people in meaningful kinds of ways, serves to keep you separate from yourself, and limits your ability to hear the voice of your heavenly Father. The problem isn't work. Work is necessary. Work is important. The problem is that many of us have allowed what we do to define our significance and to be the basis for our security. Work is inadequate on both counts.

Myth 6: Men Are the Opposite of Women

I decided to save one of the most subtle yet devastating myths for last. This myth says that men are the opposite of women. Not just a little different. They are totally different—polar opposites. You may say, "Yes, that's true. 'Opposites attract,' you know. We can't understand women because they are just the opposite of us. Right?" Wrong! But many believe the myth. When we focus primarily on our differences to the exclusion of our similarities, we set ourselves up for the divisive and antagonistic good-guy/bad-gal (or bad-gal/good-guy) mentality. Seeing each gender as totally opposite can lead to some unfortunate stereotypical distortions.

Some view men as the problem. Women are wonderful, men are jerks. They define all men as driven, irresponsible, sexually oriented (or fixated), and potentially lethal individuals who crave power, privilege, and orgasm. The flip-side of this extreme looks at women as being not only different, but wrong. They are the problem. Their differences are seen as deficiencies and weaknesses. They are inflexible, irresponsible, emotionally chaotic, interpersonally driven individuals who seek reciprocity, equality, and their kind of intimacy.

One day at work I found the following set of "rules" sitting on top of my desk, placed there by a colleague who thought I'd find the list humorous. I did, and I think you will too. Written by a man, the list shows how confusing men find male-female relationships. Here it is as it was given to me:

THE RULES

1. The Female always makes the rules.
2. The rules are subject to change at any time without prior notification.
3. No Male can possibly know all the rules. Nearly all Females are born with this knowledge.
4. If the Female suspects the Male knows all the rules, she may immediately change some or all of the rules.
5. The Female is NEVER wrong.
6. If the Female is wrong, it is because of a flagrant misunderstanding, which was a *direct result* of something the Male did or said wrong.
7. If rule #6 applies, the Male must apologize immediately for causing the misunderstanding.
8. The Female can change her mind at any given point it time.
9. The Male must NEVER change his mind without express written consent from the Female.
10. The Female has every right to be angry or upset at any time.
11. The Male must remain calm at ALL Times, unless the Female wants him to be angry or upset.
12. The Female must under NO circumstances let the Male know whether or not she wants him to be angry or upset.
13. Any attempt to document these rules could result in bodily harm.
14. If the Female has PMS, all rules are null and void.

When I have them read the above list, men invariably respond with gales of laughter. And as long as you recognize it as a joke, as long as you see it as an exaggeration of some man's perspective on male/female relationships, it really is funny. The sad part is that I have worked with more than a few men who to a great degree actually view women from this distorted perspective. That's not funny.

MEN AND WOMEN: THE SAME?

The previous six myths show how men view themselves and how they will regard and even treat women. But a variation of Myth 6 exists that I must mention as well, a politically correct variation of the "totally different" myth. Equally unhealthy and absurd, the myth says men and women are basically the same. It's origins date back twenty-five years to feminist circles, where radical feminists sought to develop research that would demonstrate that all observed gender differences were really the product of sociological influences and cultural pressure.

> Feminist researchers assert that there are few essential differences between the sexes, that most of our differences in behavior stem from our acculturation. In general feminists tend to seek environmental reasons for whatever difference there are between men's and women's behavior, abilities, and psychological makeup. However, the authors of a comprehensive text that analyzed hundreds of studies on sex differences concluded, "Feminists deemphasize and devalue biological factors in sex differences for essentially *political* reasons." (italics added)[5]

In many ways it was a ridiculous assumption, yet many intelligent people jumped on the gender-same bandwagon. The experience of generations of mothers and fathers that boys are "born" different from girls was dismissed as unscientific and therefore irrelevant. It became intellectually "chic" to downplay or ignore any evidence to the contrary.

Though some good and constructive changes have come out of the feminist movement, the political agenda of ignoring legitimate differences between men and women has had a harmful effect. The myth states that men and women are equal, but the real message is that women are more equal. They are much healthier than men and so, since all differences are really only cultural anyway, men need to become like women.

It's not just women who can suffer from this perceptual bias. Ashley Montagu, in his book *The Natural Superiority of Women*, writes: "It is the function of women to teach men how to be human." Montagu adds, "Woman is the creator and fosterer of life; man has been the mechanizer and destroyer of life."[6] Clearly some interpret the message to be that men need to be more like women. Whatever men are is unhealthy and whatever women are is healthy. And, since there is no difference between men and women, this transformation is possible. This unfortunate perspective led to what Robert Bly talks about as the "soft male":

> The male in the past twenty years has become more thoughtful, more gentle. But by this process he has not become more free. . . . He's a nice boy who now not only pleases his mother but also the young woman he is living with. They're lovely, valuable people. . . . They're not interested in harming the earth or starting wars. But something's wrong. . . . Many of these men are unhappy. You often see these men with strong women who positively radiate energy. Here we have a finely tuned young man, ecologically superior to his father, sympathetic to the whole harmony of the universe, yet he himself has no energy to offer.[7]

The answer to the male identity issues doesn't lie in men trying to be more like women any more than women assuming their problems will magically disappear if they become more like men. Yet, as Willard Gaylin writes,

> this is precisely the lunacy we seem to be adopting. Hollywood—still the best whacko index around—indulged in an absolute orgy of such gender-bendery in the summer of 1991. . . . The quintessential transition occurred in that touching story of parental love, Terminator II. Here a fourteen-year-old boy learns tenderness, caring, and affection from Arnold Schwarzenegger, a robot designed as a killer. He clings to the steel-reinforced bosom (pectorals) of the machine, since his real-life mother is the "new woman"—all muscle and ugliness. She is Sylvester Stallone in drag, with the foulest mouth this side of a Marine barracks. Tough, mean, vicious, she is too busy toting a 100-pound cannon to give hugs to her son. Hugs, you realize, are what boys "need" and don't get from their daddies. Is this what we really want: Dad as June Cleaver and Mom as Rambo?[8]

The real answer to the problem doesn't lie in a denial of male and female differences or role reversal but in the elimination of the artificial distinctions that have defined the two sexes. It's important to identify which of the differences are biological and which ones are cultural.

Carol Tavris, a social psychologist and writer, charts the similarities and differences between the sexes. She finds that studies show there are no differences between men and women in such areas as dependency, empathy, moods and "moodiness," sexual capacity and desire, and need for achievement and love and attachment and power.[9] However, studies do show gender differences in such areas as communication style, power, and status at work, in relationships, and in society.

Even international research demonstrates that, while there are definite cultural influences on how people define male and female, there are similarities that transcend cultures. John Williams and Deborah Best obtained data from fourteen countries, seeking cultural influences on masculine/feminine definitions. Their findings were sparse indeed; so much so that it caused them to "reverse" their bias for environmental shaping of gender differences. They further noted that cultures immensely dissimilar in other ways seem all to conform in their definitions of manhood and manliness.[10]

MEN AND WOMEN: DIFFERENT YET EQUAL

Fortunately there is a third option. It's more realistic, more responsible, and more biblical. The feminist movement has been correct in emphasizing that men and women are of equal value and equal worth. Unfortunately some of the more radical feminists have failed to emphasize important ways in which men and women are different. They have interpreted equal to mean same. The two are *not* synonymous.

Are men and women different? Most definitely! Are all of those differences genetic? No. Are many of the differences cultural? Yes. Are men and women opposites? No. When we regard male and female as polar opposites, with one side usually better than the other (or the "good guy"), we are setting up an unbiblical and dangerous dichotomy.

God has made male and female different. Yet we are of equal value and worth. The Bible says that we are "joint heirs in Christ."

Willard Gaylin, a medical doctor, has written that,

Boys are born with different attributes and tendencies from girls. These genetic differences are dramatic and apparent even in that stage of male development when boys are primarily attached to their mothers. Even when they are Mama's boys, they are boys. Boys are born with a potential for a larger body mass. Their verbal skills seem retarded until a later age of development. They are less analytical. They are born that way—kinetic, aggressive, with large motor skills early dominant—ready to be shaped into the form of a man, with a capital M. Still, in all, those directives are soft-wired and can be attenuated or even reversed; but we would be prudent to acknowledge honestly their existence and differences.[11]

As Gaylin notes, boy have distinct differences. However, there are certain male/female stereotypes that many people today still adhere to and are difficult to change. Consider the following:

Masculine	Feminine
assertive	passive
independent	dependent
logical	emotional
preoccupied	focused
strong	weak
silent	talkative
impersonal	personal
brave	fearful
competitive	cooperative
firm	gentle

It's true that men and women differ in the physiology of their brains. They are different. However, there is an unfortunate tendency to attribute many differences in individuals to sex/gender rather than the numerous other factors that contribute to and shape our development.

For example, I heard one speaker say that his wife is able to sum up a person's character immediately while he, with his slower adding machine brain, may take weeks or months to come to the same conclusions. That's not a function of sex. That doesn't come from a God-designed biological difference. With my wife and me it's just the opposite. I know of many other men who are able to quickly and fairly accurately sum up a person's character and are married to women who have a slower adding machine brain that takes longer to reach the same conclusion.

THE LOSS OF OUR HEARTS

The last several generations of men have to some degree been held hostage to these myths. And what has been the cost of men subscribing to these myths?

It has produced a generation of men who define themselves by the negative. Whatever women are, whatever strengths or attributes they have, whatever characteristic they possess, positive or negative, men aren't. And if women are emotional, then real men aren't. And any attempt to say they could be or should be is an attempt to "feminize" men.

By acting as if emotions and masculinity are incompatible, we have limited who God created us to be and become. The most devastating loss we have suffered by accepting these distortions is the loss of our hearts—the loss of our ability to feel, the ability to be tender as well as tough. We have lost the ability to be whole people.

These myths have produced a generation of men who are significantly out of touch with what it means to have been created in the image of an infinite yet personal God. The myths have also produced a generation of men who have little idea of how to take care of themselves. Because men don't understand and know how to express their emotions, they don't know how to deal with emotional pain. Therefore, when we do have pain we don't understand it and don't know what to do with it, so our only option is to anesthetize it. If we don't feel, then we won't feel pain or fear or grief or loss.

The anesthetic works for a while, but over time we need more and more. This leads to all kinds of destructive habits. For example, men tend to drink alcohol more to excess than women by a ratio of about four to one. Men die at a greater rate than women from both natural and external causes of death that are associated with excessive drinking.

We must reevaluate the God-given importance of emotions in our lives. That is the purpose of this book. On the following pages I hope men will find the knowledge, the understanding, and the compassion needed to help them let God heal their emotional wounds. When we do that, we can rid ourselves of misleading and unhealthy beliefs about our feelings, and learn to truly express our emotions. When we do that, we begin to become real men.

TAKE ACTION

For all you real men who ever wondered if it was OK to eat quiche, cry while watching *Terms of Endearment* (especially in front of a woman), or stay at home and watch the kids while your wife is at work, here it is, your first Inventory of Genuine Masculinity (developed by Kaye Cook and Lance Lee).

If you can answer yes to any of the next ten questions, you are probably the occasional victim of a gender-role-conflict. If you answer no to all of the questions, congratulations, you are incredibly healthy (and probably next to perfect).

Put yes or no in the blank before each of the statements.

_____ 1. I sometimes wonder if my job is "masculine" enough.

_____ 2. I question sometimes whether I'm built like a "real man."

_____ 3. I have trouble showing my real feelings, even to close friends.

_____ 4. I wonder sometimes if "real men" engage in the pastimes I engage in.

_____ 5. I hate to have a woman get the upper hand with me in a relationship.

_____ 6. I think that if I made more money, I'd feel more secure about my masculinity.

_____ 7. I wonder if I dress like a "real man" ought to.

_____ 8. I try not to cry in public, or display too much weakness.

_____ 9. I'm quite certain that most men do not have my particular hobbies and interests.

_____ 10. I get uncomfortable when a woman I am close to has more power or prestige than I have.[12]

2
BECOMING A REAL MAN

Dr. Oliver, you need to know that this is real uncomfortable for me." Ken had driven more than six hours from his western Kansas farm for his appointment. Just by looking at him I could tell that being in my office was more than "real" uncomfortable. It was *extremely* uncomfortable for him.

After a brief pause he continued. "I've always kinda made fun of people who needed to talk to other people about their problems. I figured that if you were a real man, and especially if you were a Christian, you should be able to take care of everything yourself." He paused, looked down at the floor and, with tears beginning to well up in his eyes, said, "I guess I was wrong."

Many would call Ken the typical man's man. Tall, athletic, and in his mid-fifties, Ken had grown up in the plains of western Kansas. He played football (offensive lineman) in high school and at the University of Kansas. He was a third-generation wheat farmer and obviously a hard worker. He owned a big house and more than one thousand acres of land. He had money in the bank. He had everything a man is supposed to have to be successful and happy. But in his personal life he wasn't successful and he wasn't happy.

"I've never been a real emotional kind of guy." Ken was obviously a master of understatement. "I always thought that emotions were for the women to take care of." That philosophy had worked for most of his life. But when his sixteen-year-old daughter became pregnant, the price of wheat dropped, and his wife told him that she didn't love him and if he wasn't open to counseling she wanted a divorce, his masculine and emotion-free world crumbled around him.

"I always thought that if I worked hard, did the things I was supposed to do, tried to live a good clean life—that if I did all that, things would just kinda work out." He concluded by saying, "I guess I missed something along the way."

What Ken and many other men have "missed along the way" is the fact that becoming a man doesn't start with what we do, it starts with who we are. It doesn't start with how tall we are or the size of our bank account, it starts with the fact that we are creatures that have been made in the image of God. I've talked with hundreds of men who have told stories similar to Ken's. Maybe they haven't faced as many crisis situations, but they too have ignored or suppressed their emotions. They have branded their feelings as unmanly or, even worse, as evil. And they have tried to beat their feelings down. But the result of doing this is the same as Ken's.

They feel confused, drained, discouraged, and depressed (though, of course, they don't want to admit that they feel that way). Many are surprised by the problems and their response to them. They thought that being a Christian would automatically eliminate these problems, that their lives would change.

Like Ken, they are partially right. Becoming a Christian does make a difference in our lives. Being a believer does change some things. But it doesn't change everything. And the changes that do take place don't happen overnight. Though as a believer I am now an heir with Christ and a brand new creation in Him, I don't get a new body or a new soul. Though I become a partaker of the divine nature, I still have the capability to sin, and I am affected by this sin-filled world.

Men struggle with the issues of masculinity for many reasons. However, over the years I've discovered one main reason that men, including Christians, are unsure of their manly identity. *Most men have little understanding of what it means to be made in the image of God.* Most men function as if success in life is just a matter of learning the right rules and jumping through the right hoops. Most men tend to focus on their performance rather than their person.

MADE IN GOD'S IMAGE

In the mid-sixties a nationally syndicated talk show originated in southern California called "The Joe Pyne Show." Pyne would invite controversial guests on his show and usually humiliate them. Pyne was so abrasive that he would sometimes tell those he disagreed with, "Oh, go and gargle with razor blades." On one particular program I heard him say that the Bible was primarily a collection of religious stories and not based on fact. He concluded that while it was an interesting book it was primarily fiction and had little relevance for the real world.

When I heard that I remember feeling angry. How could he get away with deceiving so many people? Pyne had a part of his program called the "Beef Box" where people from the audience could get up and talk back to him. While I was only a sophomore at Biola College I decided that I would try to get on his show and tell him what I thought. I spent much of the week preparing to defend my belief in the truthfulness of God's Word.

When it came time for the next week's show I was there and I was scared. I was allowed to be one of the speakers in the "Beef Box." When my turn came I stood before him and the cameras and said "My name is Gary Oliver, and I believe that the Bible is the inspired word of God, is fact and not fiction, and that the historicity and veracity of the Bible is supported by fact." I gave my reasons, and he listened. He didn't attack me or even disagree with me. I couldn't believe it.

Then out of the blue he asked me a question that I wasn't prepared to answer. Picture yourself as a nineteen-year-old in front of Joe Pyne and a national television audience. He asked "What does it mean to be made in God's image?" How would you answer that question? I had never thought of it before. Tough Joe Pyne was asking a question that showed he too wanted to know how people are special. I stumbled a bit and was able to give a reasonable answer but his question stuck with me. What does it mean to be made in God's image?

Can the fact that we are made in God's image make any difference in our lives? What are the implications of the fact that we are image-bearers? How can sinful human beings reflect the image of God?

Significance and Security

Knowing that you have been made in God's image can be a source of encouragement to you for at least two reasons. First, the fact that you are a redeemed image-bearer is a powerful statement as to the position God has given you. It provides a solid basis for both your significance and security.

The foundation of our identity is that we men were created by God in His image. While the fall damaged and distorted the image of God in man, it didn't destroy it. And the story doesn't end at the Fall. After the Fall comes the cross and the empty tomb. Not only are we made in God's image but our salvation was purchased with the blood of God the Son. Out of God's entire creation only man was made in His image and redeemed by His blood.

Unfortunately many men don't understand or appreciate what it means to be made in God's image. Many lean toward one of two extremes. Some focus on their sin nature to the exclusion of who we were made by and what we were made for. Others go to the opposite extreme and focus on the fact that we are made in God's image and ignore the reality and effects of sin. Both are important. I believe the biblical view involves a balance between those two extremes.

When we don't understand the basis for our significance and our security, our human nature leads us to devise our own ways of feeling significant and secure. We look for all kinds of ways to prove ourselves, to shore up our sagging sense of worth, to demonstrate and validate our masculinity.

For adolescents and young men this can involve feats of bravery, daring, and strength. Do you remember the scene in *Rebel Without A Cause* in which James Dean and another man try to show their toughness by playing chicken? Each plans to drive his car off a cliff, and the first one to jump out is chicken. As we get older the attempts can become a bit more sophisticated but nonetheless ridiculous. Many of us have become workaholics whose success is determined by the number of "pink roses" (phone messages) on our desk and how many hours of overtime we put in. Or maybe it's how quickly we get pay raises or promotions.

If you don't have a clear sense of what it means to be "in Christ," to have been made in the image of God, and to have been redeemed by the Son of God, you won't be able to build your life on that base. Furthermore, your identity is not able to be person-based, so to have any sense of significance and security our identity becomes performance-based.

Performance-based identity is an easy trap to fall into. Typically we look to an ethical or social standard—or even a church—to determine what we should know and what we should abstain from. Instead, the clear teaching of Scripture should be our guide. Scripture will show us what we should be—not do—as we model our life on Christ, the ideal man.

The Pharisees are great examples of performance-based identity. They followed all of the biblical commandments. They even added some of their own rules and regulations and followed them as closely as possible. Their focus was on head knowledge. They knew the truth in their heads but not in their hearts. Thus, when the Messiah came, they could not recognize Him. He didn't fit their mold.

In contrast, true maturity is measured by the degree to which we are "becoming conformed to the image of [God's] Son" (Romans 8:29). It is based on who we are rather than on what we do. One measure of person-based maturity is the fruit of the Spirit. This is clearly a much more difficult standard.

I believe the problem with Christian men is not that we aren't *doing* enough. The problem is that we're not *being* enough. The problem is not that we aren't *where* we should be. The problem is that we're not *what* we should be. Head knowledge is always easier than heart knowledge. Over the years I've found that it is much easier to have discussions and debates *about* the truth than it is to allow the Holy Spirit to use the circumstances of my life to help me become *conformed* to the truth.

Is head knowledge important? Do we need to understand sound doctrine? Is it valuable to know why we believe what we believe? Yes, yes—an emphatic yes. I want to be very careful to not imply in any way that head knowledge is not important. It is important and can be valuable. However, what is most important, what is foundational to the Christian life, what must come first is that we have an intimate, growing, love relationship with our Lord Jesus Christ. Head knowledge about the truth is not an end in itself. The purpose of the truth is transformation. When we are transformed, we have the courage and security to be ourselves, to be real men.

When Christ met Peter by the Sea of Tiberius he was much more concerned with Peter's heart knowledge than his head knowledge (John 21:15–17). He didn't give Peter a three-point lecture on the orthodox way to feed sheep. Christ looked Peter straight in the eyes and, man to man, asked "Do you love me?"

As a young Christian this passage in John 21 had a tremendous impact on my life. Let me ask you a question I have asked myself countless times. If Christ were to visibly appear to you today and look you in the eyes and say "Do you love me?" what would your answer be? If your answer would be yes, what would you use as proof?

Would your primary supporting evidence be your length of church attendance, number of verses memorized, the amount of your tithe, the number of boards or committees you participate in, the bad habits you don't have, the things of the world you abstain from? Christ would not acknowledge such acts. Instead, He would look at your habits of character. And if your life featured love, joy, and peace, ever increasing; patience, kindness, and goodness, often if not regularly; and faithfulness, gentleness, and self-control as part of your life—then He would say, "Ah, yes, you love me."

Knowing what it means to have been made in God's image is important for a second reason. It helps us to understand what it means to be a person and the direction God will take in the transformation process. It allows us to escape from the cultural myths of masculinity and become free from the unrealistic expectations that have bound so many of us. It provides a foundation for our growing sense of what being a man really means.

The importance of reflecting God's image is emphasized in the New Testament. God wants us "to become conformed to the image of His son" (Romans 8:29); the apostle Paul says that we are "being transformed into the same image from glory to glory" (2 Corinthians 3:18). And Peter reminds Christians that God tells us that we are "partakers of the divine nature" (2 Peter 1:4). What does that mean? What's involved in being a person?

Mind, Emotions, and Will Together

At the end of 1 Thessalonians Paul writes, "May your spirit and soul and body be preserved complete, without blame at the coming of our Lord Jesus Christ." A part of what it means to be made in God's image is that we have a soul or personality. Our personality is three-dimensional just like God's. Personality consists of our mind, emotions, and will. All three are important.

When God made us in His image He gave us a mind, a will, and emotions. God gave us a mind so that we could reason and process information. He gave us a will so that we would have the ability to make choices. He gave us emotions so that we would be able to feel. Emotions are God-given; they are a natural, healthy expression of our being made in His image.

He intentionally designed these three parts of our person to work together in balance and harmony. Like a three-legged milking stool, each dimension of our personality—our mind, will, and emotions—is vital and necessary. If any leg of the milking stool doesn't work, the stool will topple. If any aspect of our personality doesn't function the way God designed it to, it will keep us from being all that God would have us to be.

Although we often talk about the mind, will, and emotions as separate entities, we must not forget that, by God's design, they are intricately interrelated. Our choices influence what and how we feel. Our emotions influence how we interpret what we hear, what we think, and the decisions that we make. Our thoughts or the mental interpretations we make of events around us influence how strongly we feel about something and thus the choices that we make.

Most of the decisions or choices we make are based on certain kinds of information. That information comes from two primary sources. Our emotions and our mind are two different yet equally valuable ways of experiencing, understanding, and interpreting the world around us. They provide us with two different kinds of information about ourselves and our world. They can balance each other. When our mind and emotions work together in harmony we are more likely to make wise and responsible choices.

Though God designed our mind, will, and emotions to work in harmony, sin has seriously complicated the picture. Sin brought a division between God and man. It brought a division between male and female. And it produced a division within each one of us.

Due to the Fall and the effects of sin in our lives, our mind, will, and emotions have become damaged and distorted. The division is especially evident in relation to our mind and our emotions. What God designed to work together in a complementary relationship are often experienced as opposing one another.

TWO COMMON ERRORS

One of the many negative effects of sin has been to produce in each of us a tendency to prefer one aspect of personality over the other. Sometimes, especially with many men, we may emphasize one to the exclusion of the other. The common errors are to prefer mind over emotions; or the opposite, emotions over the mind.

Mind Over Emotions

Those who overemphasize the mind believe that emotions are untrustworthy and unreliable. This is error #1. I heard one well-known preacher say, "You can't base your decisions on your emotions. Emotions change, but God's Word never changes. There is no room for emotionalism in the mature Christian life." With good intentions this pastor built an artificial and unbiblical dichotomy between the mind and emotions. His interpretation was simple and clear: The mind is good, emotions are bad. Emotions are generally evil, but perhaps a necessary evil.

Do you feel that way about emotions? If so, your reasoning probably proceeds like this: *It's probably good to be aware of my emotions, but I can't take them too seriously. They are helpful for getting along with women. But when it comes to making decisions, I'm better off if I ignore my feelings. Go for the bottom line.*

Like Sargeant Joe Friday of "Dragnet," for you the only thing necessary is "The facts, ma'am, just the facts." This had been Ken's philosophy.

Unfortunately many Christians have bought into that error. From this perspective the mind is good, emotions are bad. Emotions are the "black sheep" of our personality. I have heard emotions described as something "caused by the Fall, and a cause of many people's downfall." Emotions are at best unimportant and at worst a mark of immaturity.

In my experience men are much more likely than women to fall into this error. This can bias many men's perspectives. I've worked with many men who believe that if they feel strongly about what they're saying, even if they can't give good reasons for it, they're being rational. Of course, from their perspective, if a woman does the same thing, she is being irrational, illogical, and, even worse, emotional. Why? Because she is a woman.

Many men are good at the level of the mind and the will, but due to the effects of sin and socialization they have become emotional quadraplegics. As boys we were taught that masculinity and emotionality are incompatible, and in the process many of us lost touch with a key component of what it means to be a person.

When we elevate the mind to a position of superiority and relegate the emotions to the servants' quarters, we are splitting our personality in ways God never intended. We are trading in our emotional birthright for an intellectual mess of pottage. This is a trade God never asked us to make. However, this is exactly the trade that Ken had unknowingly made. The result of this trade is what finally brought him into my office.

I've often heard women refer to men as cold, heartless, not unlike Ebenezer Scrooge in Dickens's classic *A Christmas Carol*. He was so engrossed in what he did he had little awareness of the people around him. When Jacob Marley, his deceased partner, came to visit him, he was chained to the money boxes he spent his life accumulating.

Dickens knew how easily we can replace people with performance. In Ebenezer he created a character who was lonely and functionally without a father. When other children went home for Christmas Ebenezer stayed at school, alone. He was a boy who never came close to his dad, who never learned how to trust or have a relationship, who never learned how to understand and deal with his emotions. He anesthetized his loneliness, grief, and pain by studying longer and harder, and, later, by long, dedicated hours on the job. His basis for significance and security was his performance and, as an adult, his production.

When he went to work for the warm Mr. Fezziwig, he saw a model of masculinity that was new to him. Fezziwig was a successful businessman and a hard worker. Yet he had a balance in his life. He wasn't one-sided and unidimensional. Scrooge liked what he saw in Fezziwig, but he didn't understand it. It wasn't how he had been raised. When he fell in love he didn't understand that his girlfriend was much more concerned with who he was than with how much his investments earned.

Poor Ebenezer didn't understand any of that. So he retreated in the tomb he called the office and buried himself in profit and loss statements. Somewhere along the way he ceased to be much of a person. It took the crisis of the three spirits to turn him around.

In more than twenty years of being a counselor I've met many men, many good and kind men, who have become relational Ebenezer Scrooges. On the outside they may have great communication skills and appear effective and successful. On the inside lives a frightened and isolated man who has forgotten how to dream and doesn't know how to really care. This is what can happen when we value mind over emotions.

Yes, women can suppress emotions too. In the movie *Ordinary People*, the story of a successful, relatively peaceful upper-class suburban family, everything is going well until they lose one of their sons in an accidental drowning. In the emotional crisis that follows, each family member responds differently. The mother (played by Mary Tyler Moore) deals with the crisis by trying to ignore her emotions. She goes through each day with a cold, detached, almost machine-like precision. She turns to perfectionism, control, and rigidity to anesthetize herself from facing the reality of the loss and feeling the range of emotions that come with healthy grief.

When our emotions are frozen, we miss the color of life. Everything looks black and white. When we become the prisoners of our intellect, our sensitivity decreases and we tend to develop all-or-nothing thinking. We rarely experience the highs and lows of life, we become uncomfortable with excitement and enthusiasm, we become more critical. Rather than thinking that every cloud has a silver lining, we believe that whenever we see a silver lining, if we just look hard enough, we will be able to see the cloud full of rain and hail. Without our emotions free to be expressed, we don't build or encourage. We aren't aware of our pain so we can't share it. We find it increasingly difficult to be around people who are in touch with their pain, and when we are we tend to give "answers" rather than really hear them.

Unfortunately, many of us don't know how to express our emotions. The deeper the emotion the more difficult it is to share. We may cry at the "wrong" time, laugh at the "wrong" time, or get angry at the "wrong" time. We've had years of training on how to communicate our ideas with clarity yet precious little training in clearly communicating our feelings. When we do try to express our emotions we may come on too strong or not strong enough. We get embarrassed. People misunderstand. We decide it's safer not to risk the humiliation of being rejected or laughed at, so we don't share.

Some people try to hide in their intellect to keep themselves from the pain of feeling what they never learned how to understand. David Mains, a former pastor and host of radio's "Chapel of the Air," writes with refreshing candor about the big padlock on his emotions:

> For a large part of my life I was tuned out emotionally. I wasn't aware of where others were coming from, and I didn't even understand my own feelings. I was probably extreme in that regard. I didn't know when I was tired. I seldom paid attention to whether I was hot or cold. I wasn't in touch with what I liked or didn't like. If someone would ask me what was wrong, instead of saying, "I feel trapped with no way out of this situation," I'd reply, "I'm OK, why do you ask?" Most of the time if someone accused me of expressing a negative emotion like anger or pride or frustration, I denied it. Was I stomping mad? No. Did I swear? Had my words stopped making sense because of my intense emotion? Never. What do you mean I was angry? You're accusing me of not acting the way a Christian should!
>
> "You were emoting," my wife would tell me the next day. "It was as if you were sending out waves and waves of high voltage electricity. I don't understand how everybody can sense that except you."
>
> Well, I wasn't in tune with my anger, my pain, my loneliness, my defensiveness, my fears, delights, moods, embarrassment, jealousies, whatever. I functioned relatively well in the objective world of ideas, facts, and words. But the more subjective realm of feeling was atrophying, shriveling up within me. Thank God that in recent years the Lord has been doing a major healing in me for which I'm extremely grateful. One of the signs of health is that my feelings are coming back into play.[1]

Mains adds that now when he reads the Bible he sees how much the Bible has to say about emotions. When he goes to church he often finds himself filled with inexplicable joy. He is able to shed tears when he is hurt or when he finds he has hurt someone else. He is better able to discern when he has let himself become too busy and needs a rest.

Emotions Over Mind

Those who emphasize emotions over mind make feelings the standard or measuring stick of life. All feelings are factual and valid. They don't need to be justified, explained, or proven. They have the final word. Their motto is "If I don't feel like it, I shouldn't do it. God doesn't want me to be a phony." This is error #2.

While error #1 involves ignoring the emotions, error #2 involves ignoring the mind. Those who overemphasize the mind tend to be hard, cold, insensitive, unkind, and uncaring. In contrast, those who allow their lives to be run by their emotions live on a emotional roller coaster. Feeling becomes fact. No need to check it out. They are sensitive, but can become oversensitive to the point of letting their life be thrown off balance by the smallest slight.

God designed our emotions to enrich and enhance our lives. But due to the Fall and the effects of sin in our lives, our emotions, like our mind and our will, have become damaged and distorted. For many the emotions that God gave to make life more meaningful instead make life more miserable.

It's true that feelings are important. In chapter 3 we will see that the Bible has a lot to say about God's emotions and the role of emotions in our lives. But they were never meant to be the absolute standard of truth, the infallible guide to what is right, the source of all our decisions and actions. C. S. Lewis wrote that "No natural feelings are high or low, holy or unholy in themselves. The are all holy when God's hand is on the rein. They all go bad when they set up on their own and make themselves into false Gods."[2] In a later essay he added, "Feelings come and go, and when they come a good use can be made of them: they cannot be our regular spiritual diet."[3]

Consider three biblical examples of men who let their emotions dominate them. Saul was a mighty warrior and the powerful king of Israel. However, when young David killed Goliath he became more popular that Saul. The women sang, "Saul has slain his thousands, And David his ten thousands" (1 Samuel 18:7). When Saul heard this he allowed the emotions of anger and jealousy to control him. This distorted his perspective and interfered with his ability to learn from his mistakes.

When the ten spies returned from the promised land and told about giants and walled cities, the Jews allowed the emotions of fear and depression to control them. They became so consumed by these emotions that it limited their ability to recall what God had done for them.

When Elijah allowed his fear of Jezebel and her threats to control him, he ran away from his problems and sat under a juniper tree. His out-of-control fear led to a depression that caused him to lose perspective and want to die.

Though both men and women can fall prey to Error #2, most would agree that women are more likely to fall into this category than men. Miriam Neff, in her helpful book *Women and Their Emotions*, has written,

> I've heard it said that women are more in tune with their feelings and more sensitive than men. I'm not so sure about that. I am sure about one thing: we more frequently allow our emotions to lead us. While men are thinking about what should be done, we're sorting out how we feel about it. We're likely to act based on those feelings before we've applied our minds to the issue at hand. The marriage of our minds and our emotions equals what Scripture refers to as the heart. Bridging the gap is marrying the mind to the emotions and placing them both under God's control.[4]

Which of the two errors is most characteristic of how you function? Where did you learn that this was the "right" way to be? What was modeled by your male heros? How about your same-sex parent and your opposite-sex parent? If you are married, which is most characteristic of your spouse?

THE HEALTHY BALANCE

Both Error #1 and Error #2 reveal a major misunderstanding of the biblical teaching on how God designed us to function. As Neff notes, the challenge is to regard our minds and our emotions as equally valuable and important, giving a God-intended balance to the choices we make.

By God's grace there is a third option. The only healthy response is to choose to view our emotions from God's perspective and to bring them into harmony with our mind. Maturity involves the whole person. True maturity involves a balance between our heart and our head, between our feeling and our thinking. Both are important. Both are designed by God for our good.

True spiritual maturity involves the whole person. It is impossible to be spiritually mature and emotionally or intellectually immature. It's not a matter of mind over emotions or emotions over mind. True maturity involves a balance between our heart, head, and will; among our feeling, thinking, and doing.

Unfortunately very few of the men I have worked with have understanding of or appreciation for the importance of emotions in the process of becoming a real man. The Bible regards the emotions as being very important, yet typically the role of emotions in the Christian life has been misunderstood and at times totally ignored. Recently I looked at several sets of systematic theologies in my library and was amazed to find that the word *emotions* didn't even warrant a notation in most of the indexes. One theologian, though, properly describes the relationship between facts and feelings. In *Biblical Concepts for Christian Counseling*, William Kirwan notes:

> "Facts" and "feelings" are part of the same process. The brain does not separate feelings from facts or facts from feelings. There is little distinction between the two: all feelings are psychological and neurological arousal attached to facts. . . . Nor does the Bible make a distinction between facts and feelings. . . . We deal not with facts or feelings, but with facts and feelings. . . . By seeing emotions or feelings as a key aspect of the heart we see that they are also a key part of one's being. As a key to being, they are of vital importance in the life of the Christian.[5]

A major cause of the struggles we men have and the problems we get ourselves into is a lack of understanding of our emotions. During years of counseling men, I have found that many find talking about their emotions awkward or embarrassing. For some men, *emotional* is a dirty word.

What do you think of when you hear the word *emotional*? Is your first response a positive or a negative one? Has anyone ever called you "emotional"? If so, think back to the last time it happened. What was the context? Were they giving you a compliment? You could have responded in two different ways. You could have said, "Thank you. I'm so pleased that you noticed." Or you could have regarded it as a criticism or a put-down. How did you respond? Was the person who labeled your behavior emotional a man or a woman? Did the gender of the person calling you emotional affect how you interpreted the word's meaning?

When most people use the word *emotional* they are referring to someone's behavior. "Stop being so emotional." "You're starting to sound emotional." It's also used to describe an enduring characteristic of a person. "She's just an extremely emotional person."

There doesn't seem to be any clear definition for the word *emotional*, though its uses seem to be influenced by the behavior of the person who is being described and the intentions of the one who is doing the labeling. Being emotional has something to do with the frequency, intensity, duration, and appropriateness of a response.

What is clear is that the label "emotional" is most often used in a negative context. It's often used in an attempt to influence or control a person's behavior. An emotional person is often considered irresponsible, immature, and irrational. When I play a word association game with several men's groups, *emotional* frequently receives such responses as *immature, childish, irresponsible, irrational, illogical,* and *out-of-control.* Not exactly what most of us would consider compliments.

When did the term *emotional* get this bad reputation? Is it only a bad word for men? If it's always bad to "get all emotional," what is the problem? Is it with our emotions? Or is it with how we at times choose to express our emotions? Emotional maturity is not about whether we should experience our emotions. It's more about understanding what we are feeling, determining the appropriateness of that emotion, and then choosing how to express it.

As we understand what it means to be a person with a mind, emotions, and a will, we have a foundation upon which to build a positive image of masculinity. We don't need to return to archaic rituals and outmoded ceremonies. We don't need to return to the aggressive, domineering, and emotionally disconnected male role models of the past.

"MEN DON'T . . ."

Much of who we are as men has been negatively defined. We have been reactive and allowed ourselves to be defined by what we don't do: Men don't cry, men aren't weak, men don't need affection, gentleness, or warmth, men don't rely on others, men don't need comforting, men don't admit mistakes, men don't need to be needed.

It's time for us to become proactive, to be defined by who we are and who God has created us to be and to become. We should be defined by our person and not by our performance or our production.

The essence of true manhood is not found in what a man does, in how big or strong he is, in how much money he has made. It is found in who he is and what he is becoming. It's found within his heart, his moral character, his values and integrity. It is found in personal characteristics such as courage, steadfastness, responsibility, duty, fortitude, generosity, and the fruit of the Spirit.

True manhood isn't as much a destination one arrives at as it is a direction one is going. Real men haven't arrived. Real men are becoming. They are open to change and growth. I've come to realize there is a more realistic way to look at "biblical masculinity."

Biblical masculinity is not about domination, being the boss, having all the power and privilege. It is about demonstration—being an example, practicing what we preach, walking the talk. The lives of real men are characterized by an openness, honesty, an accurate self-awareness, and vulnerability. Real men, those who know God, display consistency, integrity, and an abiding faith.

What are the characteristics of godly men? If we are becoming real men, we will be "man" enough to:

1. take an honest look at ourselves (mind, will, emotions) from God's perspective
2. have our lives characterized by the fruit of the Spirit
3. say "I was wrong," "I'm sorry," "Will you forgive me?"
4. face and deal with our own issues and allow God to heal our wounds
5. become accountable to some other men
6. love and accept those who are different from us; we can disagree with what a person does and still see them as having infinite worth and value
7. risk becoming passionate men who aren't afraid to love

8. risk being tender as well as tough, to acknowledge that there is nothing as strong as gentleness and nothing as gentle as real strength

9. model the fact that sometimes we stand tallest when we are on our knees

10. have the courage to care, commit, make a promise—and keep it!

TAKE ACTION

1. Do you tend to let your mind dominate your decisions, or your emotions dominate your decisions? Why? What can you do to change this approach to decision making?

2. Review the ten strengths of a godly man that conclude this chapter. Which one of these do you admire most and would like to achieve?

3. Of the ten traits of the godly man, which one(s) will be hardest for you to achieve and why? What can you do to develop these characteristics (for example, ask a friend to keep you accountable or look for opportunities to demonstrate that trait)?

The following poem[7] by Pastor James Ryle describes several passages of a man. It also describes a man out of touch with his emotions. What common myths of masculinity do you recognize in this poem?

When Did I Become a Man?

When did I become a man?
I really want to know.
Sometimes I wonder if I am.
Can someone tell me so?

Was it when I smoke a cigarette
Out behind the school?
Was it when I joined the other guys
And acted like a fool?

Was it when I took a drink of booze
And drove around the town?
Was it when I made myself look big
By putting others down?

Was it when I scored the final play
That gave our team the win?
Was it when I finally got the "A"
That made my parents grin?

Was it when I had a hot date
and we did it all the way?
Is that when I became a man?
Did it happen on that day?

. . . .

Did it happen in the church
When I walked the wedding aisle?
It seemed to for the moment,
If we're judging by my smile.

Did it happen on the day my kids
Looked up and called me "Pop"?
Or was it when I got the job
And made it to the top?

So now I am a man.
At least, that's what I'm told to say.
But if I am, there's just one thing
That still gets in my way.

If so, I have to ask—
And the question drives me wild—
If I've become a man, then why
Do I still act like a child?

© James Ryle. Used by permission.

3

REAL MEN
HAVE FEELINGS TOO

Kent, a successful businessman, wanted to see me soon; he would drive from western Wyoming to Denver, a nine-hour round-trip, in order to talk. I agreed, but before we met I asked him to write down his concerns and his hopes for God to help him through me. Here is a part of what he wrote:

> Most of my life I've thought that the path to spiritual maturity was to merely "set your mind on things above." I thought that if I spent enough time in the word and in prayer and was active in my church that I wouldn't have to struggle with "emotional problems." For several years that seemed to work.
>
> However, recently I have had tremendous struggles with worry and fear. This has knocked me for a loop. Anyone who knows me would tell you that I'm an optimistic and confident person. I've never focused on what might go wrong. I've always assumed the best and accepted any task that came my way.
>
> Well, for the first time in my life simply working harder or longer hasn't been enough. I've spent more time in the Word and in prayer, I've confessed every sin I can think of, I've memorized even more verses, but I still have not had victory over these emotions. I believe there must be something God wants to teach me

but I don't know what it is . . . and I'm not sure how to find it. What I do know is that I'm tired and weary, my marriage is falling apart, and for the first time in my life, I feel defeated.

When I saw Kent for the first time I could see the weariness etched on his face and hear the defeat in his voice. Somewhere along the way Kent had picked up the idea that if you struggle with your emotions it's probably because you are out of fellowship with God. I assured Kent that wasn't necessarily the case. "God often speaks to us through our emotions." By the look on his face I could tell that this was obviously a new concept to him.

"Sometimes God uses emotional pain to alert us to the fact that something is wrong with the way we are living." I continued. "It may be that we're out of fellowship with Him. Or it may be that He has something new He wants to teach us."

After another hour of listening and asking some clarifying questions, I recognized one of the root causes of his sense of discomfort and defeat. "Kent, you are facing a struggle that many Christian men face in their lives. It may surprise you, but at least part of your problem is that you don't really understand your emotions, what they are, where they come from, and why God gave them to you."

Kent is like many men who feel out of touch with their emotions. Their fear of emotions is partly due to an inadequate understanding of what it means to be made in God's image and thus an inaccurate view of emotions. I was fortunate to be raised in a conservative, fundamental, Bible-believing church; yet as I recall my early training I can't remember one message on emotions and the Christian life.

The good news is that when we ask Christ into our heart a radical transformation takes place. Yet at the same time the consequences that sin has had on our mind, will, and emotions are not immediately overcome.

We are called to have a renewed mind (Romans 12:2); indeed, that is an important part in becoming a mature man. Most of us men have a sharp respect for our minds. In fact, we equate maturity with head knowledge. Our knowledge is important, of course, but maturity is much more than what and how much we know. Many Christians who understand terms like *atonement* and *sanctification* still are influenced by old thoughts and controlled by emotions they cannot understand. Their lives are still characterized by fear, hurt, frustration, or depression.

One reason we are more comfortable with facts than feelings is because many Christian men—pastors and churchgoers alike—have emphasized that emotions aren't important; certainly they are not worth paying much attention to. Yet as you read the Bible it becomes clear that maturity is more than the acquisition of facts and head knowledge. True maturity involves the transformation of the total person. It involves becoming conformed to Christ in our mind, our will, and our emotions. (For a fuller discussion of the role of your mind in the process of becoming a mature man, see the Epilogue.)

Both the mind and the emotions are important. Alfred North Whitehead said it well when he stated that "intellect is to emotion as our clothes are to our bodies: we could not very well have civilized life without clothes, but we would be in a poor way if we had only clothes without bodies."

I believe that an equally important part of the process of becoming a mature man involves the understanding of our God-given emotions and restoring our ability to experience and express them. For most men, this part of the process is more difficult and thus more neglected. In my men's conferences I've asked men to call out words that describe where men are today. Here are some of the most frequent responses:

afraid	discouraged	inadequate
angry	isolated	stuck
misunderstood	trapped	dependent
confused	numb	apathetic
running scared	guilty	lonely
ashamed	sad	wounded

When I ask about emotions, the word catches many men by surprise. One man said, "Emotions are like a foreign language to me." Another man said, "Emotions are what women have." Some respond with, "I rarely feel any emotions." Many associate emotions with times of crisis or excitement. Most men will show joy and excitement, especially in sports, but otherwise don't express emotions.

One man replied, "I'm not even conscious of my emotions during the day. I don't even think about my emotions at work, only about my actions. If I have a bad day at work, I remind myself why I'm here. I'm trying to make a living. I'm trying to finish a task. I'm paid to move on to the next task, not to focus on how others respond to me or how I feel."

Do you remember the last time you felt something so deeply you were moved to tears? Where were you? What did it feel like? You could answer this last question several ways: uncomfortable, embarrassed, surprised, or relieved. No matter how you felt, what did you do with those feelings? Did you express them to anyone or keep them to yourself? Sometimes we enjoy having someone listen and receive our feelings, yet often we don't tell anyone how we feel. If you didn't tell anyone, how did it feel to keep those powerful emotions stuffed inside?

WHY ARE EMOTIONS SO IMPORTANT?

By now it should be clear that one of the most fundamental aspects of being a mature man involves our emotions.

However, many men are surprised to discover that the Bible has much to say about emotions. We have emotions because God has emotions. Emotions are intended by God and designed by God. From Genesis to Revelation we read about God's emotions: He is jealous, angry, loving, kind, and grieves over man's rebellion. And we are created in His image. That means, like God, we men feel, and we care. In the four gospels we read that Christ experienced and expressed anger, distress, sorrow, disappointment, frustration, fear, compassion, joy, and delight.

When Christ gave His farewell message to His disciples in the Upper Room (John 13), He knew His death was at hand. What was the most important message Christ wanted to leave with them? He told them what would identify them as followers. Interestingly, it was not an absence of mistakes or weaknesses, the number of things they abstained from, or their net worth. Instead, it was an emotion, expressed in behavior.

"A new commandment I give to you, that you love one another, even as I have loved you, that you also love one another. By this all men will know that you are My disciples, if you have love for one another" (John 13:34–35). Yes, He calls them to have love. Not the ability to be witty and clever, nor to win debates. Instead Jesus names the emotion of love.

God has designed us in such a way that our emotions influence almost every aspect of our lives. God speaks to us through our emotions. They are like a sixth sense. Emotions are to our personality what gasoline is to a car. They are the source of our passion and intensity. They help us to monitor our needs, make us aware of good and evil, provide motivation and energy.

When God told Saul that his kingdom would not endure, God showed His priorities. Through Samuel God said, "Your kingdom shall not endure. The Lord has sought out for Himself a man after His own heart, and the Lord has appointed him as ruler over His people, because you have not kept what the Lord commanded you" (1 Samuel 13:14).

Notice God's primary criterion. He did not seek someone "after His own head." His desire was not merely a rational mind or a man who could quickly calculate the bottom line and make objective decisions unfettered by emotions. No, God sought someone after His own *heart*. David was that man. Yes, David made many mistakes. He was flawed and fallible, much as you and I are (a lot like I am). But David had one quality God admired greatly. David was a passionate man who had a heart for God.

Have you ever noticed that the fruit of the Spirit aren't primarily head knowledge, works, performance, power, achievement, or financial security? The fruit of the Spirit are love, joy, peace, patience, and gentleness (Galatians 5:22–23). It includes the emotional side of who God has made us to be.

God created us with both a head and a heart. Both are important. But due to sin and socialization, most men respond to their emotions by denying, suppressing, repressing, or ignoring them. In the earlier chapters we've seen that most boys are socialized in ways that make us emotionally illiterate.

As Osherson notes,

Men don't have many opportunities to sort out what they feel and believe about being a father, husband, lover, friend, son, or worker. Men often feel an internal powerlessness when confronted by their own feelings and the dilemmas of growing up and being a man. When we try to sort out who we really are, to see ourselves clearly, we often feel on the spot, judged, and found wanting by a well-meaning wife, friend, or boss—or by ourselves.[1]

Men have paid an enormous price for ignoring their emotions. When we deny the realities of our life, it distorts our perspective, limits our perception, and leads us to distrust our experience. We often tend to deny or ignore the very things God would have us face to help us grow. Denial of our emotions only increases our pain and a sense of alienation from a fundamental part of our personality. It puts us out of touch with a third of who God made us to be. Your body and mind are incomplete, yes even paralyzed, without your emotions to empower them.

Emotional ignorance or insensitivity will cause many of us men to go through much of our lives either weighed down with or overcome by feelings of hopelessness and helplessness. Like Kent, you may have emotional pain. Though it's not physical, our inner pain can be just as draining as a headache or a wrenched back. Here are some examples of emotion pain:

- discouraged by your inability to be good enough
- overcome with guilt and shame from sinful and harmful deeds done out of lust or anger when "carried away" by the emotions you couldn't identify and didn't understand
- frustrated by repeated failures
- prisoners of your fear
- paralyzed by the prospect of rejection
- isolated by lifelong insecurities

When emotional pain strikes, we often lack the ability to understand and deal with it. When the pain becomes too uncomfortable, the only other option is to attempt to anesthetize it. As we try to deaden the pain, we run the risk of becoming addicted. And our addictions can be more subtle than alcohol or drugs.

For instance, you can replace feelings with busyness. If you don't have time to think, you won't have time to feel. The busyness becomes workaholism. Or you can turn to hobbies, television, gambling, a new accomplishment, or even a sexual liaison to quench the emptiness and pain. After all, an addiction is any substance or activity we use to medicate the emotional or spiritual pain we're afraid to face.

Our emotions are like the fall colors in New England. They add zest to life. In contrast, emotional insensitivity causes many men to experience life in black and white rather than in living color. My wife and I recently had the opportunity to visit the beautiful little state of Rhode Island to lead a marriage enrichment seminar. We were fortunate to be invited back in the month of October. I grew up in southern California and wasn't used to distinct seasons. My only awareness of "fall colors" was the color of the smog. When we moved to Colorado we learned to look forward to the fall when the aspen leaves turn to gold. It's an awesome sight to behold.

What we hadn't seen in Colorado was the wide range of colors. For years we had heard about the fall colors in New England, and Rhode Island did not disappoint. It was incredible! Bright orange, yellow, gold, green, red, and purple.

Men also pay an enormous relational price for their inability to understand emotions. They become insensitive and blind to their spouse's messages of discouragement, dissatisfaction, and resentment. Cook County Circuit Court Judge Margaret G. O'Malley commented on the behavior of these kinds of men when they are suddenly abandoned by their wives:

> I never used to believe it when a husband would come in after his wife filed and plead that he didn't want a divorce. I'd ask, "where have you been?" Now I realize they don't catch the signals until the point of no return.[2]

Without the passion and intensity our emotions were designed to give us, many men become paralyzed by the very emotions they ignore and deny. They exchange their backbone for a wishbone.

WHAT EXACTLY ARE EMOTIONS?

When I ask men's or women's groups to define emotions I often get as many definitions as there are people. The word emotion is derived from the Latin word *emovare*, which means *to move* or having to do with motion, movement, and energy. I heard one speaker say that emotion could be spelled *E-motion* since emotions are energy in motion.

Dorothy Finkelhor defines them this way:

> Emotions are the motivating forces of our lives, driving us to go ahead, pushing us backward, stopping us completely, determining what we do, how we feel, what we want, and whether we get what we want. Our hates, loves, fears, and what to do about them are

determined by our emotional structure. There is nothing in our lives that does not have the emotional factor as its mainspring. It gives us power or makes us weak, operates for our benefit or to our detriment, for our happiness or confusion.[3]

David wrote, "I am fearfully and wonderfully made" (Psalm 139:14). Nowhere is the delicate complexity of God's creation more evident than in our emotional makeup. Our emotions are complex. The experience of emotions involve sensory, skeletal, motor, autonomic, and cognitive aspects. Our emotions influence the spiritual, social, intellectual, and physical parts of our lives.

THE MOST COMMON EMOTIONS

While some people find it hard to define what emotions are, others find it difficult to name more than five or six emotions. Many emotions swirl around us, however; in fact if you were to complete the sentence "I feel—," using a dictionary you could come up with a list of almost 2,000 words.

In seminars and workshops I've asked participants to make a list of frequently experienced emotions. One group actually produced eighty-two different examples of what they considered emotions. (Interestingly that was a women's group.) Here are eighteen of the most frequently mentioned emotions:

loved	happy	anxious
indifferent	fearful	hurt
frustrated	embarrassed	humiliated
angry	depressed	excited
grieving	scared	lonely
proud	worried	sad

Of the many different emotions men can experience and express I've found that there are eight core emotions that are of special significance: love, loneliness, fear, anger, depression, anxiety, grief, and joy. These are emotions that every man faces throughout his life. Understanding and knowing how to deal with them is critical to becoming healthy, whole, and mature men. We will look at these eight emotions in detail in the following chapters, as well as conflict, a situation that evokes within us the widest range of emotions.

TEN TRUTHS ABOUT OUR EMOTIONS

Before we focus on those eight emotions, it's important for us to be aware of the ten core characteristics of emotions. So far we've seen that for most men emotions have been a wall rather than a door, a barrier rather than a bridge to a new awareness, an increased stability, and deeper relationships. Understanding these ten truths can help us to better appreciate the ways in which emotions impact our lives and help us to cross the bridge to deeper relationships and stability.

1. Everyone, including men, experiences emotions. Not only are all emotions created by God, but everyone has them. It doesn't matter if you are male or female, young or old, black or white, rich or poor—we all experience and, in one way or another, express emotions. Not only do all of us have emotions, but each of us has the capacity to experience the full range of emotions.

One of the most common misbeliefs about emotions is that there are male and female emotions. Over the years I've had several women tell me, in a humorous vein, that men have only two emotions: lust and anger. At the same time I've had several men, in a more serious vein, tell me that women have more emotions than men and that some of those emotions differ markedly.

2. Men have a more difficult time expressing their emotions. Though there aren't any distinctively male and female emotions, it is true that most women are more aware of their emotions and are more expressive of the emotions they experience. The differences become obvious in childhood, and the effects of our childhood training persists into adulthood. A comprehensive review of research related to emotional differences between men and women reveals that men tend to be both less able to identify with and feel others' pain (empathy) and less emotionally expressive than women.[4] However, several studies also revealed that men can learn these important skills as adults.[5]

One of the most devastating consequences of male role socialization is the high incidence among men of at least a mild form of alexithymia, a fancy word for a person's inability to identify and describe his feelings in words.[6] Levant says that this common male problem is

> a result of being socialized to be emotionally stoic. Not only were boys not encouraged to learn to identify and express their emo-

tions, but more pointedly they were told not to. They might have been told that "big boys don't cry." In sports they were told "no pain, no gain," and admonished to learn to "play with pain." These exhortations trained them to be out of touch with their feelings, particularly those feelings on the vulnerable end of the spectrum. As a result of such socialization experiences, men are often genuinely unaware of their emotions. Lacking this emotional awareness, they tend to rely on their cognition, and try to logically deduce how they should feel. They cannot do what is so automatic for most women—simply sense inward, feel the feeling, and let the verbal description come to mind.[7]

Thus we men can learn to express our feelings, but our early training puts us behind women in this important area. We must work at demonstrating and verbalizing our feelings, which we tend to hold in or ignore by years of habit. Here is a goal that we men will find highly rewarding in terms of bringing fulfillment and freedom in our relationships.

3. We can have strong emotions and not be aware of them. Remember Kent? As he and I continued to meet, Kent realized that his struggle with worry and fear began long before he was aware of it. "There were certain activities I stopped doing. At the time I told myself it was because I had other things to do. Now I see that I was afraid that I might fail. At one point I remember [my wife] Laura asking me if I was afraid I couldn't do it. I took her question as an insult." After a brief pause he continued, "I hate to admit it, but she was aware of what was going on inside of me before I was."

I assured Kent that he was in good company. I've talked with hundreds of men who have shared a similar experience. And I'm one of those men. Since we have not been encouraged or trained to recognize and identify emotions, it's no wonder that sometimes they have to hit us in the face for us to realize something's going on.

4. The same emotions can be healthy or unhealthy. One of the most dangerous misconceptions of emotions is that some emotions are good and some aren't. Emotions can be painful or pleasurable. However, emotions aren't good or bad; there are only "bad" or unhealthy expressions of them.

Some people view love as a totally "positive" emotion. However, if we love things rather than people, or if our appreciation for who we are in Christ turns into a narcissistic preoccupation with our uniqueness and giftedness, it can be unhealthy.

Most people view anger as the number one negative emotion. However, as we will see in chapter 5, anger is a God-given emotion that, when understood and used as God intended, has tremendous potential for good. The problem isn't that there are good or bad emotions. It's that when we don't understand our emotions we are more likely to express them in destructive and unhealthy ways.

5. *Emotions vary in their intensity.* Because we have a limited emotional vocabulary, we typically miss the flavor, intensity, and richness of emotions. Emotions are the spice of life. Our limited vocabulary will also restrict our ability to accurately communicate what we are feeling, and the intensity of those feelings, to others.

Below I list five common emotions and some examples of the different ways those emotions can be experienced and expressed: sadness, fear, aversion, anger, and guilt.[8] As you look through the list think of the clarity that would be lost if you only knew how to use those seven words. When we know and use the correct word, we help ourselves and others to understand our feelings.

	Slight	Moderate	Intense	Extreme
SADNESS	disappointed wistful regretful	dejected despondent lonely	sorrowful mournful disconsolate heart-broken	desolated anguished forlorn
FEAR	uneasy worried scared	anxious frightened aghast	dread panic nervous	terror apprehensive alarmed
AVERSION	dislike disrespect	repugnance disdain	contempt disgust revulsion	abhorrence loathing
ANGER	frustrated annoyed irritated	resentful indignant exasperated	bitter wrathful rancorous	raging furious vexed
GUILT	regretful* sheepish sorry	repentant contrite	remorseful reprehensible	self-hatred self-flagellation

* *regretful* can have either one or both meanings, *sadness* or *guilt.*

SOURCE: Dan Jones, *Words for Our Feelings*

6. *Emotions have a physical effect.* I can't count the number of times I've heard a sincere (though sincerely wrong) man say to his spouse, "Honey, it's all in your head." One of the most common misbeliefs about emotions is that "it's all in your head." Emotions impact *all* our body. The experience of emotions involves changes in our central and peripheral nervous systems that include a variety of chemicals and neurotransmitters.

When you experience emotions your heart may beat faster, the pupils in your eyes may dilate, you may have increased perspiration, you may tremble, tears may come to your eyes, you may get goose bumps, and you might experience a tremendous surge of energy—or you could feel totally drained.

Thus emotions are very important to our lives; they are not merely random feelings that affect our work or play. The ways in which we deal with our emotions can have a positive or negative effect on our health. For many years medical research has documented the role that ignoring or misusing our emotions can play in the occurrence and progression of disease. Recently, researchers have been studying the potential role emotions can play in the process of healing.

In *The Complete Guide to Cancer Prevention*, Henry Dreher discusses the results of research that suggest that the inability to express emotions may play a role in weakening the body's defenses. People prone to this problem tend to be self-deprecating, nice to a fault, and unable to express their frustration and anger. He notes that "many people who contract cancer seem to be out of touch with their emotions and their own needs and desires as individuals."[9]

7. *We can make our emotions work for us only when we understand and control them.* It doesn't matter how important or unimportant we think emotions are. It doesn't matter how much we are aware of them. Whether we like it or not, for better or for worse, our emotions play a major role in our lives. One thing is quite clear. If we don't understand and control our emotions, they will control us. Conversely, when we do control our emotions, we can make them work for us. But beware; when we overcontrol our emotions, when we suppress them, those emotions will work against us.

The first time Kent came into my office I started by listening to him. I asked him some questions and rephrased some of his statements to make sure I was understanding him. I could tell that he was discouraged and frustrated. He had said he was struggling with anxiety and fear, but he said little else about his emotions. Most of what he talked about was descriptive. He told me what had happened, when it had happened, what he had done, what his wife Laura had done, and so forth.

Finally, after a brief pause in the conversation I asked, "Kent, could you tell me what you are feeling?" My question clearly caught him off guard. He paused for a moment and then continued, "I wish I knew what I could do to help change the situation."

After a few more minutes I repeated my question, "Kent, what are you feeling?" He had been so focused on trying to figure everything out in his head that he had forgotten to take a look at his heart. He was so busy trying to understand and describe what Laura was feeling he had totally bypassed how *he* was feeling.

Many men suffer from the disease of overcontrolled emotions. Whenever we deny, repress, suppress, or ignore our emotions, they are overcontrolled. When we are out of touch with our emotions, we are out of touch with are true needs. At this point it's easy to become "other-focused" in the unhealthy sense of the word. Gradually we lose sense of who God has created us to be and can either become emotionally numb or dependent on and addicted to others.

It can get to the point that we allow others to define who we are. In these kinds of relationships our significance and security is determined not by who we are in Christ, not by what He accomplished for us on the cross, not by what God has to say about us. The basis for our sense of significance and security is determined by the "significant other" in our lives. We tend to gravitate toward unhealthy relationships where one is dependent and the other is independent. Martha Bireda lists some of the characteristics of these kinds of individuals:[10]

The Self:	The Other:
is emotionally overavailable	is emotionally unavailable
focuses on others	focuses on themselves
gives encouragement, support, money, time, etc.	gives little, if anything, to anyone
needs are rarely met	needs are being met
gives much more than 50 percent	gives much less than 50 percent

The Self (cont.):	The Other (cont.):
gives up or loses power	maintains and gains power
validates the other	validated by others
tolerates inappropriate behavior	often engages in inappropriate behavior
attaches or becomes enmeshed with the other	detaches or moves away (disengages) from the other

With the best of intentions these men become sensitive to everyone's feelings but their own. Even if they are encouraged to be aware and sensitive, it's usually to tune into the emotions and reactions of others. But then they become diverted from examining and expressing their own emotions. Men need to learn how to understand themselves as well as others. They need to be in touch with their own God-given emotions.

The opposite of the overcontrolled man is the emotionally out-of-control man. At times, we hear about such a man on the TV news, for when his anger spills out he can commit deeds of passion and rage. Let the river of emotion get out of control, and it can flood its banks and wreak havoc.

Those kinds of people bring to mind one of my favorite childhood memories—a giant wooden roller coaster. As a young teen growing up in Long Beach, California, I loved visiting the Pike, a large, noisy amusement park located downtown. At the Pike and facing the beach itself, there rose what was billed as "the World's Largest Roller Coaster." Called the "Cyclone Racer" and featuring dual coaster tracks (inside and outside), the roller coaster cost only a quarter to ride. One Saturday, after saving up as many quarters as I could, a friend and I took the bus downtown and rode the "Cyclone Race" over twenty times. It was great, a bone-jarring wild ride with twists, turns, dips, and climbs!

A roller coaster is a lot of fun to ride on. But I wouldn't want to try to live on one of them. Being married to a person who swings from overcontrolled emotions to out-of-control emotions is like trying to live on a roller coaster. When we are overcontrolled or out-of-control we are not allowing our emotions to function as God designed them too. Conversely, being close to a person like that makes life, at best, chaotic.

8. Emotional maturity can help us become more effective. When we overcontrol our emotions or let or emotions spin out of control, we display emotional immaturity. And emotional immaturity levies a high price in our lives. We can pay now or pay later, but we will pay. Whether we are overcontrolled or out of control, we will have less energy, and our creativity will decrease. Furthermore, when we are emotionally immature, our decision-making becomes impaired, we become more negative and critical, and our awareness is limited. We often will become preoccupied.

Emotional maturity can help us become more effective. Alice Isen, a psychologist at the University of Maryland, has spent more than seventeen years studying the ways in which positive emotions affect the way people think. At the annual meeting of the American Association for the Advancement of Science in 1987 Isen presented research results suggesting that positive emotions not only make people more helpful and generous toward others, but appear to improve thinking processes such as judgment, problem-solving, decision-making, and creativity.

"Good feelings seem capable of bringing out our better nature socially and our creativity in thinking and problem-solving," Isen said. Thus good feelings can be a source of interpersonal cooperativeness and personal health and growth. Her research has implications for any situation where you want to bring out the best in someone. "Positive emotions," Isen says, "encourage people to look beyond the normal problem-solving method to try different options."[11]

9. *Shared/expressed emotions are an essential ingredient in healthy relationships.* We men aren't very good at expressing our emotions. Most of us weren't taught much about emotions. Talking about emotions is like learning a foreign language. Not only is it new and different, it seems opposite to the way things should be.

Kent was shocked when Laura mentioned the word divorce. They had been married for more than thirty-five years and had four sons; he thought things were going great. With tears in his eyes Kent recalled Laura's words, "Although we've been married for close to forty years I don't feel like I even know you. And I know that you don't really know me." Kent blurted out, "How could you be married to someone for this long and then say you don't know them?"

I told Kent that people can get acquainted by sharing facts, ideas, and opinions. The more information you have the more you know about someone. But knowing about someone is not the same as truly knowing them. To become really intimate, people have to open up their heart, share their deepest longings and desires, risk exposing their doubts, fears, and insecurities. In other words, share their deepest emotions. Like many men, Kent had a hard time expressing deep emotion.

If we want to become the men God would have us to be, if we want to have deep, meaningful, and successful relationships, we must allow God to work in us to help us become whole men. Christ died in order to renew us, to help us recover from the effects of sin and our developmental disabilities, to restore us to the place He designed for us.

God wants to renew our mind. In 1 Corinthians 2:16 Paul states that "we have the mind of Christ." Romans 12:2 tells us that we can be "transformed by the renewing of your mind." In Philippians 2:5 we are challenged to "have this attitude in yourselves which was also in Christ Jesus."

God wants to heal our emotions. In Romans 14:1 we are commanded to "pursue love." In Ephesians 4:26 we see that with God's help we can be angry and not sin. In Ephesians 5:1–2 we are told that we can be imitators of God as we "walk in love, just as Christ also loved you."

God wants to direct our choices. Romans 13:12 instructs us to "lay aside the deeds of darkness and put on the armor of light." Ephesians 4:22–24 tells us that we can choose to "lay aside the old self" and "put on the new self, which in the likeness of God has been created in righteousness and holiness of the truth." In Philippians 3:13 we are encouraged not to dwell on the things of the past but to choose to reach forward to what lies ahead.

Kent had come into my office confused, defeated, and depressed. He was starting to see what had brought him to this crisis. He felt a bit of encouragement as he realized that there was some hope, both for him and for his marriage. Yet, he said, "It's hard not to kick myself for being such an idiot. Its hard not to focus on how stupid I was."

I said "Kent, someone once said 'Yesterday is a canceled check. Tomorrow is a promissory note. Today is cash. Spend it wisely.' Satan wants you to dwell on your past mistakes or live in the future. He wants you to wallow in what was, or become fixated on what might be. He'll to anything to keep you out of the present, the here and now. God wants you to learn from your past mistakes and be encouraged by your future with Him."

10. Emotional maturity is one of the marks of a mature man. I have never met a man who had true spiritual maturity who was emotionally immature. Maturity involves the whole man: his mind, will, and emotions. I've known a number of men who, on the outside, appeared to be spiritually mature. They had tremendous head knowledge, they proudly abstained from any outward form of sinful behavior, and some were gifted communicators and teachers. They appeared to be paragons of virtue. But in each case they had written off as insignificant and ignored one-third of their God-given personality, their emotions.

In Scripture Moses is a great example of the long-term consequences of ignoring your emotions. As a young man and throughout his life we find that Moses struggled with his anger. At times it doesn't seem to have been a problem, but at other times it flared out-of-control, controlled his behavior, and led him to do things he later regretted. Ultimately his out-of-control anger caused him to strike the rock and disqualified him from being able to enter the promised land.

Yes, real men have feelings. And when we men are maturing spiritually, our feelings can mature too. And that's an essential part of becoming a man's man.

TAKE ACTION

God wants us to grow up and become mature men. True maturity involves both head knowledge and heart knowledge. True maturity involves becoming conformed to Christ in our mind, our will, and our emotions. Here are a few simple suggestions to help you toward emotional and spiritual growth.

1. Recognize the importance of your emotions. Develop a vocabulary for emotions, especially the vulnerable ones (such as hurt, sadness, disappointment, fear, rejection, and abandonment) and the tender ones (sensitivity, warmth, appreciation, and affection). Take an emotional inventory. With the help of your wife, children, friends, answer the following questions:

    (1) What emotions are the easiest for you to experience/express?

(2) What emotions are the hardest for you to experience/express?

(3) What emotions cause you the most difficulty?

2. Read through the four gospels. As you read through the gospels, look at the role of emotions in the life of Christ. What are some of the emotions that Christ experienced? How did He choose to express them?

3. Name that feeling. I've worked with many men who, in the beginning of learning how to identify and understand their emotions, found it easier to write them down. It's hard for us to understand what we can't or don't identify.

Take out a sheet of paper whenever you have an emotional response and describe what you are feeling. When you write it down you don't have to worry about what someone else is going to think about you, about being criticized, or making yourself vulnerable. Thus, in this early stage, you are more likely to be honest.

I worked with a farmer in Nebraska who carried around a little tablet he'd received from a seed corn company. Every time he experienced something he thought might be anything even close to an emotion he wrote it down. When I saw him two weeks later he was surprised how many emotions he had experienced. "I can't believe that I've gone through this much of my life substantially unaware of something this significant." Writing it down is important. Many men feel free to let loose on paper what might be difficult to express in a conversation.

4. Think out loud . . . with a friend. When you find yourself sitting at your desk or driving in your car and you realize that you are preoccupied with feelings, thoughts, and decisions, find another "safe" person and "think out loud" with him. Just say whatever comes to your mind. Don't edit it. Don't think about what it sounds like. Don't worry about the fact that it might not sound logical. Don't focus on what the other person might be thinking. Just start talking. Begin with issues that aren't too personal and gradually you'll be able to talk about those that are.

5. Use the ABC method. One of the main complaints women have about men is that we don't talk enough. "If something major is happening at Tim's office I may be the last to hear about it!" one woman exclaimed. Another wife observed, "Al may tell me what happened, but that's probably all I'll hear."

There are three aspects of experiencing an event:

A = what happened
B = your feelings about what happened
C = how what has happened might affect us

Some men don't even share the "A." Many men stop with A and aren't aware of or choose to ignore the B and C. If you want to better understand your emotions and how they influence the rest of your life, you can consciously choose to go on to B and C.

By expressing your feelings about the event and your thoughts about how the event may affect you (for example, loss of job or a hurt relationship), you may not solve the problem. But afterward you will be much clearer about what you are feeling, and the friend who listens will be more able to support and pray for you.

4

FEAR

The passengers, seeking to escape a frigid week in Washington, D.C., could hardly wait to depart for Miami, but the jetliner was still on the ground due to bad weather. As the passengers fidgeted in their seats and the snow flurries tapered, the first officer noticed a thick layer of frost building on the airliner's wings. He began to think that they should have the plane deiced once more. There was still time to taxi back to the hangar for the procedure.

Finally he turned to the captain and asked, "Want me to tell ground control that we're 'temporarily indisposed'?"

The captain didn't respond. Finally, after a brief pause, the first officer began to minimize his concern. "It's not really that cold," he said. He and the captain began making jokes about being frightened by the bad weather.

A half-hour later their Air Florida jet took off. But as it started to climb, ice buildup on the wings hampered the ascent. Quickly the plane lost altitude, went out of control, and crashed into the Potomac River, less than a mile from National Airport.

Based on their recorded conversation, the captain and first officer seemed to have difficulty acknowledging, discussing, and dealing with the potentially healthy and appropriate emotion of fear. It impaired their judgment, hindered their decision-making ability, and caused them to endanger the lives of the passengers they were responsible for.

A man's inability to deal with the emotion of fear rarely leads to situations as catastrophic as the 1982 Air Florida crash, but the price for not understanding and dealing with our God-given emotions, especially the emotion of fear, is always too high.

Now to be honest, I don't like fear. I don't like what it feels like to be afraid. I don't like thinking about what others might think of me if they knew I was afraid. I don't just want to appear strong, I want to be strong. I don't want to merely appear confident, I want to feel confident. But somehow fear and strength and confidence don't seem to fit together. At least not very easily!

For many years I thought that I was one of the few men who felt this way. But over the years I've discovered through conversations with a few close male friends as well as with a wide variety of men in my counseling practice that I'm far from alone. Fear is a frequently experienced yet infrequently identified emotion.

Real men have emotions. Fear is an emotion. Therefore, real men experience fear. Fortunately God's Word can help us understand and learn how to appropriately utilize this God-given and potentially valuable emotion.

From Genesis to Revelation there are hundreds of references to various kinds of fear. In Genesis 3:10 we read that the fear of Adam and Eve caused them to hide from God. Unhealthy responses to fear have caused people to hide ever since. In Revelation we read that in the end times many will be afraid of what they see happening around them.

David experienced fear as he hid from the rage of Saul. After seeing God rain down fire from heaven and destroy the false prophets of Baal, Elijah's fear of Jezebel caused him to run and hide. His unhealthy response to fear led to his severe depression and his desire to die. Peter's fear caused him to deny three times the Christ he had defended in the garden. The disciples' fear caused them to run and hide after the crucifixion of their Lord.

KINDS OF FEAR

Fear is an unpleasant and often strong feeling caused by anticipation or awareness of threat or danger. Beyond a doubt, fear is one of our most uncomfortable emotions. Strong fear can consume your entire perspective and make it difficult for you to focus on anything else.

Most men find it more comfortable to express anger than to express their fears; it's easier to experience and express anger. That's why anger and fear often go hand in hand. For many people anger is an automatic and unconscious response to the emotion of fear. As you uncover your hidden fears you may discover one of the major contributors to your anger.

Fear comes from the Old English *faer*, which means sudden calamity or danger. It suggests a state of alarm or dread. If it is strong enough it can immobilize you. It prepares you for a key response: flight, fight, or freeze. All three responses expend energy, and you will discover your body tenses when you become fearful. But at the same time, when you are afraid you're confronted with your limitations, vulnerability, and helplessness. Anger gives you only the feeling or illusion of power and control.

When we allow our fear to control us, we tend to rehearse in our minds all of the terrible, awful, catastrophic things that might be happening. We spend our energy dealing with what might be and then don't have much energy to deal with what actually is.

Rational Fear

Fear can be rational, but sometimes it's irrational. *Normal or rational fear is a healthy and valuable emotion.* It serves an invaluable protective function. It alerts us to and helps us stay away from dangerous places, things, or people. It can be invaluable in time of crisis. If we've learned how to use it, healthy fear can provide us energy and serve as a reminder to take our time, think through what we are doing, to not panic, and, finally, to act.

Several years ago a couple of friends and I decided to climb Devils Tower, a stump-shaped cluster of volcanic rock columns rising out of the plains of northeast Wyoming. Rick, Gene, and I had been planning the climb for months and were rewarded with clear skies the morning of the climb.

Early in the morning we started, energetic and enthusiastic, and carefully made our way up that vertical wall of granite. By midday it was 70 degrees, the skies a light blue, and we were enjoying a great climb. We noticed a few clouds passing over us during the early afternoon but thought little about them as we focused on our climb.

We were almost near the top when suddenly a storm appeared above us. It had come over the Tower from our blind side and so we had no warning. We could feel the temperature drop; within an hour it had fallen into the low 40s. A cold rain began, and soon the rain turned into light hail. We were roped together, but as we tried to continue the rock became harder to hold onto, and the vegetation that grew in various places on the rock became as slick as ice.

We were tired, exhausted, and cold. It didn't take long for fear to set in. Gene felt the muscles in his arms and hands contract; he couldn't move his fingers and began to panic. And we all realized the truth: the only way to the top, a vertical route, was too slippery to navigate; the only way down was to rappel down wet ropes and on slippery rock.

As we huddled, anchored together on a small ledge near the top of the rock, our fear alerted us to the danger of the situation. Our blood was pumping, and, though we were tiring, our minds became alert. Our fear gave us the presence of mind to stop, catch our breath, assess the situation, and discuss our strategy. We helped Gene work through his panic and slowly and carefully began our descent. In a descent that took what seemed like hours we made it safely to the bottom and kissed the wonderful ground we were on. We were bruised, exhausted, emotionally drained, but in one piece. Our God-given emotion of fear had served us well that day.

Irrational Fear

Irrational fear is not helpful as is normal fear. Instead it involves an exaggeration and overreaction to a normal fear. When we don't learn how to listen to the voice of normal fear, when we ignore its "caution" signs, when we repress, suppress, deny, or ignore its alarm, we become more vulnerable to developing irrational fears. For example, an appropriate fear of rattlesnakes can become generalized to all snakes. A concern with flying in a single-engine plane during questionable weather can lead to a fear of flying in the safest jetliner that cruises above the clouds and can operate on autopilot.

Phobia

Phobia comes from the Greek word *phobos*, meaning flight, and from the deity of the same name who provoked panic and fear in his enemies. A phobia is a persistent fear of a person, object, or idea that clearly doesn't justify fear. A part of you knows it is absurd and ridiculous, but you can't overcome it.

When someone has a phobia, his fear is out of proportion to the situation. It is beyond voluntary control; it cannot be reasoned or explained away. He knows his fear is unrealistic but he can't seem to stop it. People who are phobic live on the edge of panic. They become hypervigilant, always on the lookout for their particular fear. They develop what is called "preplanned avoidance," trying to avoid fear by avoiding any suspicious setting. Their entire life can become structured around their phobia. Over time they can become prisoners of their phobia.

A good example of this is agoraphobia. This describes fears of going into public places such as cars, buses, shops, crowds, theaters, and churches. Though rare in children, agoraphobia binds thousands of adults, typically beginning between the ages of eighteen and thirty-five. It often develops after a major upset or crisis in a person's life such as serious illness, death of a loved one, an unpleasant scene in a public place, a life-threatening experience.

It often begins with recurring anxiety attacks while away from home. The intensity of the panic can be such that the person becomes glued to the same spot until the panic subsides. By this time the person wants to go back to the safety of his home. Initially the person may avoid certain places. Some refuse to drive more than ten miles away from their home. Others won't go anywhere alone. And a few actually become prisoners of their home. They come to believe that nowhere is safe.

If you've never experienced a phobia or don't know someone who has, you may conclude that it's simple to overcome. In fact, many who have phobias know their actions are "irrational," so they are afraid to share their feelings with others. They can become even more isolated and start to think that they are the only ones who have ever felt that way.

WHY MEN FEAR THE EMOTION OF FEAR

You may be thinking, "Well, if I have a fear, I should confront it like a man and beat it." But you must remember that the emotion of fear isn't the problem. Fear is a God-intended, God-designed, and God-given emotion. It is a feeling God gives to help us during times of threat and danger. The adrenaline surge that accompanies fear lets us flee or fight danger—or even to rappel down the side of a cliff to safety. The problem is not our fear, but what we do with it, or what we let it do to us.

One of the reasons fear can become a problem is that most of us men not only don't understand it but have spent much of our lives ignoring or trying to avoid it. Why? Many of us have bought into the myth that real men aren't afraid. For instance, think of some of the words you've heard associated with masculinity: bold, brave, gallant, undaunted, courageous, intrepid, valiant, adventurous, daring, and heroic. And, yes, fearless.

By running from our fears or pretending we have no fears, we fail to grow. As we'll see later, the best way to overcome fears is to face them. When we don't face our fears we stay stuck, unable to grow on the inside. Though we seek to be what we *think* we're supposed to be, we only hinder God's ability to help us to become who He's *designed* us to be—honest men who confront and deal with our feelings.

By not understanding and learning how to listen to our fear we can become desensitized to the protective warnings our fear was designed to provide. We don't grow in our ability to discriminate between legitimate and irrational fears. We don't learn how to gauge the seriousness of the potential threat.

God designed us to understand and be in control of our emotions. When we allow fear to control and dominate our lives it can lead to increased anxiety and to feelings of hopelessness and helplessness. When we give in to unhealthy fear we actually feed it, and it becomes harder to deal with.

Such fear can begin to affect our behavior and our actions. Eventually it will have a negative effect on our health. It can lessen the quality and shorten the longevity of our lives. The story has been told of Death walking toward a city. A man stopped Death and asked, "What are you going to do?"

"I'm going to kill 10,000 people," Death replied.

"That's horrible."

"That's the way it is," Death said. "That's what I do."

So the day passed. That evening the man met Death coming back, and he said, "You said you were only going to kill 10,000 people, but I heard that 70,000 were killed."

"You're right, 70,000 were killed," Death said. "But I only killed 10,000. Worry and fear killed the others."

WHAT MEN FEAR

Earlier we mentioned the unusual fear of being in public places, agoraphobia. But other fears strike men and women alike. There are personal and social fears. Fears of criticism, loss of love, old age, ill health, poverty, death, failure, insecurity, and the future are only a few that can unsettle us.

Some of our fears have fancy names, but they represent troubling aversions we have developed. You or a friend may be frightened by lightning (astrophobia), flying in an airplane (aviaphobia), bees (melissophobia), or darkness (nycotophobia). If a friend suffers from ophidiophobia, he just can't stand snakes; and someone who has brontophobia cringes when he hears the loud claps of thunder that rumble across the darkening sky.

Men and women can share many of the same fears, but some significant differences exists in the kinds of things that cause a man or woman to be afraid. A woman's fears tend to center more around relationships, abandonment, loss of love, isolation. Women don't have an overpowering need to be brave or courageous. That's not to say they lack courage or bravery. But those two virtues are not the standard by which they determine whether or not they are "real women."

What about men? Remember, one of the key myths of masculinity is that "real men are not afraid." Yet fear is a normal emotion that all men experience. So what does this myth do to them? If you believe men can't be afraid, and yet you feel fear, you must pretend you're strong. So you stuff, repress, deny, ignore, or otherwise hide from your fears. As a result, what we show people is often radically different from our true inner world.

In contrast to women, we men fear anything that robs us of our power and control, anything that might make us look less like a man. Typically this means we avoid anything that shows lack of courage or our being fearful. To be a coward is to be a wimp, not a man.

Though we can encounter physically threatening situations, most of us will feel fear when we are threatened with criticism, vulnerability, exposure of our weakness, rejection, or failure. We also fear put-downs, being abandoned or ignored, and losing control. Willard Gaylin summarizes well the nature of a man's fears:

> No new element of danger need be introduced into a man's life to make him less secure. Simply raise doubts about his strength, reli-

ability, or stature, diminish his self-respect or self-confidence, and the identical environment will seem more hazardous. It is the assault on self-esteem and self-confidence that particularly enhances our sense of vulnerability and impotence.

Men are most likely to feel threatened when they sense disapproval, deprivation, exploitation or manipulation, frustration, betrayal, or humiliation. These are the lions and tigers that stalk our civilized environment, and men have sharpened their senses so that they detect their signs everywhere.

Fear and anger were intended to serve as responses to threats to our survival. To our survival—not to our pride, status, position, manhood, or dignity.[1]

Our sexual identity and response often are associated with manliness. As a result, many men fear failure in their sexual ability. Since junior high we were told that virility, sexual ability, and masculinity were related. When some men notice a change in their level of sexual desire, their physical strength, or appearance, they may become anxious. It's easy for that anxiety to lead to fear; and if we let that fear take control, we really have problems.

Most of us have developed good skills at hiding our problems. We've learned how to fake it, how to look good, how to deny our wounds and hide our pain. However, that's difficult to do in the sexual arena. And for good reason. Several years ago one of my associates showed me an article from a popular women's magazine in which women discussed how they faked orgasm. Yet it would be impossible for a man to write an article on "How To Fake an Erection."

Indeed, at some time in their lives most married men experience some anxiety over their sexual ability. It's easy for this "performance anxiety" to turn into a fear of an inability to perform. If that fear gets out of control it can easily lead to impotence, which strikes a devastating blow to the male ego.

Impotence can take a number of forms, including the inability to get or sustain an erection, premature ejaculation, and retarded ejaculation. Years of research has demonstrated that most sexual dysfunction does not have a physiological basis. A central component to these three forms of impotence is the same: the controlling effect of powerful, dominating, and often unidentified primary emotions. The first is fear. Being fearful leads to impotence, and then to the fear of impotence.

One of the first steps in helping men overcome sexual dysfunction is to help them understand, identify, and deal with their emotions. As men learn to identify their fears and confront their irrational anxiety, the sexual drive is allowed to emerge. In treatment, we assume that confronting the man's irrational anxiety will allow the sexual drive to emerge.

After fears about our sexuality, we often have fears of financial failure. Since one of man's primary roles is that of provider (for himself and a family), the ability to adequately provide affects his sense of value and worth. Gaylin compares this fear to that of the ancient man who lost all protection and whose very survival was threatened.

> The person who destroys me financially, who takes my money, is the modern equivalent of the person who, in a previous age, extinguished my fire, raided my cave, contaminated my well, ravaged my food supply, burned my barn or stole my horse. They used to hang horse thieves. That seems incredible these days, but not to the frontiersman who knew that the survival of his family might depend on that horse. The greatest perceived threat to a man's sense of security (with the possible exception of an attack on his sexual pride) is an assault on his financial structure.[2]

Another fear that tends to plague men much more than women is the fear of being "found out." It's the fear of someday someone getting behind the facade, behind the persona or public self, and discovering the vulnerable, frightened little boy inside. We fear people will find out that we fear!

Remember Dorothy's second meeting with the grand wizard in *The Wizard Of Oz*? Dorothy has defeated the wicked witch and successfully led her three impaired male friends to see the wonderful, all-powerful, and all-wise wizard. They have incredible expectations of what he will be able to do. He is their hero. They are counting on him.

When Toto pulls back the curtain, the real wizard is exposed. He is a short, overweight, fallible, and not-too-impressive specimen of masculinity. And, even worse, he is shown to be a fraud. "You are a terrible man!" Dorothy exclaims in a mixture of anger and despair.

"No," he replies, "I'm not a terrible man, I'm just a terrible wizard."

Many of us men are like the wizard. We're not terrible men. However, we are human, fallible, and imperfect. We don't always know what to do. We're not necessarily as confident and secure as we appear—and sometimes we're afraid.

Recently one of my patients who had come for therapy in the midst of a crisis said, "I've made tremendous strides in my career. I'm successful, I'm rich, I'm powerful, and I am much more independent than I ever dreamed I would be. But when life forces me to slow down and look at how I feel about myself and my important relationships, I find that I am still being controlled by the same fears and insecurities that have ruled my life since I was probably too young to remember."

And then, after a pause of several minutes he looked me straight in the eyes, wiped away a bit of moisture from his own eyes and, with the hint of a smile and a heavy sigh of relief, said, "I thank God that He loves me enough to have brought me to this place. I think that maybe for the first time in my life I'm on the verge of discovering what it really means to be a success. To be free from the tyranny of the oughts and shoulds and expectations. To be free to discover who God made me to be and will help me become."

WHAT MEN DO WHEN THEY'RE AFRAID

What do men replace the emotion of fear with? What do *you* use to numb your fears? There are three primary responses to fear: flight, fight, and freeze.

Flight

The flight response causes us to run. We can run from the fear in two different ways. When Elijah was faced with the threats of Jezebel, he took his eyes off what he had seen God do, focused on her threats, became overcome by his fear, and he ran.

We can also run from the fear by running to something that will either numb or take our mind off the fear. By immersing ourselves in something else we are no longer aware of feeling the fear, or perhaps anything else. We can hide in alcohol, drugs, work, television, pornography, increased work, joining more organizations, working out, or golfing more.

Fight

The *fight response* causes us to go on the attack. The rush of adrenaline causes us to feel powerful. We become distracted from our pain to someone else's problem.

This common response to fear can serve to distance people. This increases our illusion of safety; we think out of sight is out of mind. The further away people are the safer we feel. If they're not too close they won't discover our blind spot, they can't remind us of our fear, and they can't hurt us; so we fight.

The fight response often involves the emotion of anger. Fear produces a sense of helplessness and vulnerability. Anger gives us the feeling or illusion of control and power. Besides, that anger seems much more masculine than fear.

Freeze

The *final response is to freeze.* Sometimes our fear can become so overpowering that it immobilizes us. Our problem-solving skills are compromised. Our decision-making becomes impaired.

Unfortunately the flight, fight, and freeze responses are not God's way for us to deal with the emotion of fear. In fact, these responses tend to exacerbate and increase the problem rather than diminish it.

HEALTHY WAYS TO DEAL WITH OUR FEARS

Before

To fight or flee fear is ineffective. And, of course, freezing in the face of fear is useless. What, then, are healthy ways to deal with our fears? We can take several steps before, during, and after fear strikes. Each has its foundation in the spiritual resources we possess if we are followers of God.

1. Have faith. If we have faith in God, we should remind ourselves of what it means that we have been made in the image of God. God has given us a mind, will, and emotions that He designed to function together in harmony.

Our faith is based on what the Bible declares about God and our relationship with Him. Therefore, we should become familiar with God's desire for us to depend on Him when fears arise. Here are just a few verses from God's Word about dealing with fear:

"Even though I walk through the valley of the shadow of death, I fear no evil; for Thou art with me" (Psalm 23:4).

"God is our refuge and strength, a very present help in trouble" (Psalm 46:1).

"Cast your burden upon the Lord, and He will sustain you; He will never allow the righteous to be shaken" (Psalm 55:22).

"Behold, God is my salvation, I will trust and not be afraid" (Isaiah 12:2).

"Do not fear, for I am with you; do not anxiously look about you, for I am your God. I will strengthen you, surely I will help you, surely I will uphold you with my gracious hand" (Isaiah 41:10).

"He has said to me, 'My grace is sufficient for you, for power is perfected in weakness.' Therefore I am well content with weaknesses, with insults, with distresses, with persecutions, with difficulties, for Christ's sake; for when I am weak, then I am strong" (2 Corinthians 12:9–10).

"For God has not given us a spirit of timidity, but of power and love and discipline" (2 Timothy 1:7).

One preacher has said it well:

> Christ does not change; he is the same yesterday and today and forever. And the truth of His teaching doesn't change either. You can count on it, indeed. You can stake your life on it.
>
> The most wonderful thing that can happen to any of us is to have that most profound of all experiences—to know Jesus Christ personally. You can hear about Him all your life and never really know Him. You can believe that He lived and respect Him and honor Him as a great historical figure and still only know Him academically.
>
> But when at last you find Him and experience His reality, when for you He comes out of the stained-glass windows and out of history and becomes your personal Savior, then you can walk through all manner of darkness and pain and trouble and be unafraid.[3]

2. Seek fellowship. The second step is to move out from our foundation in who we are in Christ and what He has given us and reach out to friends. When we are afraid we need our friends. Fear thrives in isolation.

When we experience fear, our thinking tends to be more negative than positive. We often give power to our limitations, to what we can't do, and we forget about the positive possibilities. A great example of this is Moses' response to God's call to lead the children of Israel out of Egypt and into the promised land (Exodus 3–6). When God first calls Moses, this would-be deliverer panics. On five different occasions he gives God five different reasons why he can't do it, why he's the wrong man, why God needs to find someone else.

Finally Moses agrees to do it. But when Pharaoh commands more bricks and orders the people to collect straw themselves, the people turn against Moses. In response Moses tells God, "O Lord, why hast Thou brought harm to this people? Why didst Thou ever send me? Ever since I came to Pharaoh to speak in Thy name, he has done harm to this people; and Thou has not delivered Thy people at all" (Exodus 5: 22–23). That's his way of saying, "Lord, I've had it! This is the last straw!"

God's response? He does for Moses what He often uses our friends to help us do. He helps this man put things in perspective, by having Moses focus on His nature and power. In Exodus 6:6 God tells Moses: "I am the Lord," "I will bring you out," "I will deliver you," and "I will also redeem you." Then He reminds Moses of four promises: "I will take you for my people . . . I will be your God . . . . I will bring you to the land which I swore to give to Abraham, Isaac, and Jacob . . . I will give it to you" (vv. 7–8).

The very real problems that Moses faced caused him to lose his perspective. He only saw the problems. He forgot about the promises. Friends help us to put our minds on the proper perspective and chase our fears. They can remind us of resources that we may have forgotten. They can enlarge our perspective and help us to see our fear in light of the big picture.

During

3. *Admit your fear.* When a situation actually evokes feelings of fear, what can you do? First, *admit* that you are afraid. This is much easier said than done, at least at first. Many of us men are so out of touch with our emotions that we're not sure when we are experiencing fear. Unless the fear is dramatic and overpowering, we may not even be aware of it.

Sometimes fear expresses itself in small, subtle ways. There may be an unsettled feeling, a twitch in an eye or muscle, or a sensing of a need to get busier. Or you may have stronger signals:

a pounding heart, increased perspiration and respiration. The prophet Habakkuk's response was even more dramatic. "I heard, and my [whole inner self] trembled, my lips quivered at the sound. Rottenness enters into my bones and under me—down to my feet—I tremble" (Habakkuk 3:16a, AMP*).

Even if they are aware of it, many men find it difficult to admit. Keen has written that "as we push deeper into the interior of a man's psyche, we discover that in back of the facade of toughness and control there is an entire landscape of undifferentiated fears, with all manner of beasts . . . lurking in the shadows. And to win our soul or rescue our self from its entrapment in our personality, we have to do battle with a legion of fears we never knew we had."[4]

Admitting our fear simply involves saying to ourselves, God, and perhaps others, "I am afraid." It sounds so simple, so innocuous, and yet there can be tremendous freedom in having the strength and courage to admit that we are experiencing fear.

The next part of this step is to identify your fear. Ask yourself, "What am I afraid of?" For many men this may take some time. One exercise many men have found helpful is to journal their fears. That's right, keep a record of your fears. In the journal you can record the following: (1) when you experienced the fear (is there a pattern?), (2) how long the fear lasts, (3) how intense it is, and (4) what you are aware of being afraid of.

In the journal entry, also indicate the specific characteristics of your different fears. For example, if you are afraid of dogs, are you more afraid of certain breeds, sizes, colors? Are you more comfortable at a certain distance from them? What are some of your past experiences with similar fears? Are there any promises that apply to these fears?

Then as you look at your journal entry, ask yourself, "Are these fears healthy or unhealthy? Are they rational or irrational?" You will discover that the mere act of admitting you have fear and identifying the fear will cause it to diminish.

It's kind of like being afraid of the ghost in the closet. The longer you sit and think about it, contemplate its color, size, and temperament, the more you feed the fear and the stronger it grows. Once you take the effort to grab a flashlight and look in the closet you can see that there is no ghost.

* *The Amplified Bible.*

4. Face your fear. If your fear is a legitimate fear you are ready to face it. You've laid a strong spiritual foundation. You are aware of the resources God has given you. You know you aren't alone. You have enlisted the support of your friends. You have admitted that you are afraid and have identified the fear.

Now it's time to ask yourself, "What can I do to eliminate or decrease my fear?" Usually the solution will involve facing the fear in some way. Face it, but face it gradually. Don't rush into it. Go slow. Let your confidence build. Reach out for support and encouragement.

Gaining the victory over fear can take time. Remember David's advice in Psalm 27:14: "Wait for the Lord; Be strong, and let your heart take courage; Yes, wait for the Lord."

Over the years I've realized that there is no such thing as fearlessness. There is only walking through fear with the courage that comes from God. As you begin to face the fear you will find new strength and courage. Most of the time you will discover that the reality of what you found was not nearly as bad as you thought it would be.

A classic example of finding deliverance from our fear is Jacob's dealing with his fear of Esau (Genesis 32). A major falling out had occurred between the two brothers, prompted by Jacob usurping Esau of his birthright. After being away for many years and rearing his own family, Jacob decided to return home; so he sent a message to his brother Esau that he was returning. When Jacob's messengers returned, they reported that Esau was coming to meet him with four hundred men. At this point the Bible tells us that "Jacob was greatly afraid and distressed" (32:7).

Now remember that years earlier Jacob had tricked his older brother Esau out of his birthright and Esau had threatened to kill him. Now he hears that Esau is coming out to greet him with four hundred men. What would you think? No doubt, Jacob realized the truth: "After years of my deceiving and scheming, my brother has finally decided that enough is enough and he's coming to pay me back." For perhaps the first time in his life Jacob's quick wit, clever mind, and deceitful heart weren't enough to rescue him. He was afraid. For the first time he realized his need for God.

Later on we find that Jacob wrestled with God. Have you been wrestling with God over control of a certain area of your life? Have you been struggling with fear? Maybe you have allowed fear to influence your thought life, distort your perspective, and control your decisions. Jacob allowed God to break his self-reliance and transform his fearful heart, and in that process he experienced the blessing that he had at first tried to buy and steal. He trusted God, faced his fear, and came out victorious.

In the New Testament we read about how Timothy overcame his fear. The apostle Paul had left him in Ephesus as the leader of the church there. Timothy's job was to combat heretics, to order the church's worship, to select and train its elders, to regularize the relief and ministry to its widows, and to teach the Christian faith.

He was a young man, probably in his early thirties, and had been given a lot of responsibility and authority. He was prone to illness and was fairly timid. Apparently Timothy was a bit overwhelmed by it all and had some fears and apprehensions. Paul reminds Timothy of his heritage, his call, and then he says, "For God has not given us a spirit of timidity, but of power and love and discipline" (2 Timothy 1:7). There's the resource for all followers of Christ: the Holy Spirit within, who gives us courage (power) to love and, when necessary, reprove.

After

5. *Find the lesson God wanted you to learn.* One of the most delightful aspects of being a Christian is the knowledge that, whatever happens to us, whatever our success or failure, we can learn and grow from it.

Today men are standing at the threshold of a frontier, full of new and uncharted territory. Oh, some may have gone before us but, still, that was them. This frontier needs to be cleared of obstacles. There are emotional wild beasts that must be tamed. They are different. The fear of the the unknown keeps us prisoners of what might be.

After Rick, Gene, and I had recovered from our near catastrophe on Devils Tower, we asked each other, "What can we learn from our experience?" "What could we have done differently?" "What will we do different next time?" Taking the time to evaluate our experience allowed us to learn from it.

TAKE ACTION

If Romans 8:28 is true, if God can "cause all things to work together for good," then He can even use the emotion of fear to help us learn and grow.

If you've gotten this far I assume you've read through the five steps. However, if you are like most readers, you may not have *worked* through them. I encourage you to set aside thirty minutes within the next two days, and work through a specific fear you have struggled with. You need only your Bible, a pen or pencil, and some writing paper to list that fear, study Scripture, and plan how to implement the five steps.

You may be surprised at how effective these simple steps can be. It's great to be a hearer of the Word, but it's even better to be a doer!

5

ANGER

"I would never admit this to my wife, but I've spent most of my life struggling with the emotion of anger."

"Anger? I can't remember the last time I got angry."

"I don't get angry very often, but when I do I get out of control. I say and do things I'm ashamed of. I can't believe it's me."

"The Bible clearly says that we are to put away anger and with God's help I have been successful doing just that."

Men typically have one of two responses to anger. They are either struggling with this emotion and losing, or they are struggling and winning. Either way most men struggle with anger. And they want to know how to handle it. During a national men's conference in July 1992, more than 12,000 men sat in a college football stadium late one Saturday afternoon after a full day of meetings just to learn more about how to understand and deal with their anger.

Author and counselor John Trent recently described to me a weekend men's conference he led with his colleague, Gary Smalley. They asked the three hundred men to list eight areas they wanted to work on. Trent and Smalley then asked the men to narrow their lists from eight areas to the top three. Those three were (1) how to honor my wife and kids, (2) how to handle finances and financial decisions and, (3) how to deal with anger.

Next they asked the group of about three hundred men to choose the topic of greatest interest and need and attend the workshop on dealing with that topic.

"Guess how many men went to the workshop on anger?" John asked me.

I paused and then made my guess, "Oh, 150?"

"Wrong!" John replied. Close to 250 of the men selected the group on anger.

Imagine, all but fifty of the men attending wanted help in dealing with their anger. And based on John's experience with men across the United States, he concluded, "Most men want to understand and deal with their anger."

If we are ever going to be able to handle our anger we must first understand this emotion. The less we understand our anger, the more destructive it can be. At its worst, anger contributes to wife abuse and child abuse. Men who batter their wives tend to be men who avoid feelings, who are rarely in touch with any emotion other than out-of-control anger. Often the man has himself been a victim of child-rape or other physical abuse, or had alcoholic or passive parents. Now as an adult, he still has not had the opportunity to grieve, express sadness, and work through those traumas.

SOME DEFINITIONS

Before we determine the causes of our anger and learn how to deal with this emotion, let's consider the most fundamental question, "What is anger?" We will try to define the term. Why do I write "try"? Because anger is one of the most complex and multidimensional emotions, and thus it is difficult to define.

If we consult our friend Webster, he defines anger as "emotional excitement induced by intense displeasure." Anger names the reaction but in itself conveys nothing about the intensity or justification or manifestation of the emotional state. Anger is a "hot" feeling, and when allowed to get out of control it can lead to rage. Men who are enraged can punch holes in walls, find themselves yelling or cursing, or begin plotting revenge.

Interestingly, the English word *anger* is derived from an old Norse word *angre*, which means "affliction." In German, *arg* means "wicked": thus the noun *arger* is the emotional response to *wicked* stimuli. In Spanish, *enojar* (to get angry) derives from *en* and *ojo*—something which offends the eye. In these languages anger refers to uneasiness, displeasure, and resentment.

Anger is not necessarily or wholly negative, however. Consider these seven additional definitions of anger I use, which point up the important roles of the emotion in our lives.

- Anger involves physiological arousal, a state of readiness. When we are angry our body has increased energy that can be directed in whatever way we choose.
- Anger is an intense emotional reaction that sometimes remains largely unexpressed and kept inside and at other times is directly expressed in outward behavior.
- Anger is one of many God-given emotions that can be a potentially powerful and positive force for good in our lives.
- Anger is a secondary emotion that is usually experienced in response to a primary emotion such as hurt, frustration, and fear.
- Anger is a natural and normal response to a variety of life's situations and stresses.
- Anger is a God-given emotion intended to protect and provide energy for developing solutions to life's inevitable problems.
- Anger, the ability to understand it and appropriately express it, is a sign of emotional and spiritual maturity.

TEN TRUTHS ABOUT ANGER

If we want to make our anger work for us rather than against us, there are ten truths about anger we need to understand. As you read, notice that anger is useful in helping us understand ourselves and to bring about positive change in our lives.

1. *Anger Is a God-given Emotion*

As noted in chapter 3, one of the occupational hazards of being human is that we experience emotions, all of the emotions, including the very basic human emotion of anger. From the nursery to the nursing home anger is a universal experience, especially for the American male.

I began my study of anger by opening God's Word and was amazed to find out how much the Bible has to say about anger. God acknowledges the significance of this powerful emotion: anger first appears in Genesis 4:5 and the last reference to anger is found in Revelation 19:15. In the Old Testament alone anger is mentioned 455 times, with 375 of those references dealing with God's anger.

The Old Testament reports numerous instances in which God expresses anger or is described as being angry. God is described as being angry with the people of Israel for their unfaithfulness, disobedience, stubbornness, and rebellion. His anger came out of His love for them. It resulted in acts of love, including loving discipline, designed to restore their broken relationship with Him. God's anger revealed how much God really cared. It revealed His compassion and His patience. It revealed Himself.

The Bible has different words to describe the various types of anger. In the Old Testament, the word for anger actually means "nostril" or "nose." In ancient Hebrew psychology, the nose was thought to be the seat of anger. The phrase "slow to anger" literally means "long of nose." Sometimes people's nostrils can flare as the intensity of their feelings causes physiological changes. There are numerous synonyms used in the Old Testament for anger. They include ill-humor and rage (Esther 1:12), overflowing rage and fury (Amos 1:11), and also indignation (Jeremiah 15:17). Anger is implied in the Old Testament through words such as *revenge, cursing, jealousy, snorting, trembling, shouting, raving,* and *grinding the teeth.*

Several words are used for anger in the New Testament. It is critical to understand the distinctions among these words. I've had many people remark that Scripture appears to contradict itself, because in one verse we are taught not to be angry (Ephesians 4:31) and in another we are admonished to "be angry and sin not" (Ephesians 4:26). Which is the correct interpretation and which should we follow?

The most common New Testament word for anger is *orge.* It is used forty-five times and means a more settled and long-lasting attitude of anger, which is slower in its onset but more enduring. This kind of anger is similar to coals on a barbecue slowly warming up to red and then white hot and holding this temperature until the cooking is done. But it often includes revenge.

There are two exceptions where this word is used and revenge is not included in its meaning. In Ephesians 4:26a we are taught to not "let the sun go down on your anger." Notice that the anger in the first part of this verse (*orge*) is different than the anger in the second half (*parorgismos*) where we are told not to let the sun go down upon this anger.

Mark 3:5 records Jesus as having looked upon the Pharisees "with anger." In these two verses the word means an abiding habit of the mind which is aroused under certain conditions against evil and injustice. This is the healthy type of anger that Christians are encouraged to have—the anger that includes no revenge or rage.

Another frequently used word for anger in the New Testament is *thumas*. It describes anger as a turbulent commotion or a boiling agitation of feelings. This type of anger blazes up into a sudden explosion, whereas in *orge* there is an occasional element of deliberate thought. It is an outburst from inner indignation and is similar to a match that quickly ignites into a blaze but then burns out rapidly. This type of anger is mentioned eighteen times (see, for example, Ephesians 4:31 and Galatians 5:20). This is the type of anger we are called upon to control.

Parorgismos is one type of anger that is mentioned only three times in the New Testament, and never in a positive sense. It is a stronger form of *orge* and refers to anger that has been provoked. It is characterized by irritation, exasperation, or embitterment. "Do not ever let your wrath—your exasperation, your fury or indignation—last until the sun goes down" (Ephesians 4:26b, AMP).

2. Anger Is a Secondary Emotion

Anger is an almost automatic response to any kind of pain. It is the emotion that most of us feel shortly after we have been hurt. When you trip and fall or drop a hammer on your toe it hurts, and you may experience mild anger. When your wife corrects or criticizes you in public it hurts, and you may respond to her (probably in the car on the way home) in anger.

Anger is usually the first emotion that we see. For men it's often the only emotion that we are aware of. However, it is rarely the only one we have experienced. Just below the surface there are almost always other deeper emotions that need to be identified and acknowledged. Hidden deep underneath that surface anger is the fear, the hurt, the frustration, the disappointment, the vulnerability, and the longing for connection. We will look at these deeper sources of our anger in chapter 6.

At a very early age many of us learned that anger can help us divert attention from these more painful emotions. Anger is safer. It provides a sense of protection for the frightened and vulnerable self. We can respond verbally or physically to our seeming helplessness. *If I get angry I can avoid or at least minimize my pain. Perhaps I can even influence or change the source of my anger. Besides that,* we think, *real men get angry.*

It doesn't take long to for us learn that it's easier to feel anger than it is to feel pain. Anger provides an increase of energy. It can decrease our sense of vulnerability and thus increase our sense of security. It is often a false security, but it is a kind of security nonetheless.

3. Anger Is a Signal

Anger is to our lives like a smoke detector is to a house, like a dash warning light is to a car, and like a flashing yellow light is to a driver. Each of those serves as a kind of warning or alarm to stop, look, and listen. They say, "Take caution, something might be wrong." In her book *The Dance Of Anger,* Harriet Lerner notes:

> Anger is a signal and one worth listening to. Our anger may be a message that we are being hurt, that our rights are being violated, that our needs or wants are not being adequately met, or simply that something isn't right. Our anger may tell us that we are not addressing an important emotional issue in our lives, or that too much of our self—our beliefs, values, desires, or ambitions—is being compromised in a relationship. Our anger may be a signal that we are doing more and giving more than we can comfortably do or give. Or our anger may warn us that others are doing too much for us, at the expense of our own competence and growth. Just as physical pain tells us to take our hand off the hot stove, the pain of our anger preserves the very integrity of our self. Our anger can motivate us to say "no" to the ways in which we are defined by others and "yes" to the dictates of our inner self.[1]

People who don't know how to listen to their anger are missing out on one of anger's greatest functions. As we learn to acknowledge anger's warning signs we are more likely to be able to catch and deal with an issue while it is still manageable.

Anger is an emotion that God can use to get our attention and make us more aware of opportunities to learn, to grow, to deepen, to mature, to make significant changes for the good. Anger, like love, is an emotion that has tremendous potential for both good and evil. As Tavris has written,

> I have watched people use anger, in the name of emotional liberation, to erode affection and trust, whittle away their spirits in bitterness and revenge, diminish their dignity in years of spiteful hatred. And I watch with admiration those who use anger to probe for truth, who challenge and change the complacent injustices of life, who take an unpopular position center stage while others say "shhhh" from the wings.[2]

When we don't recognize or choose to ignore the warnings of anger, we are more likely to face bigger issues and greater problems down the road. When we ignore the warning lights of our emotions, what we might have been able to deal with fairly simply will in time become a major problem.

4. *Managed Anger Can Contribute to More Intimate Relationships*

The idea that anger can lead to intimacy sounds radical, but when you manage your anger, you can draw closer to others and they can know you better. When most people hear the word *intimate* they think of words like *safety, trust, transparency,* and *security.* They think of people like a spouse or a best friend or bosom buddy, "someone who really knows me."

True intimacy takes time, in most cases a *long* time. Intimacy involves sharing not only ways in which you are similar but also sharing and working through your differences. It is through our differences that we reveal ourselves to one another as the unique person that God has made us to be. It is in working through our differences that we learn to understand and trust each other.

The emotion of anger is one of the most important ways we become aware of differences. It reveals that something is bothering me about something you have said or done. I can choose to move toward a surface and cosmetic harmony and pretend that everything is fine. Or I can risk discomfort and awkwardness by speaking the truth in love, understanding that and resolving the issue. In that process, I can increase the depth of the relationship.

In my experience most people tend to categorize anger as a sign of weakness or vulnerability. Being open about what is bothering you can lead to an increased risk of being misunderstood and being hurt. After it happens a few times you're much less likely to take that kind of chance again. Especially if you are a man. However, look at the other side. What are the costs of not communicating, of not expressing yourself, of not letting someone you love know what you are struggling with? Isolation? Loneliness? No understanding? Shallowness? Superficiality?

The road to understanding often passes through the town of misunderstanding. Rarely are we able to communicate to and understand someone else the first time, especially if it involves something as complex as emotions, emotions that we don't always understand ourselves. Often it is only in the process of trying to communicate our feelings to someone else that we understand them ourselves.

The emotion of anger doesn't strengthen or weaken relationships. Instead, how we choose to *express* our anger will affect our relationships. If you choose to sit on your anger, then the relationship is likely to remain shallow at best and, at worst, die a slow death. That's why I've had many women come into my office and say, "I've been married to this man for more than twenty years and I have no idea who he is."

As we risk expressing and then moving beyond the secondary emotion of anger to understanding its root causes, such as fear, hurt, or frustration, we will be able to identify and grow beyond the differences that divide. We can learn that it's not only safe to disagree but that without an identification of our differences and the inevitable disagreement that will follow, there is no meaningful growth. Instead, as we allow God to teach us how to use our anger-energy to get unstuck in our closest relationships, we will be free to move with greater confidence, certainty, clarity, and calm in every relationship.

5. *Anger Can Help Us Set Boundaries in Order to Clarify Who God Has Created Us to Become*

One of the most important yet difficult tasks in the process of becoming an adult is what psychologists call *individuation*. Individuation is the process by which we become distinct individuals, related to, yet at the same time distinct from, those who have come before us and those who will follow us. It involves the increasing definition of an 'I' within a 'we.'[3]

An important part of the process of individuation is the establishment of personal boundaries. A personal boundary is part of what defines and distinguishes an individual. A personal boundary is where I leave off and you begin. Boundaries provide a sense of knowing that God has made me an individual with unique needs, wants, feelings, desires, and dreams. They define what is appropriate behavior and expression of feelings.

Healthy boundaries help us to identify and clarify what is acceptable and unacceptable, appropriate and inappropriate. They let a person know when he is being violated, abused, or taken advantage of.

Sometimes our anger is a warning that a personal boundary has been crossed and we are being taken advantage of. Anger can give you the power to say no when you should say no—when your boundaries are being ignored. It is amazing how difficult that two-letter word can be for some people to say.

Christ never asked us to exchange our backbone for a wishbone. Being a godly man doesn't mean not having your own ideas and opinions. There is a bumper sticker that says "Jesus died to take away our sins, not our brains." We have the mind of Christ. God does not ask us to become conformed to what our family-of-origin, spouse, friends, or society says we should be. Instead, He calls us to become conformed to Christ. We are distinct creatures of worth, following our Creator God and His Redeemer, Jesus.

6. Anger Is a Powerful Emotion

"It's beginning to seem as if anger is our national emotion," writes Barbara Ehrenreich in an article in *Life* magazine. "You can feel it crackling along our highways, where obedience to the speed limit can get you an obscene gesture, and an obscene gesture can get you shot. It smolders in our cities, where rich and poor, often meaning white and black, face off across a gulf almost as large as the one dividing Serbs from Croats."[4]

Many people associate anger with the most painful and violent expression of anger they have seen or heard. They often associate (and confuse) anger with hostility, rage, aggression, violence, and destruction. And it's true that when anger gets out of control it can be expressed in horrible ways. But the problem isn't the anger. The problem is that people haven't learned how to understand and value their anger, how to listen to their anger, how to hear the warnings their anger provides them.

Anger involves power. When you are angry you feel "charged up" and ready for action. Physiologically anger triggers an out-pouring of adrenaline and other stress hormones to our central and peripheral nervous systems with noticeable physical consequences. Your voice may change to a higher pitch. The rate and depth of your breathing increases. Your perspiration increases. Your heart beats faster and harder. The muscles of your arms and legs may tighten up. The digestive process is slowed down. Many feel as if a war is being waged in their head and stomach.

Anger involves passion. Anger causes many people to feel alive, it gives them a sense of safety and power. It makes them feel they can do something. Many women have discovered that moving from a position of passivity, vulnerability, helplessness, and frustration to anger produces a wonderful sense of security, safety, and power. As Susan Jeffers writes,

> I remember times when my anger felt nothing short of sublime. It gave me a heady sense of power. It made leaving easier. It motivated me to make healthy changes in my life. It drove me to prove to everyone (especially myself) that I was competent and that I could do anything I wanted to do in life. Anger insidiously, but mercifully, masked the fear and pain and poison within.[5]

7. Anger Is Learned

As men and women who are made in God's image, we are designed by our Creator to express ourselves. Given the fact that we are "born to communicate," it's surprising that clear communication is so difficult for so many people.

I think there are two good reasons for this: original sin and our upbringing. Little Andrew, my three-year-old son, has few reservations about, and little difficulty in, expressing his feelings. He does it naturally. But all parents teach their children what is acceptable to express and what is not acceptable. By the time children become adults they have learned what emotions are permissible and what kinds of expressions are acceptable.

They don't just learn these emotional dos and don'ts by what we say. As part of their learning process children often imitate and then adopt the behavior patterns they see demonstrated in the adults around them. There are also external influences that contribute to a sense of what's considered appropriate behavior. These influences include friendships and role models picked up from television, movies, and books.

A good example of this is the idea that it's more acceptable for women to express emotions than men. This starts at an early age when little children learn that it's OK for little girls to cry, but that a boy needs to "be a man." And we all know that being a real man involves having bypass surgery on our emotions. This is a noninvasive procedure by which men are initially aware of their feelings but learn to keep quiet about them. After a while we have suppressed our emotions for so long we not only no longer recognize them but aren't even aware of them.

By the time many of us became men we had lost the ability to express ourselves. We learned all too well that expressing emotions is not masculine and is thus unacceptable. Unfortunately, unexpressed emotions don't just disappear. They become internalized and usually lead to an inability to understand ourselves, or to relate to and be intimate with others. Learning how to open up isn't always easy, but it's vital.

8. Anger Is the "Most Likely to Be Mislabeled" Emotion

In my counseling practice I've spent many hours with men who are confused, frustrated, and stuck in their efforts to grow and live effectively. Much of this is due to their failure or inability to acknowledge, understand, and constructively deal with anger. With the taboos on anger in many evangelical circles Christians can be particularly blind to the value of this powerful emotion. Instead of identifying the emotion and facing it squarely as a fact of life, they try to either shut out and silence their anger or they allow it to dominate their lives.

Many women assume that whenever adults experience an emotion they are probably aware of it and it can't help but show itself on their faces. At least that's the way it works for most women. But many of us men are masters of masquerade. A man who is worried usually looks and acts worried. A man who is depressed usually looks and acts depressed. A man who is overcome by fear usually looks and acts afraid. But a person who is angry may or may not look and act angry. He may appear to be worried, depressed, afraid, or there may not be any external indication of his anger.

Of all the emotions anger is the one most likely to be labeled as something else. Of all the emotions anger is the one most likely to be identified as dangerous. What are some of the most common disguises anger can take?

> When we begrudge, scorn, insult, and disdain others or when we are annoyed, offended, bitter, fed up, repulsed, irritated, infuriated, incensed, mad, sarcastic, up tight, cross or when we experience frustration, indignation, exasperation, fury, wrath or rage, we are probably experiencing some form of anger. Anger can also manifest itself as criticism, silence, intimidation, hypochondria, numerous petty complaints, depression, gossip, sarcasm, and blame. Even such passive-aggressive behaviors as stubbornness, half-hearted efforts, forgetfulness, and laziness can be evidence of an angry spirit.[6]

Not long ago I asked a group of men to call out some of the words they've heard people use to describe the experience and expression of anger. Before they were done I had filled two sheets of paper. Then I asked them to come up with a list of phrases some people use to describe the experience and expression of anger. Some of the the most common phrases included:

flew into a rage	hot under the collar	did a slow burn
boiling mad	blew up	swallow your anger
simmer down	storming mad	defuse your anger
get it off your chest	blow off steam	went ballistic
fired up	totally lost it	raised his hackles

Over the years I've found that, at times, anger can be caught peeking out from behind other safer and more innocuous expressions. Here is a sample of some that I've collected over the years. What do we say instead of saying "I'm angry"? What expressions might imply an underlying anger in people who will deny angry feelings?

You always	You never	I'm down in the dumps
I wish that	I'm disappointed	I just don't understand why

It's not fair that   I'm depressed   You should/shouldn't
I'm sick and   When will you ever   I'm fed up
   tired of

When people are asked, "When is the last time you remember experiencing anger?" they frequently have difficulty remembering a specific time. Why? Many people view anger only in its out-of-control form, so they are unaware of the subtle ways the emotion of anger can be experienced and expressed in everyday life. An important part of learning how to make our anger work for us is to be able to identify the many masks or disguises of anger.

9. *Anger Is the Emotion "Most Likely to Be Blamed" for the Effects of Other Emotions*

Think about it. Is there any other emotion that people are encouraged to avoid as much as anger? Is there any other emotion that is more likely to be labeled a sin? Is there any other emotion that people are more uncomfortable talking (or reading) about? It reveals the bad reputation that this God-given emotion has.

But many people don't realize anger is only one part of a family of emotions. Though many pastors and counselors talk about anger, the problems it causes, and how to avoid it, few talk about how to distinguish anger from ire, aggression, and related feelings. Let's take a look at some of the many different faces of anger.

Ire suggests greater intensity than anger, often with a clear physical display of feeling such as flushed cheeks or dilated pupils. *Rage* suggests loss of self-control leading to violence. *Fury* is a controlling and destructive rage that borders on madness. *Indignation* suggests a healthy anger at what one considers unfair, mean, or shameful behavior.

When we don't deal with our anger we're more likely to dwell on the causes. The more we focus on how we were wronged the easier it is for the anger to turn into *hostility.* We want to punish, hurt, or in some way repay the person who caused us the pain. Over time it's easy for the hostile thoughts to become *aggression.*

Healthy anger lets others know exactly how you feel and why. It is honest and clear. Hostility is neither honest or clear.

You know you are in trouble but you're not sure why. You know you have done something wrong but you're not clear what. And you have little idea what you can do to change it. You feel hostile, which typically leads to aggression, physical or verbal, against a person.

Rage is much more than mere anger. It is anger under a pressure that seems to demand immediate action. There's no time to think about your anger. Rage demands to be acted upon. Anger influences, but rage controls. If anger is a stream, then rage is a roaring river that's flooding over its banks. The actions we take under the influence of rage are almost always overreactions. The rageaholic shouts, yells, screams, hits, hurls painful words, half-truths, and sometimes objects, damages, destroys, and then waltzes off into the sunset with no sense of guilt or remorse. Why? Because "they deserved it."

In addition to these emotions, anger often is confused with hate. These two emotions are different. Anger is not hate, and hate is not anger. Hate is the opposite of love. Anger is the opposite of apathy.[7] However, hatred is often a cause of anger, as Oliver and Wright point out.

> With men and women, anger often arises out of bitterness and hatred. In fact, the association is so strong in some people's minds that the two are often seen as synonymous. Anger becomes a sign of hatred. This error can make it difficult to understand God's anger. There are some Bible teachers who have never clearly seen the distinction between anger and hate. They seem to teach that God is a primarily punitive God who acts out of His hate for certain people. This thinking implies a very small and insecure God—one who gets upset at every offense to His pride. God turns quickly, then, from love to hate, depending on His mood at the moment.[8]

A careful study of the Bible reveals that there is a big difference between anger and hate. For instance, when in Psalm 106:40 we read that ". . . the Lord was angry with His people" (NIV*), the psalmist makes clear that the rebellion of His people caused the anger. Further reading shows this not to be the emotion of hate. The response is not of punishment, but of discipline and correction. Yes, He did hand them over to their enemies. But then: "many times He delivered them . . . He took note of their

New International Version.

distress . . . He remembered His covenant . . . out of His great love He relented" (43–45 NIV). These are not acts of an insecure, rageaholic, and out-of-control God. Here we see that His anger arose out of love.

It's unfortunate that many people confuse the emotion of anger with the ways some people choose to express or act out that emotion. This confusion has caused anger to "take the rap" for some other emotions. The emotion of anger has never caused the breakup of a marriage. Anger is not necessarily dangerous or destructive, and it certainly is not an evil emotion. The experience of anger is not the problem. It's all in how we choose to express it.

10. *Mismanaged Anger Can Be Hazardous to Your Health*

When we do not identify or understand our anger, we carry about what is called *mismanaged anger.* Such anger is not dealt with in healthy kinds of ways; instead we will stuff, repress, suppress, deny, or ignore it. This is out-of-control anger that keeps us from knowing what we are really feeling and does damage to ourselves and others.

"Anger that isn't accepted and confronted openly can be lethal," warns Gilda Carle, Ph.D., a corporate communications specialist based in Yonkers, New York. "It leads to stress, burnout and physical illness." Recent studies of workers under stress, for example, show they have higher cholesterol levels than colleagues who are less pressured. And a recent University of Michigan study of about seven hundred men and women found that people who suppressed their anger were three times more likely to die prematurely than those who vented their frustration.[9]

People who don't get angry, get symptoms. If we bury our anger it's possible that, in time, our anger will bury us! Dr. Leo Madow, professor and chairman of the department of psychiatry and neurology at the medical college of Pennsylvania at Philadelphia, explains what happens when we "blow our top." He notes several physical effects of repressed anger:

> Hemorrhage of the brain is usually caused by a combination of hypertension and cerebral arteriosclerosis. It is sometimes called apoplexy or stroke and may have a strong emotional component, as is shown by such expressions as "apoplectic with rage" and "don't get so mad, you'll burst a blood vessel!" Anger can pro-

duce the hypertension which explodes the diseased cerebral artery, and a stroke results.

Not only does repressed anger produce physical symptoms from headaches to hemorrhoids, but it can also seriously aggravate already existing physical illnesses.[10]

A person who stays angry and hostile—even long after the particular incident that caused the anger—may be committing slow suicide. Charles Cole, a Colorado State University psychologist, suggests that the physiological effects of the mismanagement of anger and other emotions may cause blood vessels to constrict, increase heart rate and blood pressure, and eventually lead to the destruction of heart muscle. After years of studying the reactions to stress and anger in more than eight hundred patients he has concluded, "We don't have a thought that doesn't have a physiological consequence."[11]

He tells of one highly-paid man who had a falling out with his employer. He describes him as being full of anger. "He felt screwed-over and was boiling most of the time." When Dr. Cole met up with him the man had had a heart attack and was in cardiac rehabilitation. Cole ran a profile on the man, who didn't react to most stressors.

"But when I asked him to tell me about the incident (at work) his blood vessels constricted, and his systolic pressure went up to danger levels," Cole said. "You could see that even when he just thought about it, it made him [furious]."

When the man's employer wanted him back, Cole advised against it, because he didn't think his medication would protect him. The man didn't go back to work. But neither did he learn how to understand and manage his anger. Eventually he had a stroke. Just prior to the stroke, the man was so angry he had tears in his eyes. "Depression, anxiety, and anger can be very powerful," Cole said. "There are a lot of people who have surplus anger, and it's a potential health hazard."[12]

If you're like most men, most of what you've just read is not news; only a portion is new information. However, when you fit together all of these different pieces of the anger puzzle, you cannot ignore the completed picture: our response to anger is crucial to our well being. The most profound puzzle piece is the realization that the God-given emotion of anger can play a positive role in our lives.

TAKE ACTION

1. In my workshops I ask the men to complete the following statement: "If there is any one question that I could have answered about anger, it would be _____." Before moving on to the next chapter, I'd like you to complete that sentence three times.[13]

   (1) _____

   (2) _____

   (3) _____

2. How do you handle your anger? Here are some responses to anger that are unhealthy. Do you respond to your anger in any of the following ways? If so, your anger may be getting the best of you.

   (1) You find yourself having negative thoughts or frequent anger outbursts.

   (2) You experience frequent anxiety or panic attacks.

   (3) You're depressed often or for long periods at a time.

   (4) You are an aggressive person—your anger allows you to hurt others to get what you want.

   (5) You are a passive person—the anger you hold in allows other people to hurt you.

   Devon Weber has prepared an "Irritability Indicator" to measure the level of anger people feel to daily irritations and whether they need to modify their anger responses. Measure your irritability level by reading the list of twenty potentially stressful situations.[14] In the space beside each situation, estimate the degree it would anger or upset you, using this simple rating scale:

   0 = I would feel very little or no anger.

   1 = I would feel a little angry or upset.

   2 = I would feel moderately angry.

   3 = I would feel very angry.

   4 = I would feel extremely angry.

_____ (1) While carrying groceries into your house, the bag breaks, spilling the groceries all over the sidewalk.

_____ (2) You plug in your new toaster and it doesn't work.

_____ (3) Someone makes a mistake and blames it on you.

_____ (4) Your boss reprimands you for something while the actions of others go unnoticed.

_____ (5) You get a flat tire on the way to work.

_____ (6) You have a 1:00 appointment with your dentist, and you are not seen until 3:15.

_____ (7) You are being ignored.

_____ (8) You make plans to go somewhere, but the person backs out at the last moment.

_____ (9) You are trying to read, but someone near you keeps talking to you.

_____ (10) Your car stalls at a traffic light, and the guy behind you keeps blowing his horn.

_____ (11) Someone knocks a stack of important papers out of your hand, but fails to help you pick them up.

_____ (12) You are shopping and the sales clerk won't leave you alone.

_____ (13) You are trying to express your feelings to someone who will not listen.

_____ (14) You are in a hurry, but the car in front of you is going under the speed limit.

_____ (15) Your best friend asks your new romance to a party, but fails to invite you.

_____ (16) You lend a friend something of value to you, and the friend fails to return it.

_____ (17) You step on a wad of bubble gum.

_____ (18) You did not get the promotion you asked for.

_____ (19) Your friend calls you at 1:00 A.M. to tell you he can't sleep.

_____ (20) You receive your doctor bill and feel you have been overcharged.

Add up your score; then interpret the total score according to the following scale:

A score between 45 and 68 indicates that your anger response is within a normal range. However, you may not be pleased with your overall behavior and may want to change parts of your anger response.

A score between 0 and 44 or between 69 and 80 indicates that you need to work on your anger. The fact that you are reading chapters 5–7 says that you're interested in changing your behavior. You deserve a pat on the back. But if you find that the anger does not subside or you cannot express it properly, seek professional help. Here is the meaning of specific score ranges in the Irritability Indicator.

0–36: The amount of irritability you usually experience is remarkably low. Only a small percentage of the population score this low on the indicator. A score this low may mean that you are holding your anger inside. You may experience stomach cramps or muscle spasms when you are angry.

37–44: You are considerably more passive than the average person. This does not mean that you are not angry—remember, passive people hold their anger inside.

45–60: You react to life's stresses with an average amount of anger.

61–68: You experience anger often and respond to life's stresses with more irritation than the average person.

69–80: You are an intense person and have frequent anger outbursts that do not quickly disappear. You may have the reputation of hothead among people who know you. Your anger may get you into trouble in your professional and private worlds. You may experience headaches and high blood pressure. Only a small percentage of the population react as intensely to stress as you do.

If you scored very low, suggesting you are passive, yet you feel very angry inside, you're probably saying, "This doesn't fit me." Remember, the passive person is the angry person who holds anger in and lets other people dump on him. If you scored average, it simply means you're healthy with your anger, you express your anger as you feel it.

If your score is very high, this suggests you are a person who carries anger inside. You overinvest in irritating situations, and recalling past feelings gives little relief. This score suggests that you're sitting on some painful memories. You may need additional support to get to the root of your problem.

6

WHERE DOES MY ANGER COME FROM?

For some men, learning to acknowledge that they have a problem with anger can take months or even years. Being able to identify the secondary emotion of anger is an important first step. But it is just the beginning. Next, men must be able to identify the primary emotion, the source or cause of their anger.

That can be tough. Many of us men have spent most of our lives being out of touch with our deepest feelings. We have pursued excellence and actually become masters at appearing emotionally unaffected and in control. We have developed a whole armory of tactics and techniques to avoid being vulnerable.

Therefore, we need the skills and tools to uncover and identify those primary emotions many of us cannot recognize. Through my reading, research, discussions, and interviews, I've identified eight major sources of anger that, to some degree, affect every one of us. My ranking, of course, is subjective, though the final three probably are the primary sources of anger, based on my counseling experiences and the research of others.

8. CHILDHOOD EXPERIENCES

One of the most powerful factors that influences how we deal with our anger involves the experiences we had with anger when we were children. These childhood experiences influenced us in several ways. First, there is the impact of what we saw. When you were a child how did your parents communicate their anger to each other? How was anger communicated to you? Was anger negative and something to be avoided? Did anger often lead to physical violence? Numerous studies have demonstrated that children learn about dealing with their angry feelings by experience and by observing the success of others with aggressive behaviors.

Another childhood influence involves the ways in which our parents responded to our anger. How did your parents respond to you when you got angry? Was it OK for parents to be angry but wrong for children? Did they yell and scream? Were you simply ignored? Were you physically abused? Perhaps your mom handled anger one way and your dad handled it another way. If so, you may have learned that men and women have different ways of expressing anger. Perhaps as a child you discovered that anger was a way to get what you wanted.

Many men are amazed to discover how much of who we are and how we respond is related to our family of origin, to what we saw and what we heard when we were growing up. It's a common refrain from many men who have sat in my office: "As a kid I swore that I'd never be like my dad but the older I get the more I realize that I am my father's son." Understanding where we've come from is an important first step in getting where we'd like to go.[1]

7. PHYSIOLOGICAL FACTORS

When God created us He gave us a body, a soul, and a spirit. Many Christians are aware of the importance of the spiritual dimension. They spend time going to church, reading and memorizing Scripture, and being involved in various ministries. In recent years many Christians have become more aware of the importance of the soul or personality—our mind, will, and emotions.

However, it is surprising how many people still underestimate the importance of the physical. They seem almost unaware that the ways in which we treat our body can have a tremendous impact on how our mind, will, emotions, and spirit function.

When we are overworked we become tired and rushed. When we haven't received adequate amounts of sleep, when we have allowed our nutrition to suffer by skipping meals or eating junk food on the run, we become worn down. It is easier for us to get thrown off our emotional stride and become vulnerable to the emotion of anger. It's not uncommon for poor health or extreme fatigue to produce a response that may look and sound a lot like anger. Sometimes it may be anger. But it's even more of a problem because when we are exhausted and weary our guard is down but we're not always aware of it. It is easier to lose control and allow our emotions, including anger, to take control of us.

That's why one of the first things I do when working with an angry person is to take a lifestyle check. Responsible habits such as regular aerobic exercise, good nutrition, and adequate rest (to name but a few) can be influential in helping someone move from being a victim of their anger to a victor. Here are some of the questions I ask my patients. How would you answer them?

How is your general health? When was the last time you had a physical? Do you get aerobic exercise at least twenty minutes a day at least three times a week? How is your nutrition? Do you eat a healthy breakfast? How long do you sleep at night? Do you have problems going to sleep, staying asleep, or waking up early and not being able to go back to sleep? In the past two years has the amount of your sleep increased or decreased? How many hours a week do you work? How much time do you spend with your spouse and children on a regular basis? When was the last time you and your spouse went away for a weekend without the kids or other friends? How frequently do you have family vacations?

6. ACCUMULATED STRESS FROM DAILY IRRITATIONS

Busyness and exhaustion can increase our vulnerability to quickly move beyond appropriate anger to hostility and rage. When our coping system is worn-down we are much more likely to overreact, to raise our voice, to criticize, threaten, attack, or put down those we love; to stomp around, stomp on, and then stomp out.

That's right! One of the major sources of anger is normal everyday events. Why? Because they occur with such frequency. Over the years I've noticed that a common source of many marital conflicts is not major issues but a series of minor issues that were never identified and dealt with. Someone has said that the major cause of failure in marriage is not blowouts but slow leaks. Not dealing with the normal stress of everyday life can become a slow leak.

As a parent the major source of anger for me hasn't been one of my boys stealing the family car or burning the house down. Most often my anger has been the result of the bike being left out for the tenth time this week, their bedroom being left a mess, forgetting their brand new $145 (on sale) winter coat at school—and the list of seemingly insignificant incidences goes on.

Events that may on the surface seem at best insignificant can lead to irritation. Repeated irritations can lead to frustration, and continued frustration can lead to anger. How big do the irritations have to be? Not very big. Even something as simple as a series of interruptions when you are concentrating on something important can cause anger. For instance, you can be late for an appointment when a driver pulls in front of you going five miles below the speed limit, or you may lay down to take a rare Sunday afternoon nap when the neighborhood kids decide to play basketball under your window and tune their dirt bikes.

5. THREATS TO OUR SELF-ESTEEM

Gifted and intelligent, Dick demonstrated strong performance skills in the military and later became a good provider for his family.[2] Yet the West Point graduate had limited ability to function interpersonally. He had been raised in a home where there was little expression of affection or approval. Kids were to be seen and not heard. And there was constant criticism. Love was based on what one did, and Dick knew that no matter what he did, no matter how hard he tried, it would never be good enough.

As a result, Dick became an angry man. Stoop and Arterburn analyze the relationship between anger and a man's poor self-esteem (which plagued Dick):

> A man's low self-image is usually the result of threats of an interpersonal nature, such as insults or undue criticism. Studies

118

show that men with a high sense of self-worth are much less affected by criticism.

Insults and criticism are especially provocative of anger if the man already suffers from low self-esteem, instability relating to poor social adjustment, depression, anxiety and low life satisfaction. These men usually did not receive the affirmation they craved from their fathers during childhood, and they get angry when they are not affirmed and appreciated as adults. No matter how hard he tries, the man with low self-worth never quite measures up to the idealized vision of what others expect him to be. He may appear to be quite confident and secure, but in reality he is insecure and highly sensitive to the criticism of others, positive or negative.

A man's anger in response to his low self-worth serves a number of functions. It prompts him to express his displeasure at the affront he has suffered. It helps him defend himself against all his negative feelings. It encourages him to restore his wounded self-esteem and public self-image by going on the offensive. Yet in the process of trying to save his own skin, he may bring pain to others, especially those closest to him.[3]

After Dick had given his life to Christ there were some immediate changes, but his compulsiveness and perfectionism carried over to his faith. He joined the church, became an usher, started taking classes, and got involved in several committees. He only exchanged one kind of performance orientation for another. He had little idea of what it really meant to not only be made in God's image but to now be "in Christ."

Because of his biblically inadequate view of himself, the ordinary difficulties of life seemed life-threatening. Since his identity, value, and worth were always on the line it was difficult for him to accept criticism. He set high, unrealistic standards in his need to be first. When he fell short of these impossible goals, he felt inadequate, defeated, and, yes, angry. Rage was never far behind.

When his wife, Carolyn, would ask for a simple clarification of what he had said, he usually would fly off the handle. It was obvious that the cause of his anger wasn't Carolyn's simple question. His insecurity led him to interpret her question as an attack. His automatic response was to defend himself by attacking her.

The scenario was the same with his three sons, especially his oldest son, Tim. Dick's low self-esteem made Tim more vulnerable to the negative aspects of anger. His unhealthy expressions of anger to his son was a major contributor to Tim's low self-esteem and was sowing the seeds for the same kind of anger response pattern in Tim.

I had been seeing Dick and Carolyn for marriage counseling for close to six months. One day, they walked into my office and handed me a note they had found written by Tim. They were alarmed and were concerned that he might be suicidal.

"One day while I was in my room I finally realized that I was a nerd and that nobody appreciated me or wanted to be my friend," the note began. I continued to read Tim's words. "I need to try my best to do what I can and be the very best I can. Sometimes I wish I could crawl in a hole and stay there for the rest of my life. I am very different from other people. Sometimes I wish I was dead. At school I am a target to be made fun of. I don't even think my teachers like me or my work. At home I am a menace to my family. If I could I would lock myself in my room and never come out or let anyone in. Sometimes I think the work I do is useless, even a waste of my time and the teacher's. Sometimes my very best story is a piece of trash to my teacher. I even feel I am a useless piece of trash to everybody. I don't want to even go to school anymore. I think that I should run away. I will never be nothing but a failure. Nobody likes me. I wish I could hit them so hard."[4]

Feeling inadequate and unable to please his father, Tim turned his anger inward. How we view ourselves is important. Self-esteem is the value or worth we place on who God has made us to be. Biblically-based self-esteem is not some nauseating narcissism. It involves seeing ourselves from God's perspective, men and women created in His image, acknowledging the reality of our sin nature, acknowledging our strengths and weaknesses, yet seeing ourselves in light of Christ's completed work for us on the cross. It acknowledges the fact that "we are partakers of the divine nature" (2 Peter 1:4) and are "becoming conformed to the image of His Son" (Romans 8:29).

Whatever diminishes our sense of value, worth, and significance increases our sense of powerlessness. Powerless men feel especially vulnerable. This can either increase our desire for approval and thus increase our vulnerability to being taken advantage of, or it can contribute to a spirit of "I could care less" in which people give up trying, or respond by attacking the system. Gaylin writes,

With fewer sources of pride, the more likely are we to be threatened and angered by any encroachment on our self-respect. An insult from a clerk or an employer gets blown out of proportion. The loss of a lover or the "disrespect" of one's child can incite fury. Perspective is lost. A traffic dispute turns drivers into madmen. Believe it or not, people have been killed over parking spaces, being "cut off" in traffic or over places in line waiting for gas pumps.[5]

In addition to obvious threats to our self-esteem, one more subtle threat is the unrewarding work that many men are engaged in. Today many of us are engaged in work where we play an intermediary role. We know what we do is dispensable. We are dispensable. Our work is a series of intermediate and repetitive tasks whose fruits are rarely evident. Very few workers today have a part in the end result of their work with which they can identify and feel pride over. As a result we may feel insignificant and lash out in anger.

4. SHAME

The cultural expectations and social demands made on men make many of us especially vulnerable to the ravages of unhealthy shame. At a recent conference one man said to me, "I think my parents should have named me Avis because I have lived my life believing that I've always got to try harder." His humor served as a thin veil to much deeper layers of guilt and shame.

God designed the emotion of shame to lead us to Himself. Healthy shame says, "God loves me. I have been made in His image. I have value and worth. But I am also a sinner. I am not perfect. I have made and will make mistakes. I need God." Healthy shame leads us to acknowledge both the fact that we are image-bearers and that we are sinners, and that reality should drive us to the cross.

When shame becomes the basis for our identity, the shame that God intended for good can become unhealthy. A shame-based person is one who focuses on his shame to the exclusion of Christ's completed work for him on the cross. At this point shame becomes toxic and hazardous to our emotional and spiritual health.

"Perhaps the most damaging consequence of being shame-based is that we don't know how depressed and angry we really are," notes Bradshaw. "We don't actually feel our unresolved grief. Our false self and ego defenses keep us from experiencing it. Paradoxically, the very defenses which allowed us to survive our childhood trauma have now become barriers to our growth."[6]

Men who are filled with shame either ignore or are functionally unaware of the reality of who they are in Christ and of what He accomplished in their behalf on the cross. They are unaware of their legitimate needs as well as God's promise and plan for their life. They have little sense of their value and worth, have given up on the possibility of experiencing the abundant life, and because of the undercurrent of hopelessness and helplessness, they often abandon their opportunities to grow and to become all that God would have them to be.

Typically, the man who lives a shame-based life will eventually become numb to his own feelings and needs. He tells himself that what he feels doesn't matter, isn't valid, isn't important, is a sign of developmental or spiritual immaturity, or is just plain sinful. He doesn't know how to or is afraid to listen to the still small voice of the Holy Spirit speaking to him through his emotions.

He sets aside appropriate personal goals to achieve the relational goal of harmony. *After all, aren't godly men supposed to be the great peacemakers?* he tells himself. The price for peace is often his own God-given uniqueness, individuality, and identity. His unhealthy shame leads him down the primrose path of perfectionism and into the welcoming arms of a performance-based life. This is the kind of life where your value and worth is determined by what you do and how well you do it rather than who you are or, to put it more succinctly, who God has declared that you are.

Over time this unrewarding and unfulfilling lifestyle leads to an attempt to numb the pain of meaninglessness through increased busyness, even higher standards, greater guilt and shame, or the adrenaline rush we get from "losing our temper." He becomes more negative and critical of others because it is always easier to focus on the faults and weaknesses of others. If my focus is on what is wrong with everyone else I don't have time to be aware of my own stuff.

David Seamonds has written,

> I have yet to counsel a performance-based and perfectionistic Christian who was not at heart an angry person. This doesn't mean such persons are always aware of or express it openly. They often

impress us a being extremely controlled or very loving. But when we get to know them better, and they open up to share their inner selves, we inevitably discover a core of anger deep within their personalities.[7]

3. FEAR

Randy had to run a few errands, and he invited his six-year-old daughter to go with him.[8] On each one of his stops he took her inside with him. However, on his last stop he only had to run in and pick up one item. He was able to park his van directly in front of the store so he could see his daughter. He locked the doors and told her he'd be right back.

When he came back out of the store and looked at the front seat he panicked. It was empty. He had been in the store perhaps a minute, and now his daughter was missing. He ran over to the van and unlocked the door. He called her name but she didn't answer. He frantically looked all around the parking lot to see if someone had taken her.

He returned to the van to see if he had missed something. When he opened the side door he saw his little daughter hunched down in the corner behind the driver's seat. When he had looked the first time from the driver's seat he couldn't see her. She jumped up and ran to him with a huge smile on her face. "Hi, Daddy!" she exclaimed. "Did I surprise you?"

Put yourself in Randy's situation. It's a busy Saturday and you are trying to get a lot of little things done. You are at your last stop and suddenly in less than a minute your daughter has disappeared. At one moment you are upset, panicked, frantically wracking your brain for ideas on what to do next. In the next instant you see your precious daughter thoroughly delighted at herself for surprising you and anticipating your warm and enthusiastic response. What is your first response? Randy's immediate response was one of relief, and his next response was one of anger.

He gave his little girl a big hug and then in a surprisingly calm voice he took her little hands in his, looked her straight in the eyes and said, "Honey, don't you ever, *ever* do that again." He went on to explain that he thought someone had taken taken her and described the fear and terror he had felt. He told her that when she was at home she could surprise him all she wanted but when they were away from home "please, please stay where you are supposed to be."

Many things can produce fear. They include dogs, cats, snakes, lightening, fire, sudden noises, crowds, dirt, deep water, driving, heights, being trapped, elevators, new situations, airplanes, tests, tunnels, and the list goes on.

Fear can be activated by circumstances requiring physical self-protection or by emotional self-protection. Although we can encounter physically threatening situations, most of us are much more likely to experience fear when we are threatened with rejection, humiliation, failure, put-downs, abandonment, being ignored, losing control, and so on. One counselor has written,

> A men's group counselor reflecting upon his experiences with men said, "Men are very invested in not having fear, the kind that will debilitate them. So they need to surround themselves with supports from other men—that they are okay, they're powerful, omnipotent and nothing can destroy them. That is a very constant common denominator I see with men in general. Without that, they would not be able to fight wars or live life."
>
> Men are petrified, terrified of being helpless, out of control. If they acknowledge that they are helpless or terrified, they wouldn't be able to function.[9]

Fear is an unpleasant and often strong emotion caused by anticipation or awareness of threat or danger. Fear is beyond a doubt one of our most uncomfortable emotions, and we have devoted a chapter (4) to understanding it. Fear is so unsettling that most men find it more comfortable to feel angry than anxious. It's easier to experience and express anger than fear. That's why anger and fear often go hand in hand.

For many men anger is an automatic and unconscious response to the emotion of fear. As you uncover your hidden fears you may discover one of the major contributors to your anger.

2. HURT

Hurt is another one of those uncomfortable emotions that can often lead to anger. In fact, an angry man is almost always a man with pain in his life. The pain may be denied and stuffed into the unconscious, and the man may not think about it, but that doesn't mean the hurt has magically disappeared. "Out of mind" does not mean "out of memory."

Hurt can come in all kinds of packages and from many different sources. One of my earliest memories of hurt was when I was in kindergarten. As a child I had a speech problem. At times my mind would work faster than my mouth and I would stutter and stammer. It didn't take long for the kids to pick up on this and on a couple of occasions they laughed and made fun of me. I still have vivid memories of coming home from school in tears after having been ridiculed.

Eventually the layers of hurt, confusion, and misunderstanding make it more difficult to access the facts and interpretations that caused it. Unfortunately the pain of repressed hurt can simmer for years. If not dealt with it can suddenly boil to the surface, moving past the potentially positive emotion of anger to the damaging emotion of rage.

Hurt is emotionally draining. Anger can give us energy to throw up walls to protect ourself. At first the walls can keep people out and thus keep the hurt out. Anger can veil the hurt, fear, pain and sense of loss that comes from real or perceived rejection. If no one gets close to me, then no one can hurt me.

It's important to learn how to distinguish between hurt and anger. Welter suggests that for the most part hurt is the first emotion to be felt but the one that is least accessible to memory. Anger is the second emotion we experience and the one we are most aware of. If we ignore the warning sign of our anger, it can easily turn into resentment and a desire for revenge. If we allow it to have it's way, resentment will keep us imprisoned in our past, it will poison our present and ravage our future. The pain of repressed hurt can simmer for years, and eventually anger can form. If not dealt with, the hurt can suddenly boil to the surface, moving past the potentially positive emotion of anger to the damaging emotion of rage.

Many people are surprised to learn that hurt and anger go hand in hand. It's not uncommon to assume that the angry person is so insensitive they must be incapable of being hurt. That's just the point. Frequently the annoying and obnoxious person is the one who has experienced deep hurt, often in his childhood. It's a fact that we are more likely to be hurt by people who are important to us. Therefore, we are more likely to feel anger toward people who are important to us. That's just the way it is.

1. FRUSTRATION

I was on my way from Lincoln to Omaha to catch a plane to Dallas to speak to a group of pastors on ways they could strengthen their counseling skills and help their people more effectively deal with their emotions. On my way out of Lincoln I was slowed down at three different times by farmers driving tractors loaded with bales of hay pulling out on to the road going about five miles an hour. After I got around the first one, the second one pulled out. After finally getting around the second one, the third one pulled out. By that time I was frustrated and a little concerned about being able to make my flight, but I knew I could make good time on Interstate 80.

Well, I did make good time, until I got into Omaha. There was massive road construction going on, and at that point I felt my frustration and anxiety increase. I knew that if I stayed on the interstate I'd miss my flight, so I decided to take a "short-cut" across town. Unfortunately my "short-cut" didn't turn out to be short. I made several wrong turns. Construction forced me onto some one-way streets that took me in the wrong direction. But finally I knew where I was, found the street I was looking for, and calculated that if the lights went my way I had just enough time to make it to the airport.

At that very moment a large moving van pulled out of an alley and stopped in the middle of the street blocking traffic. It was a one-way street and there were cars behind me, so I couldn't turn around. All I could do was sit and wait. Up until that point I had done a fairly good job of managing my anxiety and frustration, but that was the last straw.

I lost it. In addition to hitting the steering wheel and honking the horn I found myself saying things to the driver of the moving van (that I knew he couldn't hear), my face got red, my respiration increased, I could feel my heart pounding, my hands became sweaty, and I felt like I could explode.

After a couple of minutes I realized that I couldn't do anything about my situation. Allowing myself to stay in a frustrated frenzy wasn't changing anything for the better. It was only making things worse. Suddenly I realized how immature and ridiculous I was acting. I thought to myself, *What if the men and women I'll be speaking to in Dallas could see me now?*

At that point I put my hands back on the steering wheel and started to pray. I confessed my anxiety, frustration, and anger to God. I talked to Him about my concern with missing the flight. I thanked Him for His love for me and His promises to me. As I was praying the moving van drove back into the alley, and I was able to continue.

I arrived at the airport five minutes before the plane was scheduled to leave. As I hurriedly checked in my luggage and asked for the gate assignment, the sky cap informed me that the plane and some mechanical problems in Chicago and would be two hours late. Immediately I felt a sense of relief mixed with humiliation. I was relieved that I would not miss my flight and humiliated at the immature and irresponsible way I had allowed several different frustrations to control my emotions and lead to an out-of-control anger response that I'm glad only the Lord was witness to.

Without a doubt frustration is the #1 source of anger in most men. Webster defines *frustrate* as "to balk or defeat in an endeavor, to induce feelings of discouragement in, to make ineffectual; bring to nothing nagging daily cares that frustrate a man's aspirations."

Numerous sources of frustration appear in a man's life. Most of them are caused by blocked goals and desires or unmet needs and expectations. Frustrations are those seemingly little things that, if they happen with enough frequency or at the wrong time, can become big things. Yet they need not be that way, as Hauck points out:

> Millions of frustrations are far more easily tolerated than we usually think. Children not finishing their dinner is not an awful frustration, just the waste of a few cents. If a few cents bothers you, put the plate in the refrigerator until later. A person swerving in front of you in traffic is not doing something that calls for a nuclear explosion. It isn't awful to have someone honking his horn impolitely behind you—it's only slightly annoying. Not getting your raise can hurt your pocketbook, but not you—unless you let it. Frustrations are not usually earth-shaking to begin with; they can be tolerated quite nicely if we make the effort. Secondly, frustrations, even if they are severe, don't have to lead to disturbances unless we allow them to.[10]

When was the last time you were really frustrated? Can you remember the source of your frustration? Was it something big or was it a series of comparatively small and insignificant events? How often do you experience frustration? What do you do when you get frustrated? How do you react? Are your reactions usually healthy or unhealthy? Did your mom or dad react to frustration in similar ways? How would you like to react?

Recognizing the sources of our anger is the first step in learning to properly deal with our anger. In the next chapter we will look at specific answers in dealing with our anger.

TAKE ACTION

1. Complete the following statements:
    (1) I am most likely to experience anger when _____

    _____

    (2) When I get angry I _____

    _____

    (3) When I get angry I wish I didn't _____

    _____

    (4) When I get angry I wish I did _____

    _____

    (5) I would like to better understand and improve my ability to deal with my anger because _____

    _____

2. One way to identify your anger pattern is to keep an anger log. For the next thirty days maintain an anger log.[11] Whenever you become aware of anger grab your anger log and record the following information:
    (a) The date and time of day.
    (b) Rate the intensity of your anger from 1-10, with 1 meaning the anger is barely noticeable, and a 10 meaning that you have gone beyond anger into rage. (In fact, a 10 means that you are totally out of control.)
    (c) Where possible, identify the primary emotion or emotions that led to the secondary emotion of anger.

(d) What is the issue that led to your anger? You will not always be able to identify the issue.

(e) What do you tell yourself about this situation? Does your self-talk reflect passive or aggressive re-actions or an assertive response?

Here is a sample anger log:

* *

Date: _____   Time: _____

Intensity: 1   2   3   4   5   6   7   8   9   10

Primary Emotion:
(a) Hurt   (b) Frustration   (c) Fear   (d) Other

Issue: _____

_____

_____

Self-Talk: _____

_____

_____

Stress/Pressures in past seven days: _____

_____

_____

7

ANSWERS TO ANGER

Frustration, hurt, and fear—the top three sources of anger. How do we deal with the frustrating, painful, and discouraging situations before they boil into unhealthy anger? Actually, that is the solution—deal with anger before it gets out of control. The best time to deal with anger is before you get angry. That's right, *before* you get angry.

We now consider a dual answer to anger: (1) a preemptive strike and (2) a direct response when anger strikes us. These two strategies recognize that we must acknowledge that anger does appear in our lives. When we anticipate our feelings of anger in advance and when we confront those feelings regularly, we can deal with anger effectively.

That sounds nice, but working on this anger stuff is a lot more work than I had anticipated, you may be thinking. *Is it really worth it?* Well, only you can answer that question. Many people have found that one of the most helpful ways to answer that question is to remind themselves of the benefits of understanding and learning how to appropriately express their anger.

If our desire is to become the man God wants us to be, we will make the time to learn how to make our anger work for us. When we deal with anger, we fulfill the call of Hebrews 12:15 to avoid bitterness and let God's grace work in our lives. When we deal with anger we can prevent "fits of rage," "dissensions," and "factions," three acts of the sinful nature (Galatians 5:19–20) that are at odds with the fruit of the Spirit. And the benefits of dealing with anger properly are personal, practical, and long lasting.

What are the benefits of dealing with your anger? I think that the best way to answer this question is to let some of the men I've worked with speak for themselves. Their answers, shown below, are similar to those women have given in a recent national survey.[1] Here are several of their answers:

"I'm not as afraid of this emotion now that I understand my anger and know how to express it in a healthy way."

"It gives me an increased source of energy to make the hard choices."

"It has strengthened my marriage"

"My wife feels safer and more secure around me."

"It has strengthened my relationships with the kids."

"It has decreased my fear of someone else's anger."

"Now my children have a healthy model for how to express their anger."

"It helps me keep things in perspective."

"I don't have to struggle with the guilt that came from blowing it."

"It helps me to protect myself physically and emotionally."

"I've learned how to use my anger energy to identify the real issues."

Those testimonials suggest that dealing with anger is well worth it. So let's look at the two strategies in detail: the preemptive strike and the direct response.

BEFORE YOU GET ANGRY

First, we must plan ahead for anger. As Oliver and Wright note, "It's easier to be objective about your feelings and to see them clearly when you anticipate them. Your perspective is less likely to be clouded by the intensity of your anger."[2] Many people have found that waiting until they are actually angry to try to deal with the emotion is too late.

Here are three guiding questions to help you recognize approaching anger and to deal with the feeling before it gets control of you.[3]

1. What Are the Indicators that I Am Ready to Become Angry?

With a little bit of effort you can learn to recognize the warning signs before anger appears. Remember, anger is a secondary emotion that can have a wide range of causes. Everything from stresses and daily irritations to fear and hurt can lead to anger. The eight sources of anger we explored in the last chapter can become telltale signs of tensions that can lead to anger in our lives.

Do you feel frustrated regularly, or have a deep hurt that has not disappeared after months or even years? Then you are very vulnerable to feeling and expressing anger. Do you have a lot of irritations at work—hassles driving to the job, a heavy workload, or disagreements with the boss or co-workers? Then you are likely to experience anger. All eight of the sources of anger listed in the previous chapter can lead to anger. In fact, if two or more of these causes are present in your life you are likely to be experiencing some form of anger.

Although not every man who has experienced hurt will have anger, an angry man often will have some unresolved hurt in his life. Though a man can be frustrated and not angry, an angry man often will have frustrating situations that are contributing to his feelings of anger. If you have a couple of these anger factors at work in your life, be alert to anger developing in your life.

2. When Am I Most Likely to Be Angry?

In addition to identifying indicators that anger is developing, we must recognize when we are most vulnerable to experiencing anger. For two weeks Dick also kept an Anger Log (discussed at the end of chapter 6). By faithfully using this simple tool he was able to recognize that at certain times and situations he was more likely to experience anger.

Dick discovered that he was most vulnerable during a one-hour period after coming home from work, on Sunday afternoons when he liked to relax and watch sports, and when Carolyn would make social plans for them without telling him. He also realized that when he was tired and weary he became more negative and critical and thus more vulnerable to "snapping" at Carolyn or one of the kids.

By identifying these "danger zones" he was able to prayerfully prepare his mind and his heart. This simple exercise helped him decrease the power of these situations to seemingly control his emotional response. If this is the *only* suggestion you take in this chapter, I think that you will be surprised at how helpful it will be.

3. *What's My Anger Pattern?*

What's your personal anger profile? When you are angry, does your body get more tense? Does your pulse increase? Is it more difficult for you to concentrate? Do you become increasingly preoccupied with what is making you angry?

Each of us has a specific anger pattern that can let us know when we're getting angry. Sometimes we are the last one to know when we're angry. I have a close friend whose dog knew he was angry before he did. When Norman would speak in a certain tone of voice his shelty would put her head down and slink off into another room.

An Anger Curve

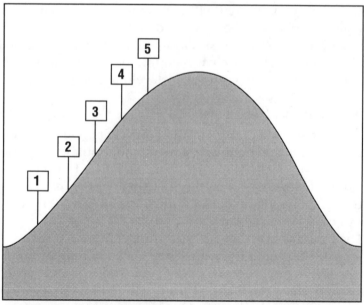

If the anger is caught at step 5, or at step 4, and so on down the line, the emotion does not get out of control. The energy can then be invested rather than spent.

Source: *Pressure Points*, by Gary J. Oliver and H. Norman Wright, p. 266. Copyright 1993, Gary J. Oliver and H. Norman Wright. Used by permission.

Often our friends can spot it, even if we cannot. How do your friends know when you are angry? How do your parents know? Your wife or your children? Perhaps you talk faster, or your face gets red. Ask them. Some men get sweaty or their stomachs start to churn. Others seem to want to hide, and purposely avoid people at work or home. It's important to identify these personal anger indicators in advance. The best way to identify them is by looking at our past experience. By keeping the Anger Log you will be able to gain invaluable information about your personal anger pattern.

It's also helpful to illustrate what you have discovered by drawing a bell-shaped curve. In the sample on page 134, I have placed what looks like road signs on the lower slope of the curve. Each numbered sign indicates one of my personal anger responses. The curve represents my anger, and as the curve gets steeper the intensity of my anger increases.

Dick's Anger Curve

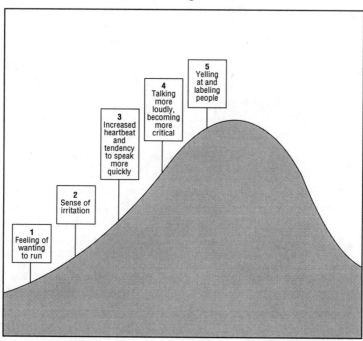

Source: *Pressure Points*, by Gary J. Oliver and H. Norman Wright, p. 267. Copyright 1993, Gary J. Oliver and H. Norman Wright. Used by permission.

On Dick's curve his first personal anger indicator was the feeling of wanting to run. The next indicator was a sense of irritation, and at this point he was aware of an increased heart beat and a tendency to speak more quickly. By the time he reached the frustration level he was also talking more loudly, was more negative, critical, and was on his way to yelling and labeling people. After drawing his personal anger pattern I encouraged him to keep a copy in his Bible. I suggested that each time he opened the Word he glance at his illustration and offer a prayer of petition for God's help in dealing with his anger.

If you are experiencing anger, that's good. Your emotions are operating the way God designed them to operate. Now the question becomes, "What can I do with my anger?"

We can learn how to be more effective in the future by better understanding the mistakes we have made in the past. Mistakes can be one of our greatest teachers, and, because we've already made them and paid for them, there is no additional emotional cost for them. Remember, it doesn't emotionally cost us anything to learn from our past. But it can cost us a lot *not* to!

WHEN YOU GET ANGRY

As soon as you become aware that you are experiencing anger you can take six simple steps that will help make this emotion work for you rather than against you.[4]

1. Acknowledge That You Are Angry

Acknowledging our anger sounds simple, but for many people it is easier said than done. Due to its negative reputation and people's tendency to deny it, anger has been called the "most likely to be mislabeled" emotion. Especially for men, recognizing that we are experiencing anger can be difficult. I encourage you to make a copy of the word list below. Then for a two-week period, put a check mark by each word that describes what you are experiencing. You may find you have checked one word fourteen times, another ten, and another three. These are words that indicate that anger might be present in your life.

Aggravated	Annoyed	Aroused	Bitter
Burned-up	Cranky	Cross	Exasperated
Furious	Grumpy	Hot	Huffy

Ill-tempered	Indignation	Irritated	Out of sorts
Miffed	Offended	Provoked	Rant
Rave	Repulsed	Riled	Sarcastic
Slow burn	Stew	Temper	Touchy
Vexed	Vicious	Wounded	Worked-up

Do you remember the story of Dick from the last chapter? When he did this assignment he discovered that for many years his anger had been disguised by terms such as *aggravated, annoyed, cranky, exasperated, grumpy, out-of-sorts* and *touchy*. By doing this simple exercise he knew that whenever he experienced any of these feelings he also needed to consider the possibility that they were a cover for anger. Over time he saw that these were often code words for his anger. "It's much more comfortable and acceptable for me to say I'm annoyed or grumpy than to say that I'm angry."

If you are like Dick, you probably find it difficult to say the "A" word (anger). You can be comforted by the fact that you have a lot of company. One of the most effective ways to work through this barrier is to start by silently acknowledging your anger to yourself. Then, when you are alone and are aware of being angry, say the "A" word; say to yourself out loud, "I think I may be angry." If you have no doubts about it, simply say, "I'm angry!" Feel free to let your volume and tone of voice accurately reflect the intensity of your anger.

Next, find someone whom you feel safe with and begin to tell him or her about your anger. It may not be someone you are even angry with. But you'll find that the simple act of acknowledging and talking about your anger with someone will decrease your discomfort and fear.

It rarely helps to "try hard" to stop being angry. What does help is to acknowledge that you are angry, identify the root causes, and redirect the energy away from attacking a person to attacking the problem.

2. Put First Things First: Prayer

Once you have acknowledged that you are angry, before doing anything else, ask yourself if you've put first things first. What do I mean by putting first things first? Take it to the Lord in prayer. He created us, He redeemed us, He has given us His Spirit to help us do in His strength what is often impossible for us to do on our own. Instead of turning on your husband or your children, turn your eyes on Jesus. Focus on what you do have, on your many blessings, on God's faithfulness and His many promises to you.

The apostle Paul exhorts us to take every thought captive to the obedience of Christ (2 Corinthians 10:5). I don't think it does any injustice to the intent of the Scripture passage to suggest that we also need to get into the habit of taking every emotion captive to the obedience of Christ. This is especially true of the emotion of anger.

At the outset we need to set aside focused time to take all of our concerns, including our struggles with our emotions, to the Lord in prayer. In Psalm 42:4 David talks about pouring out his soul, and in Psalm 62:8 David wrote, "Trust in Him at all times, O people; pour out your heart before Him; God is a refuge for us."

If you are frustrated, hurt, or discouraged and experiencing anger with someone, talk to the Lord about it. First, in silent prayer and then perhaps even out loud, ask God for His help and His guidance. It's foolish to try to do this in your own strength. In 1 Peter 5:7 we are told to cast all of our concerns on Him "because He cares for you." In James 1:5 we are told that if we lack wisdom we only need to ask for it.

Many people have found the following simple prayer to be of help:

"Dear Lord, Thank you for creating me in your image with the ability to experience and express the emotion of anger. I know sin has damaged and distorted anger in my life. I thank you that you have promised to be at work within me both to will and to work for your good pleasure. I thank you that you can cause all things to work together for good and that I can do all things through you because you give me strength. I ask you to help me to change my anger patterns. Help me to experience and express this emotion in ways that are good and that bring honor and glory to you. Amen"

3. Take Responsibility for Your Anger

Have you ever lost your temper? Does it snow in Colorado? Are there lakes in Minnesota? At one time or another all of us have lost our temper. Most of us ended up saying or doing things we wouldn't have said or done if we had developed the ability to maintain control.

When was the last time you lost your temper? If you can't remember, ask your wife, children, or a co-worker. When you lost it, what was one of your first responses? Was it similar to the response of Adam and Eve in the Garden of Eden after they had sinned? The first man and woman blamed anyone except themselves. They tried to find an excuse, shift the responsibility from themselves and blame someone else. Eve blamed the serpent, Adam blamed Eve and then God, and the rest of us have been blaming each other ever since.

As men we blame other people, circumstances, or even God. Think for a moment. What are some of your favorite excuses? Over the years I've kept a list of excuses that men (including myself) use when they lose their temper. Here are the top ten on the hit parade of cop-outs. Put a check by some of the ones you've used.

1. If she hadn't said what she did I wouldn't have lost it.
2. I warned them, but they didn't listen.
3. What I did wasn't as bad as what I might have done!
4. It's healthier to let the rage out.
5. I didn't start it. It wasn't my fault.
6. The way I behaved was wrong, but it worked.
7. Everybody does the same thing.
8. He/she deserved it.
9. He/she isn't worth bothering about, so it doesn't matter.
10. I only behaved the same way he/she did.

An important step in the process of making your anger work for you is to take responsibility for your angry and to acknowledge to yourself, God, and others that you are responsible for how you choose to express that anger. You may not always be able to control what you feel, but with God's help you can learn how to control how you choose to express that feeling.

4. Consider the Causes

Now it's time to look for the causes. Notice that I said *causes* and not *cause*. As we discussed in chapter 6, anger rarely has only one cause. It is usually the result of a combination of factors. Remember also that anger is almost always a secondary emotion.

It may be an indicator that something is wrong with the decisions I am making or in the way I am allowing others to treat me.

When considering the possible causes of the anger, be sure to rule out two possible sources. First, we must make sure that our anger is not due to sin or selfishness. That's right! One of the main effects of sin was to make meeting our own needs rather than doing God's will the most important thing in the world. When we put ourselves first we will inevitably end up last. When we put Him first (Matthew 6:33) He will take care of everything else.

Because we are all sons of Adam we are born selfish. We want what *we* want and we want it when *we* want it. When we don't always get our way, when we aren't treated the way we think we should be, when we see others who get something we think we deserved, it is easy to experience anger. If our anger is due to sin or selfishness we need to identify it, confess it, seek forgiveness, and ask the Holy Spirit for some practical steps we can take to change that part of our lives.

The second source to rule out is that of oversensitivity. Anger is an alarm, but it can easily sound a false alarm if we allow ourselves to become oversensitive. One of my good friends recently built a new home and had an alarm system installed. The first week they lived there they received eleven calls at work letting them know their alarm and gone off. All eleven alarms turned out to be false alarms.

They finally discovered that the sensitivity levels for parts of the alarm system were set too high, thus creating the false alarm. If our sensitivity levels are set too high we can take offense when none is intended. We can look for slights when they aren't really there. We can assume the worst when it may not be true.

Once you've ruled out sin, selfishness, or oversensitivity, you are ready to learn how to identify the causes of your anger. At the beginning Dick found this to be a difficult step. It's not always easy to discern what might be causing our anger. However, over time and with some faithful observation, and record keeping in his Anger Log, Dick discovered that the primary sources of his anger were frustrations that he failed to deal with when they arose. "I kept on telling myself 'It's not that important!' when obviously it was."

If you have kept the Anger Log you already have a list of the most frequent and thus the most probable causes of your anger. If you seem to be stuck and can't figure it out I'd encourage you to go back and reread the chapter on causes.

In addition to identifying some specific causes for his anger, Dick also uncovered factors that were in a more general way increasing his vulnerability to frustration. One of the main factors was the physical exhaustion that came from the high levels of stress he allowed himself to be under. Another factor was the perfectionistic demands he placed on himself and others. He had been raised with the "enough is never enough" philosophy and so his performance always fell short of his expectations.

5. *Choose to Respond in a Healthy Way*

Moving on to step 5 means that you are aware of the fact that you are angry, you have committed your situation to the Lord, and you have identified at least a couple of the causes of your anger. At this point the obvious question is, "Now what do I do?"

First, you must determine if there is anything that you can do. Unfortunately we cannot influence every situation. Three basic kinds of situations occur in our lives, and we can affect two of them: (1) situations you can control or change; (2) situations that you can influence; and (3) situations that you can do nothing about. We must remember that this third category exists. A lot of people experience increased frustration (and thus increased anger) in trying to change or influence situations they can do nothing about. If your cause falls under category three, your only choice is to, as often as necessary, give it to the Lord in prayer and turn your attention to things you can change or influence.

If it is a situation you can change or influence, get out a sheet of paper and make a list of your options. Don't worry about how practical your ideas are, just get loose and fill the sheet with as many constructive alternatives as you can think of. This may go slowly the first two or three times, but, once you become comfortable, you may be surprised at how creative you can be.

Let's assume the situation is one you can control or at least influence. What are some healthy ways for you to respond? First, determine who you need to talk to and the best time to talk to the person. Then consider the best way to communicate so that they can clearly understand your anger.

Generally the best time to talk is as soon as you become aware of the problem and have had time to choose how you can best express your feelings. Anger can vary in its intensity. If you are experiencing a mild anger, you can usually deal with the situation on the spot. However, if you are experiencing a moderate to intense degree of anger, it is usually wise to wait until you've taken time to more thoroughly think and pray it through. "He who is slow to anger is better than the mighty" (Proverbs 16:32). Why? Because the power and energy can be focused and directed. The verse continues, "and he who rules his spirit, than he who captures a city."

Ecclesiastes 7:8–9 says, "Do not be eager in your heart to be angry, for anger resides in the bosom of fools." The person who has learned to take the time to ponder and prayerfully consider important issues is the one who is best able to not only weather, but to even make progress in, the midst of a storm. A strong head wind can reveal your weaknesses or it can call forth your strength.

God's word clearly teaches that a patient spirit provides an opportunity for greater clarity and wisdom. To be "hasty in spirit" is similar to experiencing "vexation of spirit." To grow vexed or to become agitated in time of distress only makes matters worse.[5]

It's always best to express your anger to the source of your hurt. This may be difficult for you to do if you have bought into the myth that anger always destroys relationships. Challenge the misbelief by speaking the truth in love (Ephesians 4:15). Anger rarely will keep friends apart, but not dealing with the anger may separate friends.

As you meet with the person, choose to nurture a spirit of forgiveness. At some point each of us must choose to let go. Go to the person and say, "I'm angry and because our relationship is important to me I'd like to tell you why." If the other person isn't available or won't listen, write him or her a letter stating and clarifying your feelings.

Be open to being responsible for the way your life is proceeding. Be open to God teaching you what you can learn about yourself in this situation. God's promises, power, and grace are sufficient. He has given us all we need to deal with our own emotions. It's our responsibility to do something about our own pain.

6. Getting Started: Talk to a Friend

Once you have decided that you need to express your anger and you have decided on a healthy way to do it, the next (and for many the most difficult) step is actually doing it. It can be easier said than done. A good first step is to talk about your anger with someone you can trust.

Dick decided that, while he experienced anger with a number of people, the best and safest person to begin to develop his new skills with was his friend Monte. In your case I would encourage you to find someone you can trust and start with him or her. Janet Kobobel describes how the process can proceed:

> Then God placed a friend in my life who recognized my advanced case of controlled emotions. I was sensitive to everyone's feelings but my own. Wayne kept telling me I could say anything to him. Then one day he promised to phone me later when we both had more time to talk. I had had a tough day and wanted to tell him. But he never called. I decided to test the water and expressed dismay the next day. Wayne accepted it and apologized for not calling. Gee, that was pretty easy.
>
> A few weeks later, I was explaining a deep hurt to him, and he responded in what I considered a cavalier fashion. That really hurt. I got mad. So I lambasted him with the gale force of my anger and hurt, listing all the specifics. He received it all and acknowledged how right I was and how wrong he'd been.
>
> Immediately my face fell. I realized, once I'd vented my anger, that I had castigated Wayne not just because his comments were so upsetting but because I was angry at God, another friend, and my boss. (It had been a bad week.) Wayne just happened to say the wrong thing at the wrong time and ended up receiving my railing for all the Bad Guys in my life.
>
> His response to my mumbled apology was a hallmark in my emotional growth. He smiled, touched my arm, and said, "Janet, you don't trust our relationship enough to really believe it's okay to be angry. We're seldom isolated in our anger. I can handle any degree of anger you can give out, and I was wrong in what I said."
>
> So, with the encouragement of a caring friend, I found more freedom to express my anger. And I learned to make it articulate ("Why did you say _____? What I needed to hear was _____."). I not only vented an authentic emotion, but we also ended up closer friends who trusted each other more.[6]

143

A few days after you have expressed your anger and discussed the relevant issues with a friend, take a few minutes to get back to the person. Reconfirm your commitment to him or her and to developing an increasingly healthy relationship. You can do this with a word, a touch, a hug, a note, a call, or a kiss.

At times the intensity of our anger can cause us to forget that, regardless of the surface struggles, that person we have been angry with is important to us. It is because of his or her value to us that we are willing to risk the pain of compassionate and honest confrontation. It is the fact of our love and appreciation for the person that makes the relationship worth working on, fighting for and fighting about.

The best place to begin to express our anger is with a close friend, someone we can trust. Once we learn to discuss our anger with a friend (for instance, your spouse), it will be easier to discuss the anger we feel toward those we know less well. Of course, our anger is sometimes directed toward those who we don't know well. With these acquaintances, sometimes we may feel too uncomfortable to talk and may want to avoid a confrontation. This is the least effective way to deal with the tension. Handling anger is a lot like dealing with conflict; see chapter 13 for guidelines in dealing with conflict.

After You've Been Angry

Perhaps you successfully navigated that emotional rapid called anger.[7] Or perhaps you were more successful than you were in the past but still need to work on it. Whatever the result of working through the six steps, you're not quite finished yet.

The last step in dealing with anger is to learn all we can from our experience. What went well? What was different than usual? Were there any positive surprises? What could I have done differently? Over a period of several months Dick, his wife, children, and friends began to see noticeable changes in his anger pattern. They were able to see God's faithfulness in very clear and practical ways.

"What have I learned from this experience?" One of the most encouraging aspects of being a Christian is that, whatever our experience, good or bad, with God's help we can learn from it. If you've been a Christian very long you know that Romans 8:28 is true. The Bible contains the carefully recorded experiences of many men and women and nations. For more than two thousand years God protected the record of those experiences. Why? So that we could learn from them.

TAKE ACTION

1. Pull out several of your Anger Logs to help you to identify the stages that lead to your "losing it." It becomes an early warning device. For example, Dick found that his anger often proceeded through six different stages.

   Stage 1   Inability to focus or attend to what someone is saying signaled possible annoyance, irritation, or frustration (if you can identify what is going on at stage 1 you can usually keep it from progressing to stage 2)

   Stage 2   Antsyness

   Stage 3   More critical

   Stage 4   Argumentative

   Stage 5   Volume of voice increases

   Stage 6   Bombs away

2. Draw a couple of blank anger curve illustrations and do one on yourself. Then have your spouse, child, or friend do one on you.

8

LONELINESS

Loneliness

There it is again!
A twinge of pain?
Forget it. It will go away.
In the business of my day.
I've places to go and things to do . . .
A round of meetings with entrepreneurs.
Planes to catch and taxis to hail,
I have life by the tail.
But what is this painful wail?
From the depths of me I ache.
It greets me when I wake.
Even in a crowded room of people
I can hear a haunting toll from the church bell steeple.
There's nothing wrong with me.
I'm a success, as anyone can see.
I—I hurt. I feel an emptiness.
This feeling, is it loneliness?
Loneliness?
I'm married with children, three.
Yet at times I feel so alone.
Maybe it's time to come down from my throne.
It's not good for a man to be alone.[1]

Millions of Americans experience the painful emotion of loneliness. Based on a survey of a cross section of the American population in 1972, University of Massachusetts sociologist Robert Weiss estimated that more than sixty million Americans, as much as one quarter of the population, feel extremely lonely at some time during any given month. And that was twenty years ago. With longer hours and busier schedules for the 1990s man, loneliness remains one of our most dreaded enemies.

The problem of loneliness is so widespread that a billion-dollar "loneliness industry" has sprung up to meet the need of these millions of hurting people. The desire for meaningful relationships has led to singles bars, videodating clubs, health spas, singles apartment complexes and hundreds of self-help books. And for the married man, there is the feeling he doesn't know his wife or that his children will one day grow up and ignore him; or he may wonder why his busy work schedule leaves him feeling empty and alone in a home of love.

FROM THE BEGINNING OF TIME

Loneliness is not merely a recent problem experienced by those of us living in the twentieth century; loneliness has existed from the beginning of time. Many men and women in the Bible experienced and expressed loneliness.

If you read the first six verses of Psalm 142 you'll find a very lonely David pouring out his heart to God. His pain is deep and intense: "I cry," "I complain," "My spirit grows faint," (verses 1–3). "No one cares about me," he writes (verse 4), and "they are too strong" (verse 6). These are the statements of a lonely person experiencing deep pain.

Many of us aren't aware that much of the pain that we feel is due to loneliness. Even when we are aware of it and able to give it a name, it can be hard for us to admit. Thus it's no surprise that the women in our lives don't understand the loneliness we feel.

I've worked with many men who felt alienated from, angry at, or hungry for a deeper relationship with their fathers, wives, children, or other men. Osherson writes,

> A surprising number of men deep down don't feel a happy or confident sense of manhood, despite being "successful" at work or home.

. . . Neither men nor women may realize how lonely many men feel. Loneliness and shame can spiral together, each intensifying the other. Feeling lonely, we feel ashamed. Too often we take our loneliness, our yearnings for richer relationships with parents, lovers, children or friends as signs of personal failure and inadequacy.[2]

WHAT IS LONELINESS?

What words come to mind when you think of loneliness? Alone, isolated, cut-off, alienated? *Webster's Ninth Collegiate Dictionary* has all these elements in its definition of loneliness. One definition is "a sadness from being alone . . . producing a feeling of bleakness or desolation."

Have you ever experienced loneliness? How long ago was it? How long did it last? What did it feel like? One of the most common feelings associated with loneliness is emptiness. Life becomes tasteless and flat. There is a sense of hopelessness, helplessness, and despair. Nobody understands. Nobody cares. Nobody is there for you.

Most lonely people feel they don't belong. They want to feel understood and accepted. Loneliness is a signal that says you have important needs that aren't being met. God didn't design us men to live in isolation. God has revealed Himself to us as a trinity in which the Father, the Son, and the Holy Spirit are in relationship with each other.

Paul emphasizes the theme of togetherness in 1 Corinthians 12 (in the metaphor of the body of Christ) and in Ephesians 3 (in the metaphor of a household). In Ephesians Paul compares God's household to a building in which each one of us is a brick and Christ is the cornerstone. If you are a Christian, you belong to the household of faith. You are a brick helping to hold the building level and strong. Each and every brick is important. You are important, for every brick supports and at the same time is supported by other bricks.

One of the most frequent questions I'm asked is whether being alone is the same as loneliness. The answer is no. I've talked with many men who have told me that they experience loneliness even when they are in the midst of a large group of people. Loneliness isn't about whether you are an introvert or extrovert, what you do for a living, how many friends you have, or how often you are around large groups of people.

Being alone usually involves the element of choice and is time limited. Being alone doesn't tend to lead to major emotional problems. Loneliness does. One mark of a healthy balanced Christian is the ability to enjoy quality alone time. Another word for being alone is *solitude.*

Solitude is an important element in our lives. While here on earth, Christ found solitude a crucial element for balance in His life. In the gospels we find numerous times when our Lord intentionally made time to be alone. While loneliness leads to stagnation, solitude can be used of God to produce rest, provide nourishment, and can lead to a renewed perspective.

In contrast to welcomed solitude, loneliness leads to alienation. And loneliness is not a male trait alone. It doesn't matter whether you are young or old, male or female, married or single. Nor does it matter whether you are black or white, educated or uneducated. Loneliness can be a major problem for anyone. But it is a special problem for men. Why?

THE CAUSES OF LONELINESS

Many men struggle with loneliness because they have never learned how to develop close relationships. Many of us haven't developed close friendships because we did not feel a need to when we were younger. We were busy with sports or hobbies as teens, with new jobs, promotions, and perhaps transfers during our early adult years, and we found those activities sufficient, or at least too demanding to devote time to building relationships.

Our conversations were on the surface and fleeting. We did not have time to develop conversational skills, as we directed our energies toward the job. Then, as we grew older, learning how to develop friendships was more difficult, and we could easily view relationships as a threat, something we might not do well and something that could reveal our inadequacies and weaknesses.

As men we have fewer skills in and feel much more uncomfortable with developing close relationships. This lack of relational skills traces back to our childhoods, where girls are encouraged to develop relational abilities and boys are encouraged to develop a competitive and independent spirit. Young boys tend to be more emotionally unaware, and this insensitivity continues to be fostered throughout adolescence.

Often we lack close relationships because we don't know how to communicate on an intimate level. We weren't taught how as young boys. For many of us the only family time was spent staring at the TV with the most vulnerable piece of interaction being "Don't eat all the popcorn."

A second reason we men feel lonely is that many of us had few if any models for healthy male relationships. A little boy looks up to his dad, expecting him to show what it means to be a man. If his dad is physically or emotionally unavailable, distant, alienated, then the boy grows up thinking, "OK, real men are gone a lot, don't share their emotions (except anger), are distant and alienated."

If your dad was distant, though, keep in mind that many men find it difficult to reveal what they really care about, what's most important to them. And as men today, we are not much different from our fathers. We might say that our families are the most important element in our lives, yet according to surveys most of us seem unable to talk about them with our best friends. A 1989 survey by the Gallup organization and *American Health* magazine asked men and women what they talk about when they get together with their closest friends. Women talk mostly about their children and personal problems. Men talk mostly about work and sports.[3]

Still another cause of loneliness, especially among older men, is personal loss. It can come through death, divorce, or a friend moving away. If a man has only one or two people he is close to and he loses them, where does he go? What does he do? He is in the bind of not understanding what he is feeling, not knowing how to talk about it, and, even if he did, not having anyone to talk to.

THE THREE TYPES OF LONELINESS

It is important to understand that loneliness can appear in different forms. For some loneliness is an infrequent state and for others it is a way of life. Jeffrey Young of Columbia University describes three kinds of loneliness: transient, situational and chronic.[4]

Transient Loneliness

Most of us experience *transient loneliness*. The symptoms are not severe, and this feeling lasts between a few minutes and a few hours. From time-to-time almost everyone has such feelings. They are normal and can be caused by such factors as fatigue, worry, rejection or criticism at work, or realizing we have not been spending as much time with people as we would like.

Situational Loneliness

A significant event such as a divorce, a death in the family, or a geographic move can lead to *situational loneliness*. The effects can be both physical and mental—headaches, sleep problems, anxiety, depression—and can last up to a year. It often involves a temporary stepping-back or withdrawal from a person's usual levels of communication and involvement.

Situational loneliness is painful. Yet it can be a healthy response to a traumatic event. Often a person experiencing situational loneliness is choosing, for a time, to withdraw from certain relationships or activities. It can provide a much-needed "time-out" to grieve a loss, to reassess your situation, to redefine your goals before jumping back into life.

Chronic Loneliness

The most severe and debilitating kind of loneliness is that which becomes the focal point of a person's identity. The chronically lonely person is unattached, isolated, and feels stuck in a rut. He lacks a sense of belonging and believes that not only does no one understand him, but no one cares enough to try. He wants others but he feels not wanted by them.

If you experience *chronic loneliness*, over time you probably will become preoccupied with yourself and your problems. You can become rigid in your behavior patterns and tend to act in ways that increase your isolation and keep you lonely. Someone feeling chronic loneliness also has a growing fear of trying something new and of forming new friendships.

Chronic loneliness is often the result of damaging childhood experiences. It could involve a lack of bonding or attachment with Mom and Dad. When a child experiences a lack of love and acceptance at home, when he gets the message that he is merely excess baggage that is in the way, when he is not held or touched, when the only physical contact is abusive, that tender little heart can become hard.

That little mind doesn't have the ability to analyze and say, "This isn't about me, this is about my parents. They are really an unhealthy and dysfunctional pair." The only conclusion it can come to is, "I'm not loved, therefore, I must be unlovable." The child learns that the only time he is safe is when he is alone. He doesn't learn how to communicate, how to understand and share his emotions, or how to develop healthy relationships.

People who have experienced significant loneliness for at least two years and for whom no traumatic event has taken place may be considered as chronically lonely. Young says, "When people are lonely for that length of time, typically they blame themselves and their personality traits rather than circumstances." He continues, "Chronically lonely people can become convinced that there is little or nothing they can do to improve their condition."[5] In other words they become stuck.

Most people who suffer from chronic loneliness believe that they have only two basic choices. The first choice is to resign themselves to a lifetime of isolation and misery and learn how to endure it. The best they can hope for is just to survive. Their second choice is to maintain a small amount of hope by passively waiting until something happens or someone jumps in to rescue them.

In reality, those aren't the only choices. The good news is that God has given the lonely person numerous other positive options. Because much of chronic loneliness is a result of one's own doing, it is possible to do something different.

God can use the pain of loneliness to move you into a deeper relationship with Himself and others. "Loneliness is best understood as a gift that motivates a relationship with God and others," Bruce Larson says. God can use your loneliness as an opportunity to learn, grow, deepen, and mature. This is always the case with Christians. What Satan has designed for evil God can use for good. Romans 8:37 is true. We can become more than conquerors. Loneliness does not need to be a chronic condition that keeps a person imprisoned and isolated.

FIVE STEPS TO CONQUER LONELINESS

But where do you start? Here are five steps to change your feelings of loneliness. Each use the divine help of your Creator

God, combined with specific actions on your part. No matter where you are on the levels of loneliness, God can use this painful emotion for good; even if you experience only situational loneliness, you can turn this painful feeling into good.

I call these five steps the Five Looks. To subdue loneliness, we must learn to look up, look behind, look at others, look to others, and look around for options.

Step 1: Look Up

The best place to start is by looking up—developing your relationship with God. When you strengthen your daily walk with God, you know that one person, your Creator, is always with you.

Develop the habit of thanking and praising Him for His person, His promises, and His lovingkindness. Learn what it means to fellowship with Him. It's hard to "cast your cares" (1 Peter 5:7) on someone you don't know very well and aren't sure if you can trust. When David felt isolated in a cave during his flight from Saul, he found comfort by casting his cares upon God through prayer (Psalm 142). Similarly, pour out your heart to Him in prayer. Share your concerns, hurts, fears, frustrations, and discouragements.

Christ promises to be with us always, "even until the end of the age" (Matthew 28:20). In addition to Christ promising to be with, He acts as our great high priest who understands us and can sympathize with us (Hebrews 4:15). We are told to "draw near with confidence to the throne of grace, that we may receive mercy and may find grace to help in time of need" (Hebrews 4:17).

Step 2: Look Behind

As you develop your skills at looking up to God, you can then begin the task of looking behind. In the past, when you have had conversations with yourself in your mind (don't worry, all of us do it) and the topic was you, what did you tell yourself? What have those conversations been like in the past few months?

With God's help, recall those thoughts, and especially any feelings of loneliness. What have you told yourself about your loneliness? No doubt you have thought about those lonely feelings, maybe even a lot about those feelings. Here's an exercise to help you do more than think about it. Take out a sheet of paper and complete the phrase "I am lonely because—" ten times.

What did you discover? Where there any surprises? Perhaps you've been blaming yourself, God, other people, fate, or circumstances. Have you labeled yourself a loser? Perhaps you've been focusing on your weaknesses to the exclusion of your strengths. It's possible that you have made yourself the prisoner of unachievable goals and unrealistic expectations. You may have been ignoring (or may not even be aware of) what God has to say about your significance, value, and worth in Christ. Is it possible that these have merely been excuses to keep you from trusting God, facing your fears and risking growth?

Step 3: Look At

Now that you are more comfortable looking up and looking behind, it's time to develop some skills in looking at. At what? At communication, one of the essential skills needed to free you from the isolation of loneliness.

I've worked with many men who seem extroverted, comfortable in public, and had many acquaintances who, when they got away from the security of the crowds and their job description, felt inadequate, isolated, lonely, as though nobody really understood. One of the major factors that cause men to remain locked in prisons of loneliness and isolated from others is their fear of or inability to communicate about the deepest needs and longings and concerns of their lives.

Talking about what I do is one thing. Trying to find the words to describe what I don't really understand myself is something else. Furthermore, I need the courage to overcome my fear of the possibility of condemnation and rejection as I reveal what feels like an enormous black hole. For many men, talking about themselves—their hopes, fears, and failures, becomes an overwhelming task.

The confidence we have in our ability to communicate to a great degree determines our comfort level in relationships. In fact without communication there is no relationship. And, of course, this applies not only to the marriage relationship but to every relationship: parent and child, brother and sister, pastor and congregation, employer and employee, as well as friend and friend.

Why can something that seems so simple as talking be so difficult? One reason is that many people don't understand the complexities of clear communication. If you want to increase the quality of your communication here are four simple things to keep in mind.

First, remember that *quality communication takes time.* Not necessarily a lot of time; yet on a regular basis we do need to make time to talk. Most people (especially men) communicate on the run and have many other things on their mind. That is not a problem if we are discussing insignificant issues. However, it can become a major problem if for at least one of the people involved the issue is significant.

Good communication doesn't just happen. In addition to your normal daily interaction set aside at least an hour each week for focused communication with a significant person in your life. For those of you who are single, it may be a girlfriend or one of your close friends. If you are married, it should be your spouse.

Mark the day and time on your calendar. Maybe use a different color so it will stand out. I know some of you will find this last suggestion painful, but, to avoid interruptions, take the phone off the hook. Unless you are a physician who is on-call there is probably no life-or-death phone call.

Remember to pray and prepare in advance for these times together. During the week make a list of things you want or need to share. You can talk about yourself, the family, your work, things that God is teaching you, frustrations and concerns, plans for the future and anything else. You can share your schedules for the upcoming week and together prayerfully prepare for the tasks that lie ahead.

A second principle is that *quality communication involves more than words.* Many assume that what we intend to communicate and what we actually say is usually the same. Therefore, if we use the right words the other person will understand what we mean. Communication can be difficult because often what we intend to say and what the other person thinks we meant can sometimes be substantially different.

For more than ten years Albert Mehrabian researched the components of communication. He found that often the actual words we say account for only 7 percent of how someone interprets our messages. The other 93 percent involves other factors. Our tone of voice accounts for 38 percent. Other nonverbals, such as body posture, gestures, eye contact and facial expressions, account for 55 percent.[6]

Most men focus on the 7 percent and often ignore the other 93 percent. When one of these components contradicts the other, a mixed-message is sent. Confusion and frustration replaces clear communication. These lead to discouragement and the misbelief that "I knew I couldn't do it."

Third, remember that *quality communication requires that we listen.* That's right! Quality communication involves much more than talking. So we must choose to pursue excellence in listening.

One writer said that most conversations are dialogues of the deaf. Ecclesiastes 3:7 indicates that there is a time to keep silent, and Solomon says that only a fool ignores that fact (Proverbs 10:14). "What a shame—yes, how stupid!—to decide before knowing the facts," declares Solomon, who also writes, "The wise man learns by listening." (Proverbs 18:13; 21:11 TLB*)

In his best-selling book *Communication: Key to Your Marriage,* Norm Wright emphasizes the importance of listening:

> Listening effectively means that when someone is talking you are not thinking about what you are going to say when the other person stops. Instead, you are totally tuned in to what the other person is saying. . . . Real listening is receiving and accepting the message as it is sent—seeking to understand what the other person really means. When this happens you can go further than saying, "I hear you." You can say, "I hear what you mean."[7]

Make your number one objective to understand and only then to be understood. Studies have shown that most people can listen five times as fast as someone can speak. This means that during a conversation it is easy for our minds to wander. If it's an important conversation, take some notes. Learn to ask questions that clarify the issue. Cultivate the ability to restate the person's message in your own words

My fourth simple suggestion is to remember that *quality communication involves small talk.* Small talk isn't always insignificant talk. Most men like to know the facts. I'll grant you that facts are important. But don't ever forget that facts have little meaning apart from the context. It's usually the small talk that provides the context.

* *The Living Bible.*

For some of us, our first question is, "What's the bottom line?" Focusing only on the bottom line makes about as much sense as looking only at the last sentence of a love-letter from your fiancée, reading only the last chapter of the Bible, singing only the last verse of a hymn, arriving at church to hear only the last five minutes of the minister's message.

God loves us. He sent His only begotten Son, Jesus Christ, to die on the cross and save us from our sins. God designed us to be in relationship with Himself and with each other. He knows that without communication there is no relationship.

From the beginning of time God has made time in His busy schedule to communicate with us. God gave us both the Living Word and the written word. For centuries He has carefully protected His infallible written communication to us. He continues to speak to us through the "still small voice" of the Holy Spirit as well as family and friends. Conversely, God repeatedly asks us to make time to communicate with Him. He has promised to make time to listen to us. Day or night He is there wanting us to talk with Him and waiting for us to listen to Him. If communication is that important to God it makes sense that it needs to be equally important to us.

In a terrific little book entitled *Why Am I Afraid To Tell You Who I Am?* John Powell lists five levels of communication, beginning with "cliche conversation" (small talk) and "reporting the facts about others." There is little risk involved on these first two levels, and about 90 percent of the communication of men and women who suffer from chronic loneliness takes place at Level 1 or Level 2.

Level 3 involves revealing "my ideas and judgments." Here we begin to take some risk. We begin to test the waters. As I tell you some of my opinions, I will be watching you carefully to see your reaction. It's possible that as I share what I think you will disagree with me. If you respond favorably then we can probably go on to the next level. If not, then I will play it safe and stay at Level 1 or Level 2.

Level 4 involves sharing "my feelings." Sharing our feelings really tells another person a lot about us, especially as we share feelings about important things such as faith, family, and values. Due to the fear of rejection and failure, disclosing feelings can be risky, but it provides a unique opportunity for growth. If we don't take the risk and open up, we are guaranteed failure.

As we develop comfort and skill at the feeling level we can move to Level 5, which is "peak communication." This involves complete commitment and trust. We know we are safe, so there is no need to hold back. Powell compares Level 5 communication to two musical instruments playing in perfect harmony.[8]

Step 4: Look to Others

The final step involves learning how to look for and to other men who have the potential to become your friends. We all need at least one man with whom we can make a mutual commitment to encourage, rebuke, exhort, correct, and support. This is someone with whom we can share our hopes and our dreams, our failures and our fears; someone who is willing to learn to care about our person more than our performance.

Did you notice that I said someone who is "willing" to learn? It's impossible to find prefabricated friendships. In fact, real friendships aren't found, they are forged. They are developed over time. I've worked with men who have spent years praying for and searching out one or two men they could trust, men who they could care about and who would care for them. Most of them had some disappointing relationships along the way. But they learned and grew from them, and, eventually, they were able to find someone who was willing to join them in the quest of developing a meaningful male relationship.

If you pursue a good male friend, you will be on a grand quest that many men avoid. Friendships between men are an uncommon phenomenon. Goldberg explains:

> As adult males in our culture the phenomenon of being without even a single buddy or good friend is a common one—so widespread, in fact, that it is not seen as unusual nor is it even spoken about. Rather, it is taken for granted. Many men I interviewed admitted to not having one intimate male friend whom they totally trusted and confided in.[9]

Several years ago I heard several Green Berets interviewed. The interviewer asked, "What do you think about Rambo?" (The macho movie hero who defeated the enemy single handedly.) Do you know how they responded? "He could never be one of us." Why? Because Rambo is a lone ranger. If you're doing everything by yourself, if you haven't learned how to trust your buddies, you're not going to last very long. The wolf loves the lone sheep.

Every man needs at least one close male friend. Scripture abounds with examples of men needing other men, including Christ Himself. If Jesus, who was God the Son, needed twelve close friends, how much more do we need male friends. If Jesus, who was God the Son, needed the company and support of his friends, and especially his three closest friends, during his time of greatest fear, grief, vulnerability, and agony, how much more do we have that need?

In 2 Timothy 4:9–11 Paul expresses his loneliness and need for his friends. He was a prisoner, away from his friends and the support of those he loved, and he was aware that he missed them and needed them. He writes,

> Do your best [Timothy] to come to me quickly, for Demas, because he loved this world, has deserted me and has gone to Thessalonica. Crescens has gone to Galatia, and Titus to Dalmatia. Only Luke is with me. Get Mark and bring him with you, because he is helpful to me in my ministry. (NIV)

We all need friends to balance our perspective and keep us from moving in wrong directions. In Acts 19:30–31 we read that "when Paul wanted to go into the assembly, the disciples would not let him. And also some of the Asiarchs who were friends of his sent to him and repeatedly urged him not to venture into the theater." Paul's friends loved him enough to stand up to him and let him know when they thought he was making a mistake.

One of the cures of loneliness is intimacy. Although intimacy is not a feeling, it is a crucial element in ridding ourselves of the pain of loneliness. We need men that we can be side-by-side with. But we also need men with whom we can talk face-to-face. In Exodus we are told that "the Lord used to speak to Moses face to face, just as a man speaks to his friend" (Exodus 33:11).

Whenever I speak or write on male friendships I'm reminded of the moving story of Gale Sayers and Brian Piccolo. Both were running backs with the Chicago Bears; Sayers was black and Piccolo was white. When they became roommates for away games in 1967 it was a first for race relations in the NFL.

Between 1967 and 1969 their relationship developed into one of the most memorable in the history of professional sports.

During the '69 season Brian Piccolo developed cancer. Though he fought as hard as he could to complete the season, he was in the hospital more than on the football field.

Sayers and Piccolo and their wives had planned to attend the annual Professional Football Writers banquet in New York where Sayers was to receive the George S. Halas award as "the most courageous player in professional football," but Brian Piccolo was too ill to attend. As the strong and athletic Sayers stood to receive the award, tears began to flow that he couldn't hold back. He said: "You flatter me by giving me this award, but I tell you here and now that I accept it for Brian Piccolo. Brian Piccolo is the man of courage who should receive the George S. Halas Award. I love Brian Piccolo and I'd like you to love him. Tonight, when you hit your knees, ask God to love him too."

Healthy men are men who aren't afraid to need other men. Real men aren't afraid of what people will say about them if they have close male friends. Godly men aren't afraid to risk learning how to love another man.

Step 5: Look Around

Looking around you involves considering options. What are some creative options for dealing with your loneliness? What has worked for others? What has worked for some of your friends?

You don't have to suffer from chronic loneliness. Take time to develop options. On a sheet of paper complete the phrase "With God's help I can—" ten times. What haven't you tried? What have you tried that you can try again? Talk to someone you know who has overcome loneliness and find out what worked for him.

One possibility that many men have found effective comes from the apostle Paul. When he was in prison he didn't just sit around having a pity party and feeling bad. He didn't allow his problems to immobilize him. He took the initiative and wrote letters to his friends, he asked his friends to visit him, and he expressed his emotions—the joys and the sorrows—with the Lord and with his friends. He looked for ways to serve and encourage those around him.

Look around you. What are some of the concerns and needs of others? Don't just think of people you know. Consider the needs of people at your church or in your community you may have heard about but never met. What skills or interests or resources has God given you? Is there anything you could do to reach out and help others? It doesn't need to be big to be used of God in a mighty way. Little acts of kindness and little deeds of love are no longer little when God is in them.

Someone once said that the best way to have a friend is to be a friend. What are the characteristics you would like in a friend. Make a list of them. Now ask yourself this question: "How many of these characteristics do I have?" If there are any you are a little short on, dig in and start to work on those areas.

One final suggestion that many men have found helpful is to expand their areas of interests. Unfortunately many chronically lonely individuals have allowed themselves to become boring one-dimensional people. Where would they find friends? What would they have to offer a friend?

Do you have any hobbies? Are there any sports that you would be willing to try? You might be saying to yourself, "Sure, I'd like to try them but I know I wouldn't be very good at them." Don't worry about that. Remember, there are two kinds of people: athletes and athletic supporters. I'm one of those that belongs in group two. I'm not a great athlete, but there are several activities I enjoy doing. And in pursuing those interests I've made some new friends.

Perhaps you have thought about pursuing an academic or literary interest. Developing that interest can enrich your mind and bring about new friendships. C. S. Lewis observed that often friendship arises out of an encounter in which you discover that someone else shares a similar interest.

> Friendship arises out of mere Companionship when two or more of the companions discover that they have in common some insight or interest or even taste which the others do not share and which, till that moment, each believed to be his own unique treasure (or burden). The typical expression of opening Friendship would be something like, "What? You too? I thought I was the only one." . . . The man who agrees with us that some question, little regarded by others, is of great importance can be our Friend. He need not agree with us about the answer.[10]

TAKE ACTION

We've talked about looking up, behind, at, to, and around. Now it's time to stop looking and start doing. The most important step is to get up and do something. I know the steps work because I've seen the results in many men's lives. But always the men must stop the reading, thinking, and talking and take action.

The hardest step for the lonely person to take is most often the first step. Sitting around the house feeling bad and waiting for something to happen is not what the Bible means when it talks about "redeeming the time." Don't ignore your feelings, but do take your eyes off yourself and your problems and focus on specific things God will give you the wisdom, strength, and courage to do.

If you have followed my suggestions in steps 1 through 5 then you already have a number of practical options. Make a list of all of the ideas you came up with and put them in order starting with the easiest and least threatening task first and ending with the most difficult. To avoid being defeated by discouragement (one of Satan's most effective tools), begin the change process by taking some small and safe steps.

Remember that change takes time. Ways of thinking and responding that have become patterns have taken years to develop. They won't change overnight. In fact, if you experience a magic overnight transformation, it is probably only a surface or cosmetic change. Meaningful change involves a series of small steps and takes time. The process of change is often simple but is rarely easy.

You can experience deep and meaningful relationships. What God has promised He will accomplish, if we are willing, with His help, to learn to set some of our fears aside, trust Him, and by faith take a few small steps. He will reward your step of faith, your willingness to take some new risks, your resolve to face some of your old fears, in ways you may find surprising.

9

LOVE

I 've been told I'm a good lover" Jim said with a smile he couldn't conceal. "But,"—he took a long pause—"it's become very clear to me that I don't know much about what it means to love. I mean really love."

As tears welled in his eyes Jim proceeded to tell an all-too-common story. He and Carla met in college. The fell in love, or at least a reasonable facsimile of what they thought love was supposed to be. During the courtship Jim was "tender, sensitive, thoughtful, and listened to every word that fell from her lips as if they were the most profound words ever spoken." They talked almost daily. He sent her cards. They held hands when they were walking or driving. So far so good.

Then they got married. Jim was an entry-level accountant in a large national accounting firm. The first few years of their marriage he averaged sixty hours a week at work. Within fourteen months they had their first child and by the time they had been married five years they had three children. Three preschool children.

"As I moved up in the company my hours decreased a bit, but I was required to go out of town at least once a month." In addition to his travel Jim found himself spending Saturday mornings playing eighteen holes of golf with some of his friends in the company who were in management. "I told myself, and Carla, that it was something I needed to do. You know, job security, promotions, and all that."

When Jim came to see me he had been married for sixteen years. And Carla had just asked him to leave. "I couldn't believe it," he exclaimed. However as we continued to talk it became clear to Jim that this really shouldn't have been much of a surprise. "For the past several years she's asked me to go to marriage enrichment conferences, read books on communication, and in the past year she suggested that we go see a marriage counselor."

Unfortunately Jim's only response was that he didn't think there was a problem, everything seemed fine to him, and "I wasn't about to go and spill my guts to some shrink." He paused, shook his head a bit and, while looking down at the floor said, "But, here I am. Spilling my guts to a shrink."

Although I prefer not to be called a "shrink," I knew exactly what he meant. A "shrink" is someone weak, insecure, unstable men go to. Men who are strong, confident, successful, and secure don't have many problems, and the ones they do have they can solve on their own. Isn't that part of how we define masculinity? For many years it had been a part of Jim's definition. Yet here he was, a confused and broken man, asking the most basic of all questions, "What does it mean to love?"

What is it about men that brings so many of us to this point? Why are we the ones that have to be hit in the face by a two-by-four board before we are willing to acknowledge there might be a problem? Is it that *love* is a "woman thing?" Why is it that what seems to come so easy for them can be so difficult for us? Is it genetic? Is it cultural?

In chapter 1 we saw that men have the same emotions that women do. There aren't any specifically "male" or "female" emotions. We saw that before Christ ascended He told His disciples, all males, that what would set them apart, what would identify them as being His followers was love (John 13:34–35). Clearly love is foundational and essential to the Christian life. (See also Romans 13:10, 1 Corinthians 14:1, and 1 Timothy 1:5.)

Why, then, does love require so much work for us? Most of us struggle with what it means to love. Typically a man waits until he finds himself in a relationship crisis with a woman before he begins to consider what love is. Whether your girlfriend feels distant from you after the fifth date or your wife says you don't tell her you love her as you did when dating, you may be asking your-self that question: *Why is it so hard for me to give love?*

Why is it that what is clearly such a fundamental part of the Christian life takes so much work? It's not because we can't or don't love. Men have a tremendous need to receive love and have the ability to give love. The problem isn't that we're incapable of loving. The real problem is that most of us don't understand emotions. We are out of touch with our own feelings and don't have many skills in reading or understanding the feelings of others. We were not socialized in how to express emotions, especially emotions that might be considered feminine or be associated with vulnerability or weakness. Love is one of those.

Men often feel physically uncomfortable when confronted by unfamiliar emotions. Ronald Levant calls this sensation "a buzz" —the tightening in the stomach, chest, and throat, an "antsy" feeling in the legs, and increased difficulty in concentrating. In his research he found that men tend to respond to this buzz in one of four ways:

> (a) Distraction, which serves as a "circuit breaker," allowing men to disengage from the buzz; (b) the Rubber Band Syndrome, in which the buzz builds and builds until it erupts in an explosion of anger; (c) the Tin Man approach, which requires locking the buzz up tighter than a drum so that the man no longer feels anything; or (d) the Mixed Messenger, in which the buzz oozes out through the man's nonverbal behavior."[1]

Have you ever experienced the "buzz?" After first reading this piece of research I asked several of my male patients if this sounded familiar to them and, after some reflection, each agreed that this was one of the ways he experienced an unrecognized and unidentified emotion.

LOVE AND YOUR CHILDHOOD

It's a known fact that many males exhibit low expressive-ness. In fact, emotional inexpressiveness has been considered one of the key descriptors of the old male caricature. Real men were strong and silent. And there are a lot of reasons why this is the case. Look at the models we had and the ways most of us were raised. From the time we were children, thinking and talking about love, nurturing, and relationships were rarely encouraged or reinforced. In the closest of our relationships, with our fathers, most of us didn't know what to say and other fathers didn't know how to talk. In 'My Dad,"[2] Daniel Richards describes the lessons from a father who could not say "I love you," nor talk of "gentleness, caring and loving." Many of us were the recipients of neglect, criticism, or condemnation when as young boys we expressed feelings, weaknesses, and/or defeat.

When we moved into adolescence the pattern for how "young men" deal with emotions in general and painful emotions in particular was already well established. For example, when a typical high school girl doesn't get a date for the prom she is conditioned to be aware of her hurt and grief. Her method of coping with this very real adolescent disaster is to fling herself across the bed, weep, reflect on what she is feeling as she writes in her diary, and share the misery for hours on the phone with one of her closest friends. She actively seeks out the comfort she needs and probably gets it through openness and honesty. Society has given her permission to be weak and vulnerable and to express her emotions. She is not considered "less of a woman" for doing that.

Compare her with a male adolescent who may have been turned down flat when he asked a girl to the prom. Do you remember ever being turned down for a date? Do you remember what you felt when you hung up the phone? What did you you do? What did you want to do? Was your first response to shed tears and call one of your best friends and pour out your disappointment and hurt so that he could share your grief and you could be reassured that you're a worthwhile person? Fat chance!

When asked, the average male adolescent would probably downgrade the prom and shrug the whole business off with an "I didn't ask anybody this year" or "Who wants to waste a hundred bucks on an idiotic dance anyway?" His conditioning has not allowed him to develop the skills of being in touch with his emotions. Society has not given him permission to be weak and vulnerable. If he does he is considered "less of a man." The primary outlet for anguish or unhappiness allowed in the male adolescent's world is for him to kick a few garbage cans on the way home from school, slam the door of his locker, or get drunk.

My Dad

My dad, this mysterious man who is so much a part of my life,
my thinking, my very being.
You who once stood ten feet tall with hands the size of base-
ball gloves.
You whose voice could be so loud I would shudder.
You who came and went in my life with such power that I
always missed you and was momentarily happy when you
came home.
You who seemed to be so excited to have a son, but seldom
excited with me.
You who loved me, or at least they say you did.
You who taught me so many things about being a man,
strong, powerful, controlling, aggressive.
You who never talked of softness, gentleness, caring and
loving.
You whose touch I wanted, but feared.
You who carried your pain and passed it on to me.
Dad, I feel your presence in my life and all the pain you
endured.

Copyright © Daniel Richards, 1991. Used by permission

This is one of the many reasons that women are the primary
consumers of counseling services. Traditional socialization of the
male role encourages power, control, autonomy, and self-reliance. These socialized roles are inconsistent with acknowledging
needs and reaching out for help. Men are expected to be active
and achievement-oriented, dominant in their interpersonal relationships, and level-headed.

As adolescents we rarely talked about love, intimacy,
thoughtfulness, romance, and tenderness. As a young man in junior high or high school do you remember going to the library
and checking out romantic novels? Right! Many men have told
me that relationships were those messy things that made them
feel inadequate and insecure.

Instead, most teenage boys (including those who are Christians) were introduced to sex as a kind of rite of passage to prove
their manhood. While girls were interested in love, we were cur-
ious, fearful, and ultimately interested in sex. For many of us, the
word *sex* was associated with a mechanical conquest of women.
Ministers, youth pastors, and parents typically had to teach us

that sex is not the goal; love is, and sexual expression is the outcome of true love. Now as adults, we have to fight the association of sex with love.

WORKING FOR LOVE

Many men, however, still think love is something you earn by doing something, being somebody, being able to give more things than someone else. Men who still think they must "win" a woman's love also fear they can also "lose" it to someone who is better looking, more successful, bigger, stronger, smarter, and so on. Part of the reason for this prevailing attitude is a man's emphasis on achievement. Arnold Kipnis writes,

> As men, we're taught to be goal directed. Our sense of self-worth is often tied to our perception of how we perform—in the bedroom, on the playing field, on the job, in the boardroom, or in our creative expressions. We learn that it's the product, not the process that counts—making the touchdown, striking the deal, winning the prize, and being first. . . . Most of the activities men do together or alone are formulated along these lines. The joy of simply being present with our experience of the moment is often lost. That's why our achievements often ring so empty. No one was really there to enjoy them.[3]

Many men have been taught that masculinity means trying to be more than we are, giving more than we really have, and pretending we are stronger than we ever can be. Most of us didn't have much of an emotional vocabulary while growing up nor encouragement in expressing some feelings we were aware of. Those feelings we were aware of—our hope and desires, our hurts and fears—we often hid. Why? Because we feared we wouldn't be loved for who we were. In the process our public self—how people perceived us—has become more important than our private self, and, in time, our private self has disappeared.

As single men the dating process brings us face-to-face with this struggle. I didn't get married until I was thirty-three, so I had quite a few years as a single adult. Today men at singles conferences continue to tell me about the tension they feel about relationships.

On one hand single men don't want to be alone. They would like to be in a healthy relationship and eventually find a mate. On the other hand they struggle with their anxiety about relational capability, competence, and their fears of rejection. Many of them have experienced hurts they didn't understand, don't know how to deal with, and thus are afraid of being vulnerable again.

Among those of you who are married, many probably have found that trying to "do" relationships can still feel threatening and can bring out your insecurities. Perhaps when you have done things for your wife that you thought were loving, your actions either went unnoticed or you were told that you weren't doing it the "right" way.

Most men, once they feel discouraged and not affirmed in their relationships with women, turn to something where they feel they can be successful and situations where they can expect a positive outcome. For most of us, that's a job. It doesn't take long for work to consume our focus while relationships get lost in the dust. And that's happened to many of us. But we don't care. *After all, isn't this what masculinity was really about? Women do relationships and men do work.* And our models teach us the same approaches.

For example, in his best-selling autobiography Lee Iacocca describes his rise to the top of an exceptional automotive career with Ford and Chrysler. But he says little about his wife. Mary, a diabetic, had two heart attacks, each one following a crisis in Iacocca's career. In one telling section, Iacocca writes: "Above all, a person with diabetes has to avoid stress. Unfortunately, with the path I had chosen to follow, this was virtually impossible." Author Mary Gergen writes of the auto executive's attitude toward his job and his wife:

> Obviously his description of his wife's death was not intended to expose his cruelty. It is, I think, a conventional narrative report—appropriate to his gender. The book (and his life) are dedicated to his career. It appears that Iacocca would have found it unimaginable that he should have ended his career in order to reduce his wife's ill-health. As a Manstory, the passage is not condemning; however, read in reverse, as a wife's description of the death of her husband or child, it would appear callous, to say the least.[4]

In a similar vein, Chuck Yeager reveals in his exciting autobiography, *The Right Stuff*, that his wife, who had had four children in quick succession, became gravely ill during her last pregnancy. "Whenever Glennis needed me over the years, I was usually off in the wild blue yonder," Yeager wrote. Carol Tavris asks, "Would a woman write that sentence about her husband? Would she be so insensitive about her husband's needs?"[5] Of course not, but that illustrates the point. Here are two twentieth-century heroes, men who were idolized and respected by other men as what it meant to be a "successful" man. Yet these are men who, at least on the surface, appear to have had significant relational deficits.

MEN AND NURTURE

Examples like these have led some to conclude that men are incapable of any kind of meaningful love and certainly are void of any corresponding ability to nurture or care for others. Not true! Contrary to popular opinion men and nurture are not antonyms. Men can be as nurturing as women. Unfortunately men are not encouraged or taught how to nurture.

Recent studies suggest that the behavior we have for years attributed to gender often depends more on what a person is doing than his or her biological sex. In one study sociologist Barbara Risman compared the personality traits of single fathers, single mothers, and married parents. She reasoned that if one's sex or social training in childhood creates definite personality differences between men and women, then the sexes should differ in their baby care skills and nurturing talents in general, whether they're married, divorced, or single.

What Risman actually found was that having responsibility for child care was as strongly related to "feminine" traits, such as nurturance and sympathy, as being female was. She discovered that single men who were caring for children were more like mothers than like married fathers. These men were not an atypical group of exceptionally nurturing men. They had custody of their children through circumstances beyond their control—widowhood, their wife's desertion, or the wife's disinterest in shared custody.[6]

Another study looked at 150 men who were spending up to sixty hours a week caring for their ailing parents or spouses. Researchers found that the men provided just as much emotional support as women traditionally do. In our society the obligation of care usually falls to women. But when men have to do it, they are able to do it with equal care and sensitivity. Leonard Kaye, who directed the research, found that these men spent the same amount of time as women doing nurturant things—holding the sick relatives' hands, listening, and showing concern. The men were not providing this care grudgingly. In fact, they derived great satisfaction from doing it.[7]

Yes, men are loving by nature. God did not design us to be selfish and insensitive oafs. He made us to love children and to find in a sexual love the meaning of giving love. It's clear that men can be as nurturing as women, yet most men do not express love well. Why? Primarily because most of us have not been encouraged to show or feel love. In fact, to a great degree, we've been *dis*couraged from showing such feelings.

LOVE IS . . .

Thus both socialization and the male models in our lives have contibuted to many men having difficulty with relationships and with loving. We know there is a problem. So where do we go from here? What can we do about it?

The best place to start is by clarifying what love is. That's easier said than done. After all, you can love your house and dog, a car, a meal, and your mother, all in one day. And what about romantic love? Three of our great writers have shown our confusion about this emotion with their wildly varying definitions. George Bernard Shaw wrote, "When two people are under the influence of the most violent, most insane, most delusive, and most transient of passions, they are required to swear that they will stay in that excited, abnormal and exhausting condition constantly till death do them part." H. L. Menken referred to love as "a perpetual state of anesthesia." Plato is reported to have defined love as "a grave mental disease."

One of my favorite definitions appeared in a small-town newspaper in Montana: "Love is a feeling that you feel when you feel that you're going to feel a feeling that you've never felt before." Over the years, I've worked with many men and women whose definition of love isn't much more sophisticated that that.

Complicating our understanding of love is infatuation. Often we confuse the two emotions. I remember when I was in high school my friend Richard and I used to go to Huntington Beach. We'd take our back rests with us, put on our mirrored sunglasses, and then watch and wait. It usually didn't take very long before one of us would say, "Look at that blonde (or brunette or whatever) over there. I think I'm in love." If she was particularly attractive one of us would say, "I know I'm in love. This is the real thing. It was meant to be."

Now we were intelligent enough to know that we weren't really in love, but we associated that word with an attraction that sometimes led to an introduction that on occasion (if we were lucky) led to a short-term infatuation. Unfortunately what was humorous as an adolescent is not humorous when it involves adults who are laying the foundation for a long-term relationship. And I've worked with many couples who tried to build a marriage on infatuation.

Judith Viorst, in *Love & Guilt & the Meaning of Love* came up with a humorous distinction between love and infatuation:

> *Infatuation* is when you think that he's as gorgeous as Robert Redford, as pure as Solzhenitsyn, as funny as Woody Allen, as athletic as Jimmy Conners and as smart as Albert Einstein. *Love* is when you realize that he's as gorgeous as Woody Allen, as smart as Jimmy Conners, as funny as Solzhenitsyn, as athletic as Albert Einstein and nothing like Robert Redford in any category—but you'll take him anyway.[8]

Infatuation looks on the surface and often involves a projection of what you would like the person to be. Who they really are may be irrelevant. *To infatuate* means to affect with folly or to inspire with a foolish or extravagant love or admiration. People who are infatuated tend to read their most admired qualities and unrealistic fantasies onto some unsuspecting person. As soon as they realize the person is a mere mortal the infatuation goes as quickly as it comes.

During courtship couples experience the electricity of romantic love. It's new, it's exciting, it's intense, and it's unexplainable. It feels more real than anything you've ever known. You think that those feelings will last forever. But they don't.

A little girl came home from school one day and told her mom that she had heard the most wonderful story. It was about a princess who ate a poisoned apple and fell asleep. One day a handsome prince came and kissed her and she woke up. At this point the little girl turned to her mom and said, "Can you guess what happened next?" Her mom said, "Well, did they live happily ever after?" "No," the little girl paused and then replied, "They got married."

Because of people's unrealistic expectations and limited understanding of love, getting married and living happily ever after are no longer synonymous. In fact, some people believe getting married will ruin your love relationship. Real love is different. It doesn't look just on the surface. It goes beyond the public self to discover the private self, the real person underneath the initial impressions.

Love isn't just a feeling that you feel when you feel that you're going to feel a feeling that you never felt before. Love is a decision and a choice. Real love involves an unconditional commitment to an imperfect person. Love is not a commodity like toothpaste. Love is like a plant that needs to be watered and taken care of.

C. S. Lewis observed that many people have the mistaken idea that,

> if you have married the right person you may expect to go on "being in love" forever. As a result, when they find they are not, they think this proves they have made a mistake and are entitled to a change—not realizing that, when they have changed, the glamour will presently go out of the new love just as it went out of the old one. In this department of life, as in every other, thrills come at the beginning and do not last. . . . Let the thrill go—let it die away —go on through that period of death into the quieter interest and happiness that follow—and you will find you are living in a world of new thrills all the time.[9]

Love involves learning who your spouse is, learning what she needs and desires. Love also involves learning how to pray with and for her and how to recognize when she is hurting or discouraged—and asking when you're not sure. The best way to learn about your spouse is to talk with her. Not at her or to her but with her.

LEARNING HOW TO SAY "I LOVE YOU"

For us men to express more effectively our affection for our wives, children, and friends we need to *cherish and nourish*. I discovered this principle several years ago while preparing a series of messages on marriage based on Ephesians 5. The apostle

Paul says in verse 29, "for no one ever hated his own flesh, but nourishes and cherishes it, just as Christ also does the church." *Cherish* is what I feel about someone. *Nourish* is a behavioral term that looks at what I actually do. The attitude of cherishing and the activity of nourishing are two of the key dimensions of giving love. A healthy relationship needs both.

In my experience most men find it easier to cherish (feel or think love) than to nourish (effectively and creatively express love). I can't count the number of men I've worked with whose relationships died the death of good and sincere intentions. What does it mean to nourish, and how can we do it?

In the mid-1970s I moved from California to Nebraska. I didn't have much furniture, so the large, old farmhouse I rented seemed rather bare. A friend suggested that I go to a nursery and purchase some plants. "Plants add warmth and character and are attractive. And they're cheaper than furniture." It sounded like a good idea.

I went to the nearest plant store and selected about ten different plants. As I chose each plant the clerk explained the uniqueness of that plant to me. Things like when to prune and fertilize and how much water and light each plant liked. Unfortunately, for me and the plants, I didn't listen to her. *I have other, more important things on my mind,* I thought. *Besides, everyone knows that plants are plants. To nourish and help them grow, just give them some water and light and occasionally fertilize them and they will grow.*

On my way out the door I picked up some fertilizer spikes. The package said that you should use one spike for an eight inch pot. I decided to really nourish my plants, so I put in three spikes rather than one. Knowing that plants need water I gave those plants more water than any plant deserved. I knew that in no time those plants would be growing and I would be seeing new buds and leaves.

In several weeks all of my plants were dead. I couldn't believe it. I had spent my hard-earned money on them. I gave my plants what I thought they needed and I gave them a lot of it. I had faithfully nourished each one of those plants—or so I thought. Obviously I hadn't nourished them. I had killed them. What had I done wrong?

I returned to the nursery and told the clerk what I had done. At first she thought I was kidding and started laughing. I let her know that I wasn't kidding and that I didn't think it was funny. Especially with the price of plants.

She then explained that I had not given the plants what they needed. I gave them what I *thought* they needed. "Each plant is different," she told me once again. "What may nourish one plant can kill another. Learn the unique need of each plant and treat it accordingly."

This time I listened. I purchased more plants, and I wrote down everything the clerk said about each plant. I followed the instructions on the fertilizer spike package carefully. Guess what? My plants grew and flourished because I had truly nourished them.

Many of us are like I was during my first visit to the nursery. One of my mistakes was that I thought I knew more about plants than I really did. In relationships many of us men tend to think we know and understand our spouses better than we really do. We believe that we can nourish our spouses by giving them what we think they need. Often this involves us giving them what we would like and assuming that if we would like it they should too.

You may give your wife more, give her bigger and give her better. It doesn't seem to work. You become frustrated, disappointed, and discouraged. The desire of your heart is to nourish, but that isn't the result.

Nourish does not mean giving someone what you think she needs and wants. Quality nourishment involves stopping, looking, listening, and studying that special person you love. Taking the time to do this will help you to know what she needs and wants. Nourish means investing the time to learn the love language of your beloved and to love them in ways that are meaningful to them. Often what says love to you, what excites you, what brings you great joy is different than what says love to your partner.

What are some practical ways that we can nourish those we love?

Speak Their Love Language

One of the most powerful ways we can tell someone we love him or her is to learn how to speak the person's love language. We need to communicate in ways that are meaningful to the other person. It is amazing how little quality time most married couples

177

spend communicating with each other. Most communication takes place on the run as we pass each other. A little comment here, a short observation there, a concern, a frustration only partially heard. Tournier said that the communication of most couples are "dialogues of the deaf."

For example, men and women tend to communicate differently. Most have a different emotional language and mode of expressing intimacy than most women. Men are usually more comfortable with a side-by-side way of relating. Here intimacy means sharing the same activity together. This is what they have become used to as they work on a project, hunt, fish, watch or play sports together. On the other hand, most women are much more comfortable with a face-to-face kind of intimacy where they share ideas and emotions in an in-depth heart-to-heart exchange. For many men a face-to-face interaction implies confrontation, a kind of squaring off or sizing each other up.

I've talked with many men for whom an "intimate activity" can be doing something together that they both enjoy. It may even involve little conversation. To them words are irrelevant. This kind of "intimacy" is difficult for most women to understand. Even introverted women. Unfortunately, many of us bring this same style of relating into our opposite-sex relationships, usually with drastic results. As one woman said,

> My husband and I have a custom of reading the papers and having coffee together every morning. He loves to listen to music in the background, so the radio is usually on. I don't like the music especially—I'd rather have quiet—but I know how much he does. One morning, though, the radio was annoying me, so I got up to read the paper in the other room. My husband protested immediately— "Where are you going?" I said I was leaving so he could enjoy his concert. "Never mind the music," he said, rather crossly, "come back here and I'll turn it off." His tone made me feel cranky, until I realized what he was really saying—he'd rather share the morning with me than with the radio.[10]

Set aside at least a half-hour a week for some face-to-face conversation. Ask some open-ended questions that will draw them out. Remember that what may seem like "small talk" to you is probably "important talk" to your spouse. In conversation many men like to get to the bottom line. For women the bottom line isn't a conclusion or summary statement; the bottom line is the process of interacting and revealing themselves to one another.

Do Things That Say "I Love You"

Something as simple as remembering birthdays, anniversaries, and Valentine's Day means a lot to most women. Though I have suspected that women purchased more greeting cards than men, I learned recently that 85 percent of all Valentine's Day cards are purchased by women.[11] That's an astonishing difference —only 15 percent of all Valentine cards are purchased by men.

Abigail Van Buren, better known as "Dear Abby," once published the pleas for attention of one women, who probably represents the desires of many wives:

> Dear Abby: Another St. Valentines Day has come and gone without flowers, candy or any kind of a valentine from my husband. I'm 25 and he is 26, and we've been married for three years. I'd have been thrilled if he had brought me a flower—or even handed me a valentine—but he ignored the day completely. . . . He's a super guy, hard-working and decent, so maybe I shouldn't complain. But it sure would have felt great to have been remembered on St. Valentines Day.[12]

A little greeting card. It doesn't have to be very expensive. It doesn't even have to be Valentine's Day. In fact, you can make the card yourself. But it is a way of saying, "I value you, you are important to me, and I'm thankful to God for giving you to me." The card is one way of saying, "You are important enough to set aside my 'work' long enough to think about you, put feet to my thoughts, and purchase, write in, and send a card."

There are other little things you can do to say "I love you." Take her to dinner on a special occasion; hide a love note in the kitchen before leaving for work, give her an unexpected kiss after dinner. Of course, flowers or candy are always acceptable.

Before you read any further I encourage you to grab a calendar and schedule a time, this week, to go to a card store, spend at least ten minutes reading different cards, pick one out (or if you get on a roll, pick several), write in it (don't just sign it, although that's better than nothing), and mail it to your wife. And don't tell her you got the idea from this book. And before you put the calendar down, turn to a date three months from now and write in "Send _____ a card."

Tell People That You Love Them

Throughout the Bible, from Genesis to Revelation, God tells us that He loves us. I know that some of you grew up in homes where love was not verbally expressed. Other men have told me, "If you have to tell someone you love them, something is wrong." I disagree.

I've had many grown men weep in my office as they told me that they had never once heard their dad say, "I love you." I worked with one man who had been estranged from his father for close to fifteen years. His dad had been a workaholic and alcoholic. He had been physically and emotionally unavailable most of his life. There was a lot of hurt, bitterness, and resentment. Early in his therapy Tim said, "If that old S.O.B. wants to get together he'll have to make the first move. [There's no way] I'm going to call him." Yet he loved his dad and longed for some connection with him.

Toward the end of our work together I encouraged him to fly back to the East Coast to spend some time with his dad. He debated the pros and the cons. He had endured many painful memories and had released much bitterness and resentment—but facing his dad after close to fifteen years apart? That was a different story. One of the factors that helped Tim decide to visit his dad was reading a little book, *Why I Can't Say I Love You*, by Jack Balswick. I loaned him the book and asked him to read the following section.

> I was privileged to have a son for ten years who was warm, loving and expressive of his feelings. Jeff died a few days short of his tenth birthday after a three-month fight with cancer. My warmest memories of Jeff center around the times when we were intimate with each other. A bedtime ritual which I established with him was to tuck him in bed and before turning the light out to tell him that I loved him. He would invariably reply, "I love you too, Dad." Sometimes he would even beat me to the punch and would say, "I love you, Dad" before I had a chance to express my love to him.
>
> If any circumstance can be found for making the dying of my son more bearable, it was that I knew his heart. Because of Jeff's openness I knew that he knew that I loved him, and I knew that he

loved me and that he loved Jesus as his personal Lord and Savior. The comfort came in being able to hear his expression of love.

We often erroneously believe that to die like a man is to die without showing any feelings. Jeff died like a man, not because he did not show his feelings, but because he expressed them.[12]

In the story, Jeff called out one evening to his mom. "Mom, I'm going to die! Mom, I'm going to die!" He asked questions about dying and heaven, and he knew heaven awaited him. His father also assured Jeff that God was waiting for him.

Later that night Jeff died peacefully in his sleep. A few days later while his parents were cleaning out Jeff's dresser drawers they found a note he had written sometime in the past. The note read, "I love you, Mom and Dad, even when you get mad at me. I will always love you." Balswick writes that, "I am grateful to God for having given me a boy who could say, "Dad, I love you.""[14]

Tim read the passage. A couple of weeks later he decided that he needed to make the trip. We rehearsed what he wanted to say. God had given him the freedom to forgive his dad for many things. The pain was still there, but the bitterness was leaving, the wound was starting to heal. When he went back he was able to talk to his dad, hug him, and tell him that he loved him.

Several months after making this trip he received a call that his dad had died in his sleep. Tim called me and in tears of grief and of joy he asked for prayer and expressed thanks for my encouraging him to make peace with his dad. He said "I thank God that my last memory of my dad was my being able to say "Dad, I love you," and to hear him say, for the first and last time, "Tim, I love you too."

You don't need to become a mushy, huggy-kissy person to let people know how much they mean to you. The simple words "I love you" along with a look in the eye, a hug, a squeeze, a gentle touch can make a big difference in the life of your girlfriend, wife, your children or even your friend.

TAKE ACTION

Do you want to be a man whose life is characterized by Christlike love? Here are a few simple steps that will help you.

1. Develop an understanding of what real love is all about. This involves taking a fresh look at the best example of love we have, our Lord Jesus Christ. He is the source of love, and we are the objects of His love.

   A simple way to do this is to turn to the textbook for love, the Bible. Start by reading 1 Corinthians 13 in several different translations or paraphrases. Each time you read it ask God to give you one insight on love. Then go to your church library and borrow *Vine's Expository Dictionary of New Testament Words* and look up the word *love*. Look at the various definitions. Have your Bible handy and look up several of the references and mark them in your Bible. Take a special look at the passages that deal with Christ and His love for us. Ask the Holy Spirit to help you to see these passages with new eyes and a heart sensitive to what you can apply in your life.

2. Discover the nature of a biblical marriage. What makes for a healthy and growing marriage relationship? What makes for effective and enjoyable communication? How can you better understand and appreciate individual differences?

   This step involves learning from what God has taught other Christians. Pick up books such as *Romancing Your Marriage*, and *Quiet Times for Couples* by Norm Wright, *Self-Esteem: Gift From God* by Ruth Ward, *Love Life* by Ed Wheat, and *His Needs, Her Needs* by Willard Harley. At the end of each chapter write down one principle or idea that you can use to help you better understand and appreciate your spouse. Make note of new and more creative ways to say "I Love You" in her love language.

3. For the next twenty-one days begin each day by asking for God's help and guidance as you pursue excellence in not only cherishing but also nourishing your beloved. Commit yourself to this goal and then take action, putting feet to your good intentions and prayers. Not everything you try will work. We all have our "bombs." But with God's help even when something doesn't work you can learn from that. God can cause "all things to work together for good."

10

WORRY

I want to get married. I want to have a family . . . but I'm scared to death that I will marry the wrong person." Greg was a bright, successful, and attractive thirty-seven-year-old. But he described himself as a "prisoner of my worries and fears of making the ultimate commitment and getting married."

Both his mom and dad had gone through several marriages and divorces "and so I was concerned about my ability to maintain a relationship." Greg had become a Christian in his midtwenties and seemed to have a good knowledge of the Bible. This had increased his appreciation of the value and seriousness of the marriage vows. During his early adult years Greg had experienced the normal healthy concerns about marriage. But over time, building on the foundation of his parents' failed marriages and those of some of his friends, he found himself moving from concern to worry. He started asking himself, "What if?"

"What if I marry the wrong person?" "What if I wake up one morning and find out that I don't really love her, or worse, that she doesn't really love me?" "What if I get married and we can't have kids." "What if we have kids and I turn out to be a lousy father like my dad was?"

That list of "what ifs" may sound silly to you, but they were very real to Greg. Greg isn't that different from many of us. Most of us like to think of ourselves as concerned and compassionate.

Concern is a constructive and healthy emotional attitude that consists of three phases. Concern begins with the awareness of a present or potential need or a problem. When we care about a person or issue and we sense the possibility of a threat or problem, typically we become concerned. Next we move from the awareness of a threat or problem to a search for and consideration of possible solutions. What are the resources available? What can be done? What needs to be done? How can I help?

In the final phase of our concern, we try to take some kind of action. In fact, taking action is one of the distinguishing characteristics of concern. We have identified a concern, we have looked at the possible options, and now it's time to do something. Concern leads to action.

Whereas healthy concern is good, it is easy for it to turn into unhealthy worry. For most of us the problem of worry usually begins in the second phase of being concerned. While we are considering the available solutions to a legitimate concern, we also tend to become more aware of all of the terrible, awful, horrible things that might take place. If we aren't careful, we can start to feel as though all of those terrible, awful, and horrible things have already happened.

It's easy to lose our problem-solving focus and let our perspective become distorted. When that happens, like Greg we get stuck in the rut of asking "What if _____." Our minds operate like the tires of a car stuck in the mud: we let them spin quickly, hoping to free our concerns with some solution, only to find we are deeper in the muck. Our concerns slide into worry, and if we allow the activity of worry to dominate our lives long enough, we can end up with a full-blown anxiety disorder.

We look at worry in different ways. Among the words men and women have used to describe worry or anxiety in their lives are *tense, apprehensive, shaky, terrified, wound-up, nervous,* and *scared.* Some say they're uptight or on edge. A few describe their worry as feeling panicky. What do you think of when you hear the words *anxiety* or *worry*? What are some other terms you use to describe this emotional state?

Worry and anxiety are terms that for the most part can be used interchangeably What exactly is anxiety? It is a universal emotion that, like all other emotions, can be experienced in healthy and unhealthy kinds of ways.

> In its mild form it is experienced at one time or another by everyone; in more extreme forms it leads to fears of impending death or catastrophe. The feeling of anxiety may occur without physical symptoms, or it may be accompanied by numerous overwhelming symptoms affecting many organ systems; it may cause no change in behavior or it may lead to immobilization or chronic avoidance. The unpleasantness—and universality—of the symptoms are evidenced by the fact that over 80 million prescriptions for anti-anxiety drugs are dispensed in the United States each year. Despite its importance, the nature of anxiety remains elusive.[1]

Over the years I've found that one of the most effective ways to understand anxiety is to look at it as a continuum:

Healthy Anxiety   **Unhealthy Anxiety**

concern————————worry————————anxiety disorders

On the healthy end of the continuum we have concern. By giving this feeling our continued attention, however, concern can soon turn into worry. Notice how easily concern became worry for Greg. When we allow worry to dominate our mental activity it can lead to a variety of anxiety disorders, including phobias, obsessive-compulsive disorders, and panic attacks. Though it's fairly easy to distinguish between concern and worry, I've found that it is often difficult to draw a clear line between worry and clinical anxiety, which is often referred to as unhealthy anxiety.

Here is a list of characteristics common to most definitions of clinical anxiety:

> (1) it is an emotional state with the subjectively experienced quality of fear or a closely related emotion; (2) the emotion is unpleasant; (3) it is directed towards the future; (4) there is either no recognizable threat, or the threat is by reasonable standards, quite out of proportion to the emotion it seemingly evokes; (5) there are subjective bodily discomforts during the period of the anxiety; (6) there are manifest bodily disturbances.[2]

The English word *anxiety* comes from Latin and Greek words that mean "to press tight," "to strangle," "to be weighed down with griefs." Reading the above qualities, we can easily understand why anxiety comes from words meaning "to press tight."

Are you uncomfortable yet? Well, here's the good news. Like all other emotions, anxiety is designed by God for our good. In this chapter we will see how anxiety can be healthy and valuable. But we must recognize the down side first. When we allow it to run wild and to control our emotional lives, worry can wreak havoc.

What exactly is neurotic or unhealthy worry? It is a feeling of dread or apprehension and involves spending great amounts of time dwelling on a real or imagined problem. For many people worry is a common experience. It is so automatic for them that they aren't even aware that they are worrying. However, left uncontrolled, such worry can lead to unhealthy anxiety and anxiety disorders. Here are some symptoms of anxiety disorders: difficulty in concentrating, difficulty in reasoning, inability to remember important things, confusion, distractibility, and obsessive thoughts. In addition, those having anxiety disorders may become increasingly irritable or preoccupied, and have heightened fears, such as fear of losing control, of going crazy, of physical injury/death, or of criticism.

THE ROLE OF HEALTHY ANXIETY

As indicated earlier, anxiety is normal and God-designed. It is even healthy to have a degree of anxiety; the feeling can prove to be valuable. As Osborne writes,

> . . . . not all anxiety is destructive. There is a creative form of anxiety which causes a man to get out or bed in the morning and go to work. A mother answers the cry of her child in response to an inner anxiety which is also creative. [Sudden danger] stimulates the secretion of additional adrenaline into the bloodstream and prepares for "fight or flight." This is a God-given instinctual response to fear. It is only when fear becomes an all-pervasive anxiety which impairs our effectiveness that it ceases to be creative and becomes destructive.[3]

Anxiety helps us as workers and leaders to do our jobs effectively, as Hyder writes,

A little [anxiety or tension] in normal amounts can enhance performance. Athletes would be unable to perform successfully without it. Businessmen do better in their competitive world than they could do without its stimulus. It definitely strengthens concentration and spurs imagination, thereby producing more creative ideas. It stimulates interest and develops ambition. It protects from danger. Too much, however, can actually decrease performance.[4]

Numerous researchers have found that when anxiety levels are low people tend to be poorly motivated.[5] Life can be boring, dull, and unrewarding. However, when our levels of anxiety are too high or when anxiety turns into worry and becomes a way of life, the results can be devastating. The results of their research are summarized in the graph on the next page. Notice that when anxiety is low, a person's efficiency and satisfaction with life are also low. When high anxiety exists, efficiency in life and personal satisfaction are still low. However, when a person feels a medium amount of anxiety, efficiency of behavior and satisfaction with life are both high.

Dr. Irving Janis describes a study he did on the role of different degrees of anxiety on recovery for surgery patients. Several hours before their surgery he interviewed the patients to assess the degree of their anxiety. Based on these interviews he was able to divide them into three groups. Group one were comprised of non-anxious patients who were cheerful and optimistic about their impending operations. They expressed no anxiety about their upcoming surgery, claimed to have slept well the night before, watched TV, and exchanged jokes in the hours prior to their operations.

Group two were comprised of moderately-anxious patients. While they were outwardly calm and apparently not overly concerned about the upcoming operation, they wanted information about the surgical procedures, needed some reassurance and admitted to feeling a degree of tension.

Group three was comprised of highly-anxious patients. They were constantly edgy and worried about their upcoming operations. They had difficulty sleeping the night before and were worried about possible medical complications and even death. Reassurance did little to calm their worries.

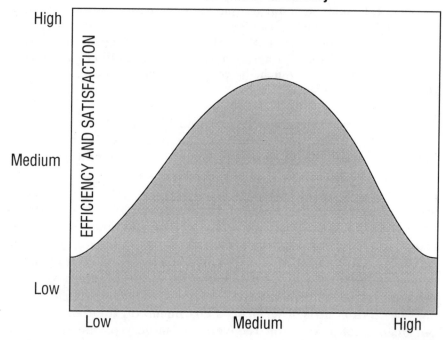

The Effects of Anxiety

High

Medium

Low

EFFICIENCY AND SATISFACTION

Low   Medium   High

SOURCE: Gary R. Collins, *Overcoming Anxiety*
(Wheaton, Ill.: Key, 1973), 17.

After the surgery Dr. Janis interviewed these patients again. Can you guess which group of patients showed the quickest recovery and the best postoperative morale? If you guessed Group Two you're correct. The moderately-anxious patients were able to tolerate the discomforts of the surgery process and were able to recover most quickly. The nonanxious and highly anxious patients showed slower recovery, poorer morale, inability to get along with others, an increased tendency to criticize, and both a fear of and intolerance for treatment.[6]

THE ROLE OF UNHEALTHY ANXIETY/WORRY

Beyond healthy anxiety is worry. Almost always worry is assuming the worst about something that has not yet happened. When we allow ourselves to worry we are trying to cross our bridges before we come to them, and we are assuming that they are all going to break while we are in the middle of crossing them.

Worry magnifies our problems and then distorts our perspective so that we can't think logically or clearly about them. Then worry tends to paralyze us from taking constructive action. The energy we have wasted on worry cannot be used to help us solve the legitimate problem that first attracted our concern. When we worry we are focused on the negative, we become more critical, we are threatened more easily and can take offense at something that hasn't even happened. When we don't catch worry in the early stage, we become more vulnerable to fear, depression, and anger. Things go from bad to worse.

When we worry we literally divide the mind. The word *worry* comes from a combination of two other words, *divide* and *mind*. As John Haggai writes,

> Worry divides the feelings . . . therefore emotions lack stability
> Worry divides the understanding . . . therefore convictions are shallow and changeable
> Worry divides the faculty of perception . . . therefore observations are faulty and even false
> Worry divides the faculty of judgment . . . therefore attitudes and decisions are often unjust and lead to damage and grief
> Worry divides the determinative faculty . . . therefore plans and purposes if not scrapped altogether are not filled with persistence[7]

Worry Versus Fear

We must distinguish between worry and fear. The emotion of healthy fear is consciously recognized and stimulated by a real threat or problem. When you mix worry with fear the result can be an irrational fear that can lead to the development of phobias and panic.

If you should have one fear about worry, that fear should be that unresolved worry leads to many other problems. I've read studies from a variety of medical journals suggesting that between 55 percent and 75 percent of our hospital beds are filled with people suffering from very real physical ailments caused by the lack of healthy, biblically-consistent functioning of their emotions, especially the emotion of worry.

Worry isn't just a contemporary problem. People have struggled with worry since the beginning of time, and the Bible has much to say about worry. Here we find examples of the problem and the practical solution that God offers.

A Case Study: The Twelve Spies

One of the classic examples of worry involves the people of Israel after they heard the report of the twelve spies who surveyed the Promised Land. In Numbers 13, the spies report that the land is just as God said it would be (verses 26–27). They give confirmation that they found exactly what God had promised.

But there is also concern, shown by the first word of verse 28, "nevertheless." There are some large walled cities that are highly fortified. Some of the people are big and strong. Ten of the twelve spies have some concerns.

Still one of the spies, Caleb, says "Lets go for it. We can do it." He knew God's promises. He knew God's character. He kept his focus on what he knew to be true rather than allow himself to be sidetracked by the "what ifs." Too bad the rest of Israel did not follow his lead; instead, they allowed themselves to become sidetracked. They took their eyes off God and what they knew to be true, and instead focused their attention on the negative possibilities. They didn't just cast a glance at the possible problems, they started staring at them. They chose to interpret then negatively.

"We are not able to go up against the people, for they are too strong for us" (verse 31) they tell the people. Obviously when they used the word "we" they were totally forgetting about God. The same God who in Exodus 23:20–33 and 33:1–2 had told them this was the land He would give them. The same God who had brought the plagues on Pharaoh, parted the Red Sea, destroyed the mighty Egyptian army and protected them and provided for them.

From their observation arose a negative *interpretation*. A short time later came the *exaggeration* (verse 32). Not only does this land have walled cities and some large people, but now the spies report that the land "devours its inhabitants; and all the people whom we saw in it are men of great size." The text tells us that ten of the spies gave out a "bad report."

Their worry, their negative interpretation, their exaggerations carried over to the children of Israel. The confident and hopeful voices of Joshua and Caleb were drowned out by the anxious and fearful voices of the ten other spies.

By this time the ten spies were emotionally paralyzed and the decision has already been made. They were not going in. Who knows what terrible things might happen to them? Their distortions led to discouragement, which led to even greater distortions. In verse 33 we read that the spies regarded themselves as "grasshoppers in our own sight, and so we were in their sight." They became victims of the Grasshopper Complex. What's that?

The Grasshopper Complex occurs when we choose to look at our life, our needs, our concerns in light only of who we are and not in light of who He is, and who we are in Him. It happens when we try to live life on our own. When we try to fight the battles in our own strength. When we lose perspective our problems appear bigger than they really are . . . and we appear smaller.

Now if the story were to end here it would be bad enough. But it doesn't. The people have picked up on the spies' worries, and they start to whine and weep (14:1–4). Their worry leads them into depression. That can happen to us too. The more we focus on the negative, the more we dwell on our problems, the more we allow ourselves to wander in the land of "what if?" the worse things will get.

The people become so out of touch with reality that they wanted to go back to Egypt. They totally forgot how hopeless and helpless they were in Egypt. Because of their lack of faith upon hearing the spies' report, they were forced to wander in the wilderness for forty years. They had seen God's power, His glory, His signs, His faithfulness and yet they still chose to test Him (Numbers 14:22, 33). Because of their lack of faith, only two adult males who left Egypt, Joshua and Caleb, were allowed to see the promised land. Over the next forty years almost 600,000 other males would die. That's about one funeral every twenty minutes, twenty-four hours a day for forty years. Now that's depressing!

Some of you who are reading this chapter may this very day be facing your own Grasshopper Complex. The giants of difficulty and discouragement are around you, and, looking at the weeks and months ahead, you may not be able to see how you will overcome. The answer is to look beyond the size of your giants to see the size of your God. It's who He is—and what He has promised—that will sustain you and keep legitimate concern from becoming unwholesome worry.

The Negative Effects of Worry

In this one example from the book of Numbers we can see several of the negative effects of worry on our lives. First of all, *worry magnifies our problems.* The more we dwell on something, the bigger it appears to be. At first the spies had some legitimate concerns about the walled cities and a few large people. By the time their story ended their observation had led to exaggeration—now the land was filled with giants.

That can easily happen to each of us. My friend Greg, thirty-seven and single, started out with legitimate and even healthy concerns about marriage. But as he allowed worry to consume a larger place in his thought life, his perception of the problems grew and grew.

Second, worry distorts our perspective so that we can't think logically or clearly about them. Our mind gets overwhelmed by so many different possibilities and options that it's easy to forget what's really important and become sidetracked. In his classic book *The Screwtape Letters*, C.S. Lewis, through the senior devil Screwtape, explains Satan's desire to keep a man as confused as possible.

> We want him to be in the maximum uncertainty, so that his mind will be filled with contradictory pictures of the future, every one of which arouses hope or fear. There is nothing like suspense and anxiety for barricading a human's mind against the Enemy. He wants men to be concerned with what they do; our business is to keep them thinking about what will happen to them.[8]

A third effect of unhealthy worry is that it *tends to paralyze us from taking constructive action.* This is exactly what happened to Greg. As he became overwhelmed with negative possibilities, he could easily become fearful of making any decision because, whatever choice he made, something could go wrong. His worry led to a clinical anxiety that produced a voluntary paralysis. He became afraid of doing anything.

Fourth, worry drains us of energy. You might be surprised how much physical and emotional energy is consumed by worry. Unfortunately, the energy we have wasted on worry cannot be used to help us solve the legitimate problem that first attracted our concern.

Fifth, worry also tends to make us more impatient. After a while the pressures of our situation can become overwhelming, and we want to take things into our own hands. This increases our vulnerability to being reactive and making unwise decisions. As Greg grew older his fear of spending his entire life single began to overwhelm his fear of making a wrong decision, and he "came unbelievably close to making what my friends told me and what in my heart I knew would have been a terrible decision [about marrying someone]."

If we don't catch worry in the early stages and apply some sound biblical principles, we become more vulnerable to fear and depression. Things will have gone from bad to worse. The worry that led to the children of Israel spending forty years in the desert wilderness today keeps many Christians wandering in an emotional wilderness.

What are the biblical principles for defeating worry? For many of you who have spent your life struggling with worry it may seem as if there aren't any options. Be of good cheer, the Scriptures offer hope—and direction.

WHAT TO DO BEFORE YOU WORRY

The best time to deal with worry is before you find yourself worrying. Don't wait until you are in the midst of a worry session to deal with this pesky and potentially dangerous activity. In Matthew 6:25–34 Christ Himself gives three things people can do to help prevent worry; as part of His Sermon on the Mount, they remain good suggestions today.

The first is to recognize God's involvement in your life, so that your spiritual values are in control. Remind yourself of God's many promises to comfort and help you. Write key verses and passages on 3x5 cards and carry them in your coat pocket or brief case. Recite them and meditate on them. Helpful passages include Psalm 37:1–9, Matthew 6:33, Romans 8:28–29a, 1 Corinthians 10:13, Philippians 4:4–9, 13, 19.

Second, we can ask God to help us accept what can't be changed. There are three categories of circumstances in life: circumstances we can control or change; circumstances we cannot change but can influence; and circumstances we cannot change or influence—things that we can do absolutely nothing about.

Many of us spend time worrying about things we can't change, and we get so worn out worrying that we don't have any energy left to figure out if we can even influence the problem and, if so, what we can do.

The third way to prevent worry is to live one day at a time. This key principle is articulated by our Lord in His Sermon on the Mount, "Therefore, do not be anxious for tomorrow; for tomorrow will care for itself. Each day has enough trouble of its own" (Matthew 6:34). I find it interesting that "one day at a time" has become the motto of many recovery programs.

Remember that worry usually involves reaching into and borrowing potential problems from tomorrow. One friend told me, "Yesterday is a canceled check and tomorrow is a promissory note. Today is cash. Spend it wisely." That's sound, biblical advice.

FIVE WAYS TO DEFEAT WORRY

Unfortunately, at times we allow worry to slip past our guard. We're seeing all the giants in the promised land. We've thought of all kinds of terrible, awful, and horrible things that could happen. Our list of "what if's?" is growing longer and longer. What can we do when worry has already invaded our feelings?

Even at this point you can take out those 3x5 cards with the promises on them and read through the verses. When you come to the Philippians 4:4–9 passage, hold on to that card. In this passage Paul has given us the plan for victory. Here are the five things you can do when worry has you on the run. All are based on Philippians 4:4–9.

1. Start by rejoicing and praising God. The apostle Paul tells us to take our eyes off the problem and turn our focus on God, His character, His promises and His love for us. "Rejoice *in the Lord* always," (verse 4, italics added).

At one point the people of Israel and their king are in a dangerous situation. Surrounded by "a vast army" (2 Chronicles 20:2 NIV), they are outnumbered. Things look hopeless—they feel helpless. The outcome will surely be terrible. But the priest Jahaziel tells them, "You need not fight in this battle; station yourselves, stand and see the salvation of the Lord on your behalf." King Jehoshaphat and the people then bow to worship God. The next day they sing to the Lord and shout praises as they go to battle.

When they had begun to sing and praise the Lord, *then* the Lord provided the victory (verses 18–23).

As we rejoice, we do not ignore the problem or pretend it does not exist. Instead, to escape the worry trap we begin to re-orient our perspective. The best way to do that is to focus on who God is and what He has promised.

2. Continue to choose to not worry. Now after reading that last sentence you might be saying to yourself, "C'mon Oliver, get real. How in the world are we supposed to do that! If it's that easy, why do you have a whole chapter in this book telling me how to overcome worry?"

Well, it's not that easy. In fact, for many people it is very painful and difficult. However, a key to overcoming worry is to choose, to purpose in your heart to make the God-given emotion of anxiety work for you rather than against. "Be anxious for nothing," Paul declares (verse 6).

Before Christ was able to heal the paralyzed man at the pool of Bethesda He asked him, "Do you want to be made whole?" That's the same question He asks each of us today.

3. Seek the divine perspective. In the second part of verse six Paul encourages us to discuss the issue with God in prayer. Many have changed the motto "Why worry when you can pray?" to "Why pray when you can worry?" Doesn't make much sense, does it?

In prayer God can help us to identify and clarify our worries. We can weed out the outrageous and irrational fears from the legitimate and rational concerns. He can help us identify the real issues.

4. Look at your worries in light of what you know to be true, honorable, right, pure, lovely, and of good repute (verse 8). We are to fill our minds with that which is healthy.

There are many ways to do this. We can read good Christian books or have friendships and good conversations with people who love and honor God. One powerful way to fill our minds with healthy thoughts is by listening to Christian music. Today we are fortunate to have an abundance of Christian praise music that can remind us of God's grace, goodness, power, and majesty. By listening to the radio or the cassette player in the car, at work, or at home, you can lift your eyes and heart to God.

When we take a few minutes to focus on God's promises, on His perfect provision for our needs, on the ministry of His Holy Spirit in our lives, we cannot easily believe that things are terrible or awful. Instead, we begin to be empowered to move back into the healthy response of concern and begin to work on some constructive alternatives.

5. *Practice what you know to be true* (verse 9). This final step involves making realistic plans and then acting on those plans. Remember, with worry we review an issue over and over in our mind; in contrast, concern leads to action. One of the best ways to abandon the merry-go-round of worry is to jump off and do something.

If you can change the situation, consider specific changes you can make. If you can influence the situation, look at the ways that your influence can be applied. If you decide that you can't change it or directly influence it, then obviously you can still pray about it. Once you have prayed about it, turn your efforts and energy into concerns that you can change or influence.

Here's a nice surprise—somewhere in the middle of taking this last step you will become aware of something returning that your worry had taken from you. It's called peace (verse 7). When we choose not to worry, when we choose, with God's help, to break the worry habit, we find that our lives are increasingly characterized by focus, clarity, increased effectiveness—and by peace.

The change won't happen overnight. But with God's help, over time you can change unhealthy, destructive patterns of dealing with your anxiety to healthy and productive patterns. You can experience the God-given emotion of anxiety the way God intended for you to experience it.

Greg did. It took time for him to work through his long-standing worries, but seven months after our last counseling session I received a wedding invitation. And about a year after the wedding I received the following note. I've kept this encouraging note, and with Greg's permission I can reprint part of it:

Dear Gary,

When you first told me that God could help me be victorious over my anxiety my first thought was "This guy obviously doesn't understand how serious this is!" Well, I was wrong.

The problem wasn't that you didn't understand my worry. It was that I didn't fully understand what it meant to be made in God's image and how to apply the specific truths of His word to this area of my life.

As you helped me understand the difference between concern and anxiety as well as the principles in Philippians 4 I remember thinking "It can't be that easy." This time I was right. It wasn't easy, but it was simple. It was just a matter of being faithful, keeping at it, and not giving up.

I still worry. But not as much as I used to, and not for as long as I used to. The bulk of my life is characterized by healthy concern and not unhealthy worry. By the way, I still use the 3x5 cards. In fact I wore out the first two sets and had the third set laminated.

As a young man I memorized 1 Peter 5:7, "Casting all your anxiety upon Him, because He cares for you." Now I can say that I not only know that verse in my head, but I have proven it in my heart and life and marriage.

TAKE ACTION

One of the best ways to take action is to apply the principles you have just read. First, however, take a few minutes and answer the following questions:

1. What are the three things you worry about the most?

2. About how much time do you spend each day in worry?

3. What is the cause of your worries?

4. What has worry accomplished in your life?

5. List three of the biggest benefits of worry.

Now ask yourself, "In what way can I apply these five principles from Philippians 4 in my life today?" Don't wait for tomorrow or next week; begin to apply them today. Take them for a test drive. You may be surprised at how well they work!

11

DEPRESSION

Don't turn away from me in this time of my distress. Bend down Your ear and give me speedy answers, for my days disappear like smoke. My health is broken and my heart is sick; it is trampled like grass and is withered. My food is tasteless, and I have lost my appetite. I am reduced to skin and bones because of all my groaning and despair. I am like a vulture in a far-off wilderness, or like an owl alone in the desert. I lie awake, lonely as a solitary sparrow on the roof.

Psalm 102:2–7 TLB

Obviously the man who wrote this psalm was having a very bad day. From time to time we all have bad days. However, for many people the bad days run together and become bad weeks, which can turn into bad months and for some even bad years.

Ernie started our first session by saying, "I can't remember a time in my life when I haven't been depressed." He continued, "As I've gone through life I've learned not to have very high expectations. It seems as if whatever can go wrong will go wrong.

"My wife and kids think I'm depressed and wanted me to talk to someone. I *told* them that I wasn't depressed. 'This is the way I've always been,' I said."

"Then why did you come to see me?" I responded. "How are you hoping I might be able to be of help to you?"

Ernie then explained that he had read an article on depression and that when the article listed some of the many symptoms of depression, "It described me. I couldn't believe it. I've been a Christian most of my life. I can't be depressed." From his tone of voice I could tell that his last statement was really a question. And his question reflected some common misconceptions about depression.

Many men go through life experiencing depression totally unaware of it. Their family and friends are aware; their co-workers may notice it. But frequently the depressed individual is the last one to acknowledge his depression. And by the time he does identify and acknowledge it, he has been robbed of joy, drained of energy, compromised of creativity, and basically been a real drag to be around.

Have you ever known someone who is frequently depressed? What are they like to be around? One of my favorite illustrations of a depressed person is the character in the old comic strip L'il Abner, Joe Bifstick. Whenever he appears in the strip he always has a dark cloud over his head. That's what a depressed person is like. They carry this perpetual dark cloud with them. The deeper their depression the bigger their cloud. If you spend too much time around them you may end up walking away with a bit of their cloud.

Some people have the motto, "Every cloud has a silver lining." The depressed person's motto is, "Every silver lining has a cloud." If you just look for the negative long enough, you'll get "lucky" and find it.

A COMMON THEME

The Bible has much to say about this emotion. Martyn Lloyd-Jones has written,

> It is interesting to notice the frequency with which this particular theme is dealt with in the Scriptures and the only conclusion to be drawn from that is that it is a very common condition. It seems to be a condition which has afflicted God's people right from the be-

ginning, for you find it described and dealt with in the Old Testament and in the New. That in itself would be sufficient reason for drawing your attention to it, but I do so also because it seems in many ways to be the peculiar trouble with many of God's people and the special problem troubling them at this present time. . . . It is very sad to contemplate the fact that there are Christian people who live the greater part of their lives in this world in such a condition. . . . In a sense a depressed Christian is a contradiction in terms, and he is a very poor recommendation for the Gospel.[1]

When Christ was on earth He experienced and expressed the full range of human emotions, including depression. Consider the account of Christ in the Garden of Gethsemane (Matthew 26:36–38).

Then Jesus went with them to a place called Gethsemane, and He told His disciples, Sit down here while I go over yonder and pray. And taking with Him Peter and the two sons of Zebedee, He began to show grief and distress of mind and was deeply depressed. Then He said to them, My soul is very sad and deeply grieved, so that I am almost dying of sorrow. Stay here and keep awake and watch with Me. (AMP)

Jesus knew full well what He was facing. He had known from the beginning of time that His journey on earth would end at the cross. From a human perspective He was facing the prospect of the excruciating physical pain of the crucifixion. From a spiritual perspective He was facing separation from His Father. And these realities caused Him to experience depression. His depression didn't control Him, but it was there. He experienced it and expressed it—to His friends and to His Father.

Depression affects millions of people every year. I've heard statistics suggesting that one of every seven individuals will need professional help for depression at some time during his life. It has been estimated that American industry loses four to six billion dollars of productivity due to the effects of depression that is either unacknowledged and/or untreated. Dr. David Burns describes depression as,

the world's number one public health problem. In fact, depression is so widespread it is considered the common cold of psychiatric disturbances. But there is a grim difference between depression and a cold. Depression can kill you. The suicide rate has been on a shocking increase in recent years . . . in spite of the billions of antidepressant drugs and tranquilizers that have been dispensed during the past several decades.[2]

It is unfortunate that some Christians find it hard to admit that they experience depression. Many have the wrong idea that the Bible teaches that Christians should not be depressed, and so depression must be a sin. Instead of identifying their emotion as depression and using the resources God has given us for dealing with it, many Christians prefer to deny their depression or say that they are sad, discouraged, or just feeling a bit low.

At the outset of our work together, I reminded Ernie of the clear biblical teaching that every human has been made in the image of God. Although the image of God in men and women has been damaged and distorted by sin, we are still image-bearers, I explained. "Part of what it means to be made in the image of God is that we have emotions. God has a mind, a will, and emotions. Man has a mind, a will, and emotions. One of those emotions is depression."

I told Ernie what is a theme of this book: Emotions are not in themselves good or bad; there are only good or bad uses of them. The good news is that all of our emotions were given to us by God to enrich and enhance our lives. The bad news is that just as sin distorted and damaged our spiritual life, it also distorted and damaged our emotional life. But the good news is that part of the process that the apostle Paul describes in Romans 8:29 as "becoming conformed to the image of His Son" involves God removing the distortions and healing our damaged emotions. That includes the emotion of depression.

THE MANY FACES OF DEPRESSION

Though Ernie had been depressed for some time, he wasn't sure how to define depression. How would you define depression? Is depression a sin, an illness, or an appropriate mood experienced by people with certain kinds of stresses?

It's clear that depression affected some of the leaders of Israel; thus depression is a common emotion that traces far back into history. Moses was so depressed that he asked God to take his life (Numbers 11:10–15). David fought despair while being chased by

King Saul and told God, "I am helpless, overwhelmed, in deep distress" (Psalm 25:16 TLB).

Elijah was physically and emotionally drained after confronting King Ahab and 450 false prophets at Mount Carmel (1 Kings 18–19). When one person, Jezebel, threatened him, he assumed the worst, ran away, crawled under a juniper tree, had a one-man pity party, and allowed his perspective to become so distorted by severe depression that he asked God to take his life. Elijah had an almost terminal case of what might be called the "Juniper Tree Blues."

Elijah was more than just sad, he was depressed. What's the difference? Burns notes that depression differs from sadness in that the depression is more intense, it lasts longer, and it significantly interferes with effective day-to-day functioning. Depression involves the loss of perspective and the inability to experience joy and feel pleasure.[3]

The simplest definition of depression is that it is a specific alteration of one's mood downward. But from that point on it gets a bit more complicated. In fact, Christian psychiatrist John White has written that in some ways depression defies a single definition and that it has many different faces and can wear many different masks.[4] However, when we don't understand depression and when we allow it to control us, it can have destructive and devastating effects. When we experience anxiety or anger these emotions trigger mechanisms that provide us with energy to meet the threat. Depression is not an energizing emotion. Just the opposite. Depression drains us of energy.

THE CHARACTERISTICS OF DEPRESSION

Because depression can be so draining, we must be able to recognize and deal with this emotion. Indeed, depression can become more than an emotion when we allow it to consume our lives—it can become a way of life. In fact, many experts classify chronic depression as a disease:

Clinical depression is not an emotion, but a specific disease. One of the ironies of that disease is that feeling depressed—i.e., dejected, blue, down—is not necessarily an indication of being depressed. The true "feelings" of clinical depression are hopelessness, helplessness, agitation, despair, self-loathing, a sense of the corruption

203

and degeneracy of the world, a constriction of feelings, or worse, anhedonia—no "feeling" at all.[5]

Depression has many symptoms. Elijah, who experienced many of the classic characteristics, is a good example of how depression can affect men. He withdrew from normal activities, he isolated himself, was discontent, gloomy, and despondent, and felt hopeless and helpless. Notably, Elijah developed a distorted perspective and lost his confidence in God. A few of the other characteristics of depression include a lack of motivation, changes in normal sleeping and eating patterns, oversensitivity and increased anger. Here's a classic description of the depressed person, written more than seventy years ago:

> Thinking is difficult to the patient, a disorder which he describes in varied phrases. He cannot collect his thoughts or pull himself together; his thoughts are as if paralysed, they are immobile. His head feels heavy, quite stupid. . . . He is no longer able to perceive, or to follow the train of thought of a book or a conversation, he feels weary, enervated, inattentive, inwardly empty; he has no memory; he has no command of knowledge formerly familiar to him, he must consider a long time about simple things. . . . He feels . . . "a creature disinherited of fate": he is skeptical about God, and with a certain dull submission, which shuts out every comfort and every gleam of light, he drags himself with difficulty from one day to another.[6]

Sounds pretty depressing, doesn't it? The only good news for men is that the risk of depression continues to be two to three times higher among women than men. However, the gap appears to be closing. As more of us men are becoming secure enough to embrace the emotional side of our masculinity, we are finding it easier to identify, admit, and deal with our depression.

For all of us who experience this emotion, though, its manifestations are not comfortable. Depression produces changes in how our body functions, how we emotionally feel, and how we think. In the physical arena one of the stops on the road from depression to clinical depression is an increased sense of "being tired." As men we are especially likely to misinterpret this psychological warning sign as merely a physical condition that more exercise would cure. Yet a man can feel tired and not experience hopelessness and helplessness.

When we feel tired, then we are feeling temporarily spent; when we feel depressed, we feel permanently spent. When we are tired things may look bad. When we are depressed things look terrible, and even catastrophic. Furthermore, when we are depressed we believe that tomorrow will be as bad if not worse than today.

Depressed patients frequently complain of being "exhausted," "drained," or "wiped out." From time to time many of us feel tired. This is a normal transient physical experience that warns us that, for some reason, our energy reserves are low. But when someone feels chronically tired and drained an alarm is sounding that in some way he is "spending" more energy than he is "earning," and he should heed it. As depression continues it can lead to changes in our eating and sleeping patterns, our weight, and in our sexual relationships.

As an emotion, depression also involves many other emotions. A depressed person may also feel hopeless, guilty, angry or hostile, and fearful. Other symptoms of depression include feelings of shame, worry, irritability, or a loss of affection. Sometimes the depressed person experiences uncontrolled crying and oversensitivity. If you find yourself experiencing any of these emotions in ways that are out-of-proportion to your usual experience, chances are good that you may have a mild to severe level of depression.

Depression can also have a profound effect on how and what we think. When we are depressed our perspective becomes distorted. Positive things appear neutral. Neutral things appear negative. Negative things appear to be terrible, even catastrophic. Our negative ideas appear to us to be an accurate representation of reality, even though our family and friends tell us we're wrong. Some of the cognitive symptoms of depression include: self-criticism, all-or-nothing thinking, indecisiveness, overgeneralization, and difficulty concentrating. In addition, depression can result in short-term memory loss and lessened ability to solve problems.

WHAT CAUSES DEPRESSION?

When Ernie came to see me, some of his first questions were, "Where did my depression come from?" and, "How and when did I get depressed?" A variety of factors can contribute to the development of depression, ranging from physical ailments to unemployment and even the letdown that follows success. Furthermore, what may be a source of depression for one person may not have any effect on another person.

Some of the causes involving physical factors are genetic predisposition, biochemical factors, reaction to medication, menstruation, menopause, and hypoglycemia (low blood sugar). The risk of depression is about two to three times higher for people who have family members who have experienced depression.[7]

Other causes include poor eating habits, not enough rest or exercise, unresolved grief due to a loss, disappointment, self-pity, unemployment, low self-esteem, stress, any positive or negative change, unconfessed sin, unfair comparisons, or even the letdown after reaching an important goal.

Recent research suggests there has been an increase in depression among the "baby boomers." This increase could be caused by their expectations concerning economic well-being not being fulfilled, increasing urbanization, people moving more and not developing personal attachments, a decrease of common social standards and beliefs, and changes in family structures and the roles of men and women in the workplace.[8]

Among men, our relational isolation and lack of emotional development can make us increasingly vulnerable to depression and suicide. Because many of us have based our identity on what we do rather than on who we are, financial and vocational losses put us at risk much more than women. As noted in the introduction, men commit suicide at a rate four times the frequency of women. "They do it invariably because of perceived social humiliation that is almost exclusively tied to business failures. Men become depressed because of loss of status and power in the world of men."[9]

When a woman has a financial loss or loses a job, she is much more likely to be able to understand and describe what she is feeling, and she is more likely to have several friends with whom she can share her sense of anger, grief, loss, discouragement, or depression. In contrast, many men who experience a similar kind of loss feel a kind of emasculation. "I'm a failure. I can't even hold a job and make a decent living," several men have told me. "I don't know how my wife and kids can ever respect me. I sure can't respect myself."

Can you imagine those words coming from a woman? It's possible, but highly improbable. Women don't struggle with the same cultural myths that men do. And when men haven't identified and dealt with the myths we discussed in chapter 1, they open themselves up to an increased frequency and levels of depression.

When a man loses a job or suffers a financial setback, he fears becoming dependent. Many men have difficulty dealing with dependency for the same reasons they struggle with other emotions that put them in touch with their weakness. These feelings threaten the tenuous construction of their fragile male ego.

DEALING WITH DEPRESSION

So much for the characteristics and causes of depression. Are there any solutions? Yes! There are specific steps that most people can take to deal constructively with depression. I say *most people* because there are some whose depression is so severe that they need immediate professional help from an experienced Christian psychologist or physician. God has given us tools and resources to deal with most experiences of depression, but when depression has continued too long and becomes severe, it can disable a person. At that point the individual needs professional help.

Here are six steps to deal effectively with the emotion of depression.

Step 1: Acknowledge the Emotion and Identify the Level of Your Depression

The first step in dealing with unhealthy depression is to admit that you are depressed. Acknowledge your depression to yourself, to God, and to others. It's no sin to be depressed. However, if we don't acknowledge and deal with our depression, if we allow our depression to control us, it can lead to sin.

Once you've acknowledged your depression, identify the level of your depression. In comparison to your past experiences of the emotion, is your present depression mild, medium, or severe? The chart on the next page summarizes the characteristics of the three levels of depression.[10]

With mild depression you may feel a little down with a decreased interest in things you would normally enjoy. You are probably aware of a little less energy than usual. You might be aware of feeling more discouraged and a greater desire to be

DEPRESSION
THREE INTENSITIES

Light	Medium	Heavy
LOW MOOD	←THESE SYMPTOMS INTENSIFIED FEELINGS OF HOPELESSNESS	VERY INTENSIFIED
MINOR LOSS OF INTEREST		SPIRITUALLY EITHER WITHDRAW OR OBSESSIVE PREOCCUPATION
THINKING OK	THINKING PAINFUL AND SLOW	
KNOT IN STOMACH	MORE PREOCCUPIED WITH SELF	
EATING AND SLEEPING OK	SELF BLAME	
SLIGHT SPIRITUAL WITHDRAWAL	EATING AND SLEEPING A BIT DISTURBED	

DEPRESSION

Light	Medium	Heavy

alone. There may be a few physical symptoms, but your eating and sleeping habits are normal. Many people with mild depression also experience some slight spiritual withdrawal. If your depression is mild, you can still continue with steps 2 through 6.

In moderate depression you may have all of the symptoms of mild depression, plus you may start to experience a growing sense of hopelessness. You find it takes more energy to process information, solve problems, and make decisions. At times you may find yourself crying for no apparent reason. You will probably start to experience changes in your eating and sleeping patterns. Your appetite may increase but will probably decrease. You may have problems going to sleep, waking up in the middle of the night, or waking up early in the morning and being unable to go back to sleep. If your depression is moderate, you may still go ahead with steps 2 through 6, but if you don't begin to experience some significant change rather quickly you should consider getting professional help. Because depression involves a loss of perspective, many moderately depressed people need someone else to help them handle the depression.

With severe depression the symptoms of mild and moderate depression become intensified. At this level it can become hard to even function. You may be isolating yourself both physically and spiritually. It can be difficult if not impossible to perform even the most basic daily tasks. I've worked with severely depressed people who could not even motivate themselves to get out of bed. They felt flooded with feelings of fear, guilt, dejection, rejection, discouragement, helplessness, self-pity, and self-blame. If your depression is severe, especially if you are having any suicidal thoughts, *immediately* contact your pastor and a qualified Christian therapist.

Most who experience mild depression don't want it, but they don't know how to get rid of it. If we allow God to teach us how to identify and deal with our mild depression, it will rarely move into moderate or severe depression and it will be much easier to deal with.

Step 2: Choose to Yield Control to God

Next you must choose who or what to give control to—the depression or God. This is a fairly simple yet critical step. It's a matter of saying to yourself, "Yes, I am depressed. My depression is telling me that something is wrong with the way I am living my life. Depression is a God-given emotion that I can learn from." We have a choice to let go of the depression and give it to God or to hold on to the depression. If we learn how to deal with and "let go" of mild depression we won't plunge into the depths of long-lasting and heavy depression.

Wright provides an excellent illustration of this "letting go" process:

> Imagine that you are treading water in a deep pool while holding a heavy rock. The weight of the rock begins to pull you down. "I'm sinking," you say to yourself, but you do not let go of the rock. In time the surface of the water is over your head. You continue to sink lower and you think, "I'm going down and down and down." Are you causing yourself to sink? No! It is the rock. Let go of the rock, and you then have the opportunity to begin the journey back up to the surface.[11]

Step 3: Tell God About Your Concern

The third step is to go to God. You can do this by talking to Him in prayer, seeking His guidance and direction, and being open to the ministry of the Holy Spirit. This step can take the form of a simple prayer such as, "Lord, I thank You that I have been made in Your image. I thank You that in Your wisdom You gave me the ability to experience depression. I thank You that You can use my depression to help me learn and grow. I give my depression to You. With Your help I choose to make my depression work for me rather than against me. Thank You for Your faithfulness to what You have promised."

You can also turn to God's Word. A good place to start is the Psalms. Look at Psalms 55, 58, and 59. Here we find that David, a man after God's own heart, both experienced and expressed the emotion of depression. In addition, look up some of the many promises God has given you. Choose to utilize the resource that God has given to you. Choose to focus on who you are in Christ and on what God has promised to those who are His children.

Consider also the words of Psalm 42:

> Take courage, my soul! Do you remember those times (but how could you ever forget them!) when you led a great procession to the Temple on festival days, singing with joy, praising the Lord?

Why then be downcast? Why be discouraged and sad? Hope in God! I shall yet praise him again. Yes, I shall again praise him for his help. Yet I am standing here depressed and gloomy, but I will meditate upon your kindness to this lovely land where the Jordan River flows and where Mount Hermon and Mount Mizar stand. All your waves and billows have gone over me, and floods of sorrow pour upon me like a thundering cataract (4–7 TLB).

Step 4: *Ask Yourself, "What Might My Depression Be Trying to Tell Me?"*

Most of us tend to view depression as negative, painful, a sign of weakness, and something to be eliminated as soon as possible. It's true that depression can be all of those things. But if we catch it early and listen closely, our depression can also be a friendly messenger.

Theodore Rubin has written that depression can serve as a signal or warning sign that something in our lives needs to be changed. If we heed this warning sign it can lead to one of the most productive and constructive times of our lives. Dealing with our depression can help us clear the air and discard years of accumulated hurt and anger. As a result, we can move toward once again experiencing warmth, affection, and love. We can reevaluate our expectations of ourselves and others and set new and more realistic goals.[12]

Without a doubt, our depression can have a positive side. We need to understand that fact and develop the ability to look for that positive side. This potentially constructive role of depression is clearly stated by Archibald Hart:

Depression is a symptom which warns us that we're getting into deep water. It is, I believe, designed by God as an emotional reaction to pull us back so we can take stock. I would even say that it is designed to drive us back to God in terms of trust and resources. It is a protective device which removes us from further stresses and gives us time to recover.[13]

Later, Hart suggests a reason that God might allow sad emotions to enter our lives instead of allowing only happy emotions in our experiences:

As humans, we have been designed to experience emotion, not just joy, but sadness as well. Perhaps the dark side of our emotions is to drive us to God. If we were happy all of the time, maybe we wouldn't feel we needed God. With depression there is certainly a positive side. God has created us with the ability to experience depression for a very good reason, I believe.

Depression is like pain. While pain is inconvenient, it is a warning system, essential for our survival. We wouldn't ask, "Why does God allow me to experience pain?" If I felt no pain, I'd be killed the first day I walked out my front door. God also has created me with the ability to experience depression so that I can have a very important warning system to tell me when things are wrong. But He doesn't allow me to be depressed in the sense of sending it my way as a form of punishment. He has taken all my punishment on the Cross. But He has given me a wonderful gift in depression which I should be able to use as an important warning system. If we can make that distinction, I think we will avoid reacting in an unhealthy way to the depression itself. This will only intensify it.[14]

Step 5: Identify the Causes

The fifth step is to identify the causes. Usually there are several causes. Review the partial list of causes mentioned on pages 206–07. Ask yourself, "What might I be doing that could be causing my depression?" "Is there anything that I might be dwelling on that might have contributed to my depression?" "Have I been allowing myself to focus on my problems to the exclusion of the solutions?" "Have I been spending adequate time in the word and in prayer?"

Like the children of Israel in Exodus 5 and 6, you may be operating with a distorted perspective. Although God promised and provided the Israelites freedom from their despair, despondency, and depression, they continued to live with a "bondage mentality." They ignored what God said and they ignored what Moses said. They chose to dwell on their discouragements, remain prisoners of their problems, and wander in a wasteland of whininess. They chose defeat, discouragement, and depression.

Look over the last four to six months of your life. What has your schedule been like? Has it been busier than usual? Has your job been consuming most of your time and energy? Have you allowed the tyranny of the urgent to keep you from doing the important things in your life? How much time have you had for yourself, your wife, your family, and your friends?

Consider physical causes. Have you made time for regular (at least three times a week) aerobic exercise? Have you maintained good nutrition? Have you made sure you have received adequate rest? Have you had any physical problems that appear out of the ordinary? How long has it been since your last physical?

Step 6: Get Busy and Just Do It!

Once you have identified the causes the sixth step is to identify what you can with God's help directly change or at least influence. Areas of change might include your thought life, how you spend your time, and some specific behaviors or habits. Make a list in order of importance of those changes and start with the first one. Then move ahead—choose to do it. Don't wait until you feel like it. It could be a long wait. If you need some encouragement, take a good look at Philippians 1:6; 2:13; 3:14; and 4:13.

One of the first steps for any depressed person to take is to increase his activity, or, to be more precise, different kinds of activity. When a man feels tired or depressed he doesn't feel like doing anything. Yet in this case you will only get some energy as you spend some energy. Energy must be invested, not conserved, in exercising, loving, and playing.

Throughout the recovery process continue to maintain your perspective by reminding yourself of what you know to be true. Write the following verses on 3x5 cards and read them several times a day. Add to the list other verses that God may give to you.

I have set the Lord continually before me; because He is at my right hand, I will not be shaken (Psalm 16:8).

For Thou doest light my lamp; the Lord my God illumines my darkness (Psalm 18:28).

The Lord is my light and my salvation; whom shall I fear? The Lord is the defense of my life; whom shall I dread? (Psalm 27:1).

God is our refuge and strength, a very present help in trouble (Psalm 46:1).

Create in me a clean heart, O God, and renew a steadfast spirit within me (Psalm 51:10).

Cast your burden upon the Lord, and He will sustain you; He will never allow the righteous to be shaken (Psalm 55:22).

My soul waits in silence for God only; from Him is my salvation (Psalm 62:1).

If you still feel that you can't do it, remember that Romans 8:37 says that "we overwhelmingly conquer through Him who loved us." Not through our own strength but through Him. You do not need to be controlled by your depression. Remember that emergence from depression is usually gradual and that feelings are almost always the last thing to change; but even feelings can change.

GIVE IT TIME

We find that God dealt with Elijah in part by allowing him to express his emotions, by temporarily relieving him of responsibility, and providing him with nutrition, rest, and exercise (see 1 Kings 19). Time is essential for recovery. The result was a refreshed Elijah with a renewed perspective. God wants you to be refreshed and your perspective renewed. God has provided exactly what you need for that to be accomplished.

Healthy people experience depression. Christians experience depression. Spirit-filled Christians experience depression. Depression is a God-given emotion that He can use in constructive ways for our growth. It is not healthy to allow ourselves to be controlled by our depression or by anything else apart from the Holy Spirit. For those of you who have struggled with depression there is help and there is hope.

Remember that emergence from depression is usually gradual, it takes time. Feelings are almost always the last thing to change.

TAKE ACTION

1. If we ignore the warning of depression, if we fail to learn from our depression, it may become a way of life. It's time to take an inventory to see if you have depression and to look at the effects, positive and negative, in the lives of people, including yourself. As you answer these questions, consider the lessons depression can teach you.
   (1) What depresses you?
   (2) When are you most vulnerable to depression?
   (3) Is there any history of depression in your family?

    (4) What are some of the models you've had for dealing with depression?

    (5) How did God use depression in the life of David and Elijah?

    (6) How has God used depression in the lives of godly people you have known?

    (7) How has God used your depression in the past?

    (8) What has your depression taught you about the commitments you make, the things you choose?

2. Sometimes reading about the experiences of others can help us gain better perspective on own conditions. To understand depression and the proper responses more fully, you may want to read one of the following books.

D. Martyn Lloyd-Jones, *Spiritual Depression: Its Causes and Cure*. Grand Rapids: Eerdmans, 1966.

John White, *The Masks of Melancholy: A Christian Physician Looks at Depression & Suicide*. Downers Grove, Ill.: InterVarsity, 1982.

H. Norman Wright, *Beating The Blues: Overcoming Depression and Stresss*, ed. Ed Stewart. Glendale, Calif.: Regal, 1988.

12
CONFLICT

Part I—Extracts from Adam's Diary

Monday: *This new creature with the long hair is a good deal in the way. It is always hanging around and following me about. I don't like this; I am not used to company. I wish it would stay with the other animals. . . . Cloudy today, wind in the east; I think we shall have rain. . . . We? Where did I get that word?—I remember now—the new creature uses it.*

Part II—Eve's Diary

He talks very little. Perhaps it is because he is not bright, and is sensitive about it and wishes to conceal it. It is such a pity that he should feel so, for brightness is nothing; it is in the heart that the values lie. I wish I could make him understand that a loving good heart is riches, and riches enough, and that without it intellect is poverty.

from *Diaries of Adam and Eve*, by Mark Twain[1]

Mark Twain no doubt uses some literary license as he tries to recreate the early days of the first man and woman in Eden. But he has a point. Conflict started long ago with Adam and Eve, and it's been going on ever since. Man with woman, man with man, and woman with woman. We don't understand it. Most of us don't like it. But day-in and day-out all of us experience some degree of conflict.

For many people *conflict* is almost as negative a word as *anger*. Most of us haven't learned the value of conflict. We misunderstand the potential of conflict and automatically interpret it as an attack. We view conflict as a rude and unwelcome interruption in our lives rather than a normal and necessary part of being in relationships.

But conflict is common and not necessarily bad. Conflict happens because we are all different. And we are all different because God, in His infinite wisdom, chose to make each one of us different. In 1 Corinthians 12–14 and numerous other passages, it is clear that God designed differences. In fact, the strength of a marriage and family is largely related to the diversity of the individuals that make up those relationships.

Yes, the Bible tells us to "be of the same mind," to "accept one another," and to "admonish one another" (Romans 15: 5, 7, 14). But as we work toward becoming one in Christ, reflecting the unity Christ prayed for in John 17, we find that at times our differences produce problems. They can lead to disagreements that may result in conflict.

Relationships aren't destroyed by our God-given differences. They are destroyed by the immature, irresponsible, and unhealthy ways in which we view those differences and our unwillingness or inability to take them to God and allow Him to help us use them for His glory and our growth.

HOW MEN RESPOND TO CONFLICT (POORLY)

Of all the experiences we can have in life, conflict is the one that tends to elicit the widest range of emotions. Conflict provides us with a unique opportunity to better understand and more appropriately express our emotions. However, most men don't "do" conflict very well. Some of us may be able to handle conflict on a professional level, but I've worked with many men who, while they could stand eye-to-eye and effectively disagree with anyone at the the office, were reduced to Jell-O when faced with a personal conflict with their spouse, child, or close friend.

When only your thinking is involved, conflict may be easy. When your feelings get involved, many men run. When the conflict involves how I communicate, why I don't talk more, how I express affection, why I say I love my wife and kids and yet spend the vast majority of my time at work—when it involves talking about emotions I don't understand and haven't had much experience talking about, the tendency is to run, shut down, or go on the attack and scare everyone away. Why is it so difficult for many men to deal with personal conflict?

First, many men find it difficult to accept criticism. Rather than viewing criticism as an opportunity to learn and grow, we see criticism as an attack on our adequacy. Many men are threatened by conflict because they assume it will involve an admission of failure, inadequacy, or incompetence.

> In modern life, no new element of danger need be introduced to make a man feel less secure, less manly, less worthy. Simply raise doubts about his strength, his ability or stature, and you will diminish his self-respect or self-confidence. The same environment is then perceived as more hazardous. The extremely insecure man in today's society will receive any criticism as a threat. There need not be rejection, humiliation, abandonment; it is enough for someone to raise questions about his essential worth to produce a sense of stress, introducing either a frightened or an angry response. In the ghettos of our cities, "disrespect" is offered as an excuse for "wasting" an opponent, and "turf" is a leading cause of gang wars. Any criticism can be interpreted by a man as questioning his power and his competence.[2]

When our power and competence are questioned many of us feel like our value and worth are at stake. One woman told me, "Ryan acts like that because he's the man of the house; he always has to be right." Many of us grew up with the myth that real men have all the answers, real men aren't weak, real men don't lose.

A respected Christian leader came to see me for counseling a few years ago. About halfway into our first session he told me that for several years the Lord had been telling him that "I needed to get some help. But going to counseling seemed like an admission of failure. I've encouraged others to do it, but I told myself 'I'm a leader. I shouldn't need it.'

"I'm not sure what I expected," the leader continued, "maybe to be criticized and condemned or that you would immediately go for my emotional jugular vein. As I sit here in your office I realize that it's not as bad as I thought."

A major cause of conflict in men is their dynamic relationship with women. Women are different from men. I know, you've noticed that. But Mark Twain's diary accounts of Adam and Eve highlight a key element of the difference—perception. Your differences from women are not exclusively physical; and in terms of conflict, the differences are not even primarily physical. Men and women communicate differently, respond to problems differently, and, when wrong, even apologize differently.

Deborah Tannen, professor of linguistics at Georgetown University, notes that many of the conflicts between men and women are caused by basic misunderstandings of the opposite sex. For example, while driving in the car a woman asked her husband, "Would you like to stop for ice cream?" Her husband thought about it for a minute and said, "No." Later on he became frustrated because he realized that his wife was annoyed. Why? Because she had wanted to stop. "If you wanted to stop, why didn't you just say so?" he asked.

What had happened is that they each had misread the other. She had incorrectly assumed that her husband's no was a nonnegotiable and irreversible position. Her husband had misconstrued his wife's question as a request for a decision rather than the beginning of a discussion about what both of them would like.[3] It's no secret that many of us men are much more comfortable giving a one-word decision such as "yes" or "no" rather than entering into a discussion whose direction is unclear and whose length is uncertain.

Many men and women differ in their ways of coping with problems. When many women talk about problems, they are more likely to be seeking understanding and sympathy and not trying to find "the solution." They want to discuss their situation with someone they can trust. The support they get from the process of someone interacting with them may be more meaningful than getting to the answer. Many of us men are different. We don't talk about problems unless we want advice. Therefore, we often frustrate women by offering advice and trying to solve the problem rather than taking the time trying to understand. We are much more likely to move to "the bottom-line." We think that we are loving our wives by giving them the "solution" to the problem. Then we're often caught off guard and surprised when our wives don't seem to appreciate our response.

Another difference that is a major source of hurt and anger to many women involves making apologies. Many women say "I'm sorry" as a way of making a connection and joining with the other person. It can be another way of saying "I'm sorry this happened to you" or "I'm sorry you feel so bad—I do too."

For many men saying "I'm sorry" means admitting that they were wrong and they need to make an apology. They believe this puts them in a one-down position, and for many men that is unmasculine and unacceptable. Over the years I've concluded that one of the main reasons men struggle with conflict is that we don't understand it.

When you experience conflict it means that *someone has a different value or opinion than you do.* Most of us assume that our position is the correct one, and we try hard to help the other person see things as clearly as we think we do. Of course, the other person feels exactly the same way. He or she invests an equal amount of energy trying to help us see things as clearly as he/she does.

Rather than working at listening and understanding, most of us attempt to change the other person. We spend most of our time trying to help the person see things from our point of view. I've worked with many conflicting couples who weren't too sure what the real issue was. But they were sure that whatever the issue, their position was the correct one. To add more muscle to their argument, some would say that their view was the most biblical one. Who would dare argue with that?

I've known some Christians who think that other believers, if truly mature, will agree almost all of the time. Every decision made must reflect the unanimity of those involved. Conflict is viewed as a sign of immaturity and carnality. But in many ways the exact opposite is true.

Whether on a committee, conferring with a co-worker, or consulting your mate, your relationships will have conflict. All marriages, families, and friendships experience stress and problems, and all have conflict. Someone once said that when two people always agree and think alike, one of them is totally unnecessary. Healthy men value conflict and have the ability to handle problems in a constructive way.

Men who don't face and deal with their problems will have problem relationships. Strong men understand that conflict is inevitable. It is a normal part of being in a healthy relationship. In fact, it is not only normal but also essential for the development of understanding, intimacy, and unity.

To summarize the positive side of conflict and to correct some of the confusion about it, here are seven truths about men and conflict:

1. Conflict is a natural phenomenon and is inevitable.
2. Conflict provides opportunity for growth in a relationship.
3. Most conflict is not dealt with openly because most people have not been taught effective ways of resolving conflict.
4. Unresolved conflicts interfere with growth and hinder satisfying relationships. The more we try to deny, hide from, overlook, and otherwise avoid conflict the greater the problem becomes. When we ignore problems they only get worse.
5. It is normal to feel somewhat defensive when challenged or criticized, thus conflict often involves the emotion of anger.
6. Conflict is neither good or bad, right or wrong—conflict simply is. It is how we choose to respond to conflict that produces the growth—or creates the real problem.
7. Conflict involves both personal needs and relationship needs.

Knowing all this, we are able to recognize that conflict is an essential part of the process of learning how to understand and appreciate another person. Conflict, in fact, is an essential part of developing a trusting and intimate relationship. However, most of us haven't been taught the value of conflict or good conflict resolution skills. Thus when many people think of conflict they think of terms like *frustration, dead-end street, out-of-control anger, waste of time*, and *"I'll only lose again."*

STAGES OF CONFLICT

Conflict develops through predictable stages. If we can identify and understand the underlying patterns that lead to conflict, we are much more likely to be able to make conflict work for us rather than against us. The four stages are acceptable differences, uncomfortable differences, unacceptable differences that bring conflict, and resolution. In the illustration "How Conflict Develops" (p. 223), we can see that conflicts occur as people try to move closer to each other, becoming more intimate.

How Conflicts Develop

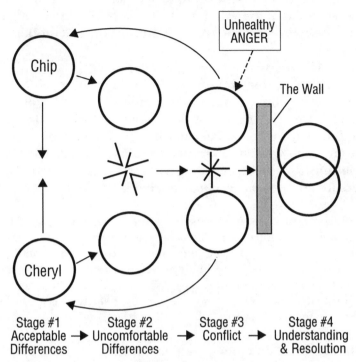

Stage #1 → Stage #2 → Stage #3 → Stage #4
Acceptable   Uncomfortable   Conflict   Understanding
Differences   Differences   & Resolution

Stage 1: Acceptable Differences

The first stage in the development of conflict arises because every human being is different. At first those differences can be a source of attraction. Do opposites attract? Yes! For how long? In most cases, not very long! When we make an effort to get closer and try to develop a meaningful relationship, conflict is sure to appear. We can call this *the stage of acceptable differences.* Such conflict is normal and healthy.

For just a moment think of your spouse or your closest friend. What are some of the ways in which you are different? Do you come from different ethnic backgrounds? Were you raised in different parts of the country? Did one grow up in the country and another in a large city? How were your childhoods different? What were your parents like? How many brothers and sisters did you have? What were your birth orders? This is just the beginning of the ways in which people can differ.

Earlier in this chapter we saw that there are some significant differences in the ways men and women tend to communicate. In the dating relationship the couple spends so much time together and is so focused on what they have in common and in how unique their love is that these differences aren't noticed or are overlooked.

In addition to male/female differences in communication there are also significant differences in their approach to conflict. Many women believe that for years men have had all of the privilege and power, and thus they don't stand a chance when engaged in conflict with a man. Perhaps in the areas of politics and finances men have had the privilege and power. But when it comes to relationships most men feel vulnerable and one-down. This can create an unusual response during men-women conflicts:

> Many woman feel powerless in conflicts with men, and therefore believe men must feel powerful. However, because men believe they must appear heroic and infallible to women, conflict with a female partner is more likely to leave a man feeling rejected and that he has failed in some way. When men react in anger and with dominating behavior, it is to defend against this threat, rather than from a feeling of power.[4]

In addition, differences in personality types can play a powerful role in conflict. Imagine two men—one an extrovert, the other an introvert—having a disagreement. Their personality differences will surely affect how they will express their differences and when they will express them.

Such a personality difference affected Chip's relationship with Cheryl. When Chip first met this woman, he was attracted to her fun-loving, extroverted style. She loved to talk with people and had a way of drawing him out. Cheryl was attracted to Chip because he seemed like "the strong, silent, and thoughtful type. He was so different from all of the other guys I had dated." So far so good.

Stage 2: Uncomfortable Differences

However, the more they dated the more the differences they only partially understood became a problem. As they spent more time together they found themselves disagreeing more and more. At this point they had left acceptable differences and entered *stage two: uncomfortable differences.* Chip and Cheryl, who were falling in love, chose to gloss over them, and for a season, they were successful in ignoring them. Their romance felt so good they didn't want anything to spoil it. They went ahead and got married.

For the first two days of the honeymoon everything went great. Eventually, however, their differences led to disagreements they could no longer ignore. Unfortunately neither one of them grew up in homes where they had learned healthy styles of conflict resolution. It didn't take them long to develop a dance that only after several years they were able to identify. It went something like this:

1. Cheryl shares an emotion or feeling. Chip (a) feels threatened or criticized and, in turn, challenges the "logic" of her feeling; or, (b) he hears what Cheryl says as a message that he needs to be responsible and tries to "fix" the problem
2. Cheryl tries again.
3. Chip feels like he has failed to understand or help her, so he withdraws into activity to avoid his rising anger or discomfort.
4. Cheryl's frustration leads to anger that she expresses by criticizing Chip. She continues to "push" Chip to get him to interact with her.
5. Chip starts criticizing her as a way to protect himself and in his anger he calls her names.
6. Cheryl feels put down, and Chip feels rejected and unhappy with his own behavior, though he isn't willing to admit it or be vulnerable.
7. Chip or Cheryl "lose it" and attack each other with generalizations such as "you always," or "you never," or "you're just like your mother/father."
8. The situation is so disappointing and painful that their fear of conflict and belief that nothing good can ever come from conflict is reinforced and they simply work harder to suppress, repress, deny, and ignore problems until, once again, they grow to the point of threatening the relationship.[5]

Stage 3: Unacceptable Differences

In stage three the couple hits the wall of conflict (see chart, page 223). Men become threatened by their own vulnerability and the increasingly assertive behavior of their wives, and women experience fear of rejection or even physical abuse at the hands of their husbands. Unhealthy and out-of-control anger often takes center stage, and the issues that led to the conflict are forgotten in the wake of the deeper fears and anxieties they have struggled with for years.

At this point what many couples do is to cycle back to stage one. There may be several hours or days of silence; they may kiss and make up and then pretend that everything is "fine." Nothing was clearly identified or resolved. They've lost another opportunity to explore, understand, and learn from those differences.

Stage 4: Understanding, Growth, and Resolution

With help and over time we can learn to break through the wall of conflict and move to stage 4, which is understanding, growth, and resolution. However, to find a satisfactory resolution, we need to identify our dysfunctional styles of dealing with conflict and replace them with healthy styles.

STYLES OF DEALING WITH CONFLICT

Whenever there is a conflict there are two levels of need that are at stake. First, personal needs are involved. Part of the reason for the conflict is that what I think or want differs from what you think or want. On their honeymoon, Chip wanted to spend more time snorkeling. He was fascinated by the beautiful fish and was thoroughly enjoying exploring the beauty of this new underwater world with Cheryl. On the other hand, Cheryl thought that snorkeling was fun but she wanted to explore the island, visit the shops, discover different restaurants, and talk with Chip about their experiences.

Although Chip and Cheryl had different personal agendas they both wanted to nurture their relationship. They had personal needs, but they also had relationship needs. Chip said, "I knew that it was important for me to deal with this issue in a way that wouldn't seriously injure or destroy our relationship." That, of course, is the challenge of effective conflict resolution. How can we deal with issues in ways that take into account both our personal and relationship needs?

In his practical little book, *When You Don't Agree*, James Fairfield has identified five different styles of dealing with conflict.⁶ As you read through them you probably will see yourself in at least one or two of the styles.

The first and least effective style of dealing with conflict is to *withdraw*. In Style 1 we say, "I'll get out." We refuse to discuss the situation and stonewall our partner. Withdrawal is the least effective style because we lose out on both our personal and relationship needs.

Style 2 is *winning*. We say, "I'll get what I want or I'll get him/her." This was Cheryl's preferred style. She was bright, verbal, confident, assertive, and competitive. When she wanted something she went for it. She was usually able to do it in ways that were healthy and appropriate, ways that showed sensitivity and respect for the other person. However, when her sense of significance or security was challenged or threatened, she would go for the win.

In this mode her motto was "take no captives." In the win mode she was able to get her personal needs met but at the cost of the relationship. Over time she learned that, in any relationship, whenever one person wins what really happens is that both lose.

There are some people whose predominant style is #2 and who aren't as healthy as Cheryl was. They must always win. They must be the best, brightest, and most frequently acknowledged. They are people who have become legends in their own mind. They must dominate, and they must win.

While Cheryl's predominant style was #2 Chip's was #3: *yielding*. Style 3 is the opposite of style 2. Style 3 says, "I believe in peace at any price, so I'll give in." For a time Chip was able to do this. Having his relationship needs met were at that time more important than getting his personal needs meet.

But after Cheryl's repeated attempts to draw him out, the nagging, the criticism, the implicit and explicit ("Why don't you act like a man?") messages of inadequacy and inferiority, Chip would kick into style 2 and go for the emotional jugular vein.

As you can see, the first three styles are unhealthy and can be destructive. They lead to circular arguments that produce more heat than light, that build more walls than bridges, that increase the hurting rather than the healing.

In style 4 we come to one of the two healthy styles. Style 4 is called *accommodation*, and it says "I'll meet you halfway." Some people use the word *accommodate* as a synonym for sell out. *Accommodation* means an adjustment of differences or a settlement. In conflict it means that I am willing to bargain some of my personal needs for some of my relationship needs. Legitimate love always requires some accommodation. In my experience more than 90 percent of our conflicts can be dealt with through accommodation.

In style 4 we are able to solve the issue at hand. Chip and Cheryl frequently disagreed about what TV shows they felt the kids should watch. They finally developed enough conflict resolution skills that they were able to solve most of these kinds of problems.

Style 5 is similar to style 4, but it goes one additional step. Style 5 says, "I'll grow with you beyond this problem." In *resolution* we are able to solve a specific issue. As we talk, listen, and ask questions, as we better understand our spouse, child, or friend, we are at times able to go beyond the specific issue at hand and arrive at a solution that deals with the whole category of issues.

As Chip and Cheryl talked about their concerns with various TV programs, their discussion soon extended to movies. They began to clarify both for themselves and for their partner the deeper values that underlie the opinions they had expressed. Over the course of several conversations, some of them rather animated, they discovered that not only did they understand each other but they had arrived at a mutual policy regarding all movies and TV programs for their kids.

The following chart uses minus and plus signs to show the effectiveness of the five styles of conflict. Withdrawal is completely ineffective; and whereas winning meets one's personal needs, it is a failure in dealing with relationship needs. Study the chart below.

EFFECTIVENESS OF THE FIVE CONFLICT STYLES

	Personal Needs	Relationship Needs
1) Withdrawal	-	-
2) Winning	+	-
3) Yielding	-	+
4) Accommodation	+	+
5) Resolution	+ + +	+ + +

SEVEN STEPS TO CONFLICT RESOLUTION

Though most people try to avoid conflict, we all know that conflicts are inevitable. Some conflicts can be dealt with quickly and easily, and some take much more time and energy. Regardless of the severity of the conflict, however, you'll find that constructive conflict resolution is much easier (notice I didn't say easy) when you have a plan. Many men and women have found that the following seven simple steps have helped them make conflict work for them, rather than against them. You'll find the steps worth your time too.

Step 1: Acknowledge, Discuss, and Define the Problem

The first step is to acknowledge the problem, set aside ample time to discuss each other's perception of the issue, and work toward a definition. Frequently when people disagree the temptation is to try to solve a problem that's only partially defined and not understood.

During this time, you may need to agree to disagree with the other person. Some issues can be taken care of in one discussion and some may take seven or eight. Disagreement may continue for a while. If you place pressure on yourself to "solve this thing," you will only increase the level of frustration.

In this first step, it will also be helpful to make a mutual decision as to which style you both will use to reach a solution. In her practical book, *The Dance of Anger*, Harriet Lerner has listed twelve additional suggestions that are important to keep in mind. Her Dos and Don'ts are practical advice:

1. Do speak up when an issue is important to you.
2. Don't strike while the iron is hot.
3. Do take time to think about the problem and to clarify your position.
4. Don't use "below-the-belt" tactics.
5. Do speak in "I" language.
6. Don't make vague requests.
7. Do try to appreciate the fact that people are different.
8. Don't participate in intellectual arguments that go nowhere.
9. Do recognize that each person is responsible for his/her own behavior.
10. Don't tell another person what he or she thinks or feels or "should" think or feel.
11. Do try to avoid speaking through a third party.
12. Don't expect change to come from hit-and-run confrontations.[7]

Step 2: Ask Yourself, "What Is My Contribution to the Problem?"

Whenever there is a conflict we usually have little difficulty identifying the other person's contribution to the problem. It is amazing how clearly many of us can see how "they" need to change, what "they" could do differently, and how "they" could listen better. Instead, we must recognize how we have contributed to the conflict and what we can do better.

Of course, it's easier to pray, "Lord, please change them. Please help them see things as clearly as I do. Please give them the same wisdom and insight you've given me." It's easy for us men to pray "Change my *wife*, oh Lord" rather than, in the words of a popular praise song, "Change my *life*, oh Lord."

Proverbs 25:12 says, "It is a badge of honor to accept valid criticism" (TLB). Those are sound words. Listen to what the other person has to say. Even if 90 percent of what they are saying is invalid, look for the 10 percent that might be true. Look for even the 1 percent that God could use in your life to help you deepen and mature.

Step 3: Identify and Develop Alternate Solutions

By this time you know what doesn't work. Ignoring the problem won't make it go away. Make a list of what you have done that hasn't worked. Then make a list of what you haven't tried.

Talk to some other individuals or couples who have been in a similar situation. What worked for them? What did they learn as they worked through their conflict? In step 3 be careful not to ignore a potential solution just because you don't think it will work. Get as many ideas as possible on your list. Look them over and talk about them. You may find that pieces of two or three different ideas come together to provide a solution neither one of you had considered.

Step 4: Discuss and Decide on a Mutually Acceptable Solution

Deciding on a mutually acceptable solution can sound easy. Over time it can become easy, but in the early stages of changing your conflict patterns it may be difficult. Don't be upset or disappointed; that's normal.

Be sure to set aside ample time for discussion and prayer. Find a quiet place with no interruptions. Take the phone off the hook. Remember that you are choosing to bargain some of your personal needs for some of your relationship needs. Read 1 Corinthians 13 out loud.

At this point in workshops men have raised their hands and asked, "But what if we can't agree on a mutually acceptable solution?" After a brief pause I usually smile and respond by saying, "Well, if you can't agree on a solution, reach into your pocket, pull out a coin, ask the other person if they want heads or tails, and flip it."

This usually brings a lot of laughter. "I'm serious," I quickly add. "If you can't decide, it's better to try something that might work than something that is a proven failure." Then I quote my definition of crazy: "*Crazy* is to find out what doesn't work and keep on doing it."

If the first solution you try doesn't work, then move on to the next option. It may take three or four attempts before you find something that works. But if you follow through with my suggestions, over time you'll be able to deal with almost every issue.

Step 5: List the Specific Steps Involved and Who Is Responsible to Do What

Most people leave out an important step, listing the specific steps in resolving the problem and assigning who does what. So determine the specific steps involved in the solution. Then ask, "Who is going to do what, and when will they do it? For how long will they do it?" Then determine when you will let each other know that you have done what you agreed to do.

Step 6: Just Do It!

You've run from it, hid from it, fought about it, cried over it, and now you have the opportunity to resolve it. Once you've agreed on a plan and detailed who is going to be responsible for what part of that plan, then do it. Don't wait for the "best" time. Put your plan into action.

"Just do it!" say the Nike star athletes who typify the active, take-charge guy. When it comes to dealing with conflict, at some point you just have to do it.

Step 7: Review It!

When you've given your plan adequate time, it's important to get together and discuss the results. Evaluate the solution.

Here are some questions you can ask: Were there any surprises? How could we improve it? What did I learn from this conflict about myself? What did I learn about our relationship? What did I learn about God's faithfulness?

Finally, consider what you could do differently the next time conflict arises.

TAKE ACTION

Here are several ways you can prepare for future conflict. (Remember, conflict *will* come; it's unavoidable.)

1. Start by asking God to help you become a listener during a conflict situation.

2. Find another man to be accountable to. Talk about your conflicts and your struggles in dealing with them, and ask him about his conflicts. Become "prayer warriors" for each other.

3. An attitude of love will go a long way to shortening and focusing your disagreements. Effective conflict resolution will look for the other person's well-being as well as your own. Meditate on the following passages about love and acceptance *before* conflict comes. Then put them into action when conflict arises: Romans 12:10; 16–19; 1 Corinthians 13:5–7; Galatians 5:14–15; Ephesians 4:15–16.

There also are things you can do during and after the conflict to respond properly:

1. Caring about the other person during the confrontation is very important. When the confrontation begins, check your attitude. Remember that caring and confrontation go hand in hand.

2. Remember that a mistake is not a failure. Mistakes only become failures when we fail to learn from them.

13

GROWING THROUGH GRIEF

It caught me totally off guard. I never dreamed that it would affect me in that way. Numerous friends had visited it and they told me of the profound effect it had on them but, for some reason, I wasn't prepared for the overwhelming sense of grief and loss that emerged from somewhere deep inside and swept over me like a tidal wave.

Several of my friends served in Vietnam in the late '60s and early '70s. A couple of them died there. I still have vivid memories of the struggles our nation went through during that horrible war. I remember watching the nightly newscasts showing the bodies of young men, many of them my age, being taken out of the jungle.

I didn't go to Vietnam. But in respect to my friends and in memory of the turmoil and loss in this undeclared and divisive war, I went to Washington, D.C., to visit the Vietnam Veterans Memorial. My reaction caught me by surprise.

The Vietnam Memorial is merely a series of polished black granite blocks with mostly men's names inscribed on them. The long columns of names stare forward—names of men who were killed. Young men.

I looked up a couple of names that I knew. Then I began to read some of the letters and poems that loved ones had left at the base of the memorial. Some family members had left the pictures of these brave and at the same time frightened men. The photos, many more than twenty years old, showed the men with their friends and family. And suddenly, I couldn't stop the flow of tears. Even as I write this story tears come to my eyes.

I still don't fully understand it. But I understand it now better than I did then. What was I experiencing? What am I experiencing even as I write this sentence? It's an emotion that many of us men aren't very good at. It's the emotion that can cause us to feel the weakest and most vulnerable. It's the emotion of grief.

When men experience a loss, their grief may not show; they may appear to work through the feelings rather quickly. People may look at a man who is grieving and be amazed at "how well he took it." Some may even make the comment that "he really took it like a man." That used to be a compliment. But rarely do men truly take it well. Instead, we either stuff, repress, suppress, deny, or ignore our grief. And instead of taking it like a man, we take it like a non-person. We withhold a truly human response—grieving. As Carol Staudacher observes,

> It is generally true that the man who expresses, releases, or completely works through grief is the exception rather than the rule. He is less likely to talk about, cry about, and appear to others to think about his loss. He'll probably be reluctant to seek the support of others, either individually or in a group. Instead, he's more apt to assume full responsibility for his bereaved state and depend only upon himself.[1]

Grief in our lives can be triggered by some kind of loss. A long-time friend moves, or an active, cheerful co-worker gradually becomes sluggish and pessimistic; one day he announces he is leaving work at the end of the week to begin therapy after being diagnosed as having multiple sclerosis. Your sister dies at age forty-five. All of these situations result in a loss of something valuable in our lives. The role of loss is discussed further on page 237. For now, let's ask ourselves, "How do we deal with such losses?"

Men typically have been socialized to deal with loss by (1) taking charge, (2) taking care of others as we "bear up under the load," and (3) accepting the task of dealing with the loss and keeping it together as a challenge, a kind of test of our masculinity. Rather than having permission to feel our pain and work through our grief, the task becomes one of how to be a "manly man." We tell ourselves, "I can't cry"; "I can't feel the pain"; "I can't let them see me hurting."

Though we regard grief as an "unmasculine" emotion, our needs and drives call us to express this God-given emotion. The more we allow our behavior to be controlled by how we've been trained to respond or how others expect us to act, the more we get out of touch with and can eventually become totally insensitive to our need to experience and express the healing emotion of grief.

When loss brings grief, most men are uncomfortable with the powerful emotions associated with grief. *They're unmasculine*, men think. But those feelings are natural, and to keep them in check requires an enormous amount of energy. For instance, a man must be careful to not be afraid, to not be weak, to not hurt, to not cry, and to not appear out of control when everything that's happening to him actually causes him to feel that way.

As a result of trying to rigidly control their feelings, some men begin to "feel" numb; from childhood they learn to feel little. Other men "have been overwhelmed with feelings for years and have engaged in a losing battle for control. Still others have all the 'unmanly' feelings under 'control' but are extremely angry individuals who often act out their angry feelings in inappropriate ways.²

WHAT IS GRIEF?

Significantly, grief describes both an emotion and a process. Though Webster's Dictionary describes grief as "a deep and poignant distress caused by or as if by bereavement," it also refers to grief as a process, a part of suffering.

That grief is an emotion is clear from the words that my friends, patients, and experts use to describe the word. For instance, many describe grief with one of the following words: *sorrow, hurt, lamentation, despair, anguish,* or *pain.* Others use similar words loaded with feelings that are considerably downbeat: *heavy heart, desolation, torment, ache,* or *mourn. Sadness, melancholy,* and *crushing* are three other words I've hear used to describe feelings.

In addition to being an emotion, grief is also an emotional process whereby we gradually detach or slowly let go of a person, place, or thing that has been significant to us. This process is necessary before we can reattach to a person and continue living a more meaningful life.

Grief isn't a single event. Grief is a process that consists of several stages that can last from one to two years (and even longer) depending upon the significance of the relationship and the source of the loss. It is a process that involves a wide range of emotional experiences.

Grief is one of the most transforming of the emotions. Over the past twenty years in my clinical work I've found that grief is the doorway to many men's emotional lives. At one of my conferences a man in his mid-thirties came up to me during a break. Though slightly overweight, he was tanned and nicely dressed. Lenny introduced himself and thanked me for the weekend and then, after taking a deep breath, he added, "I used to be one of those men you talked about this morning. I didn't express any emotions until four years ago when my son died." Even as he spoke of the death of his son, tears began to well up in his eyes.

Lenny continued, "I cried buckets and buckets of tears. God used his death to force me to reevaluate my life. The loss of my only son helped me learn what it means to be a real man." This is a real man—one who expresses his feelings, including tears of sorrow. Grief and masculinity are not incompatible. In fact, in the warrior tradition, you don't trust a warrior who can't or won't grieve.

When we don't understand the emotion of grief and the process of grieving we are more vulnerable to getting stuck in the grief process. If we stay there too long the healthy depression we experience as a part of the grieving process can begin to take over our lives and turn to deep despair. Gaylin describes the ultimate consequences of improper grieving—deep depression.

> Depression is a macabre and grotesque parody of grief. It persists too long; it becomes self-destructive; and to the traditional forms of grief it adds a few irrational emotions. The depressed patient seems almost masochistic in demeaning himself, in blaming himself, in finding fault with his life, his functions, and his persona. He seems devoid of all self-esteem and is excessively involved in self-

accusations. He has passed beyond the sense of a loss into a state where all is lost.[3]

THE ROLE OF LOSS

We usually think of grief as being associated with death, but the pain of grief can be brought on by many different circumstances. Although death is certainly the ultimate loss in the course of our lives, there are many different kinds of losses we can experience. The loss may be tangible, such as a home, a job, or a loved one. Or it may be intangible, such as loss of respect, hope, joy, or meaning and purpose. The amazing thing is that it doesn't matter whether the loss is tangible or intangible; the grieving process can be similar for both.

We experience loss whenever we lose or are deprived of something or someone we value and have become attached to. The loss may feel like a tap on the shoulder or a two by four across our forehead. The severity of the impact depends on the significance of the loss.

The loss is like a "blow," and we are thrown off balance. Even if we have been able to anticipate the loss, it can still have a powerful effect on us. Grief is the process by which we are able to survive our loss, regain our balance, and move ahead with life. By grieving our losses, we come to accept that a change has occurred in our external world and that we are required to make corresponding changes in our internal world.[4]

Again, the losses can be varied—divorce, the death of a dream, a father finding out that his daughter is pregnant, being fired from a job. All these circumstances will throw us off balance. And we need to grieve in order to restore the balance. Having to move for the fourth time in seven years, recognizing you never had a childhood because of new responsibilities you were forced to take on due to alcoholic parents are losses too, and we must grieve.

Whenever we suffer a personal loss, grief is the normal response. Several years ago a friend of mine was betrayed by someone he worked with. This person was kind to John's face, but behind his back he told half-truths and lies in an attempt to turn co-workers and friends against him.

He was someone John had cared about and trusted; John had poured himself into the person. John felt many emotions:

hurt by the betrayal, shame at not seeing it sooner, foolish for having trusted him, angry at his deceit and deception, and, yes, grief over the loss.

How did John respond to these feelings? At first he tried to minimize it—the typical male response. "These things happen," he said. "It's all part of leadership. If you can't stand the fire then you'd better get out of the kitchen." But these platitudes didn't work for long. Over a period of a couple months the hurt, shame, and anger hadn't gone away.

Finally he talked with God about it. Then as John gained a clearer understanding of what was going on, he revealed his feelings to his wife, Sara. Eventually he was able to share his feelings with me and a few other close friends. "Gary, this doesn't seem like it should be that big a deal. I don't know why I can't just let go of it and get on with things."

I explained to John some of the principles we'll be looking at in this chapter. Only as John trusted God and a close friend to help him work through this process was he able to experience healing, learn from the experience, and move on. John recently told me, "When I think of this I still feel some pain. To a degree I'm still letting go. But I can honestly say I'm wiser and stronger because of it."

WHEN SOMEONE CLOSE DIES

Without a doubt the ultimate loss is the death of a loved one. The experience of losing someone you love can't be compared to any other life event.

> Death brings obvious and profound sadness and yearning, along with a flood of other less obvious reactions such as emptiness, agony, fear, loneliness, and despair. The feelings which well up in the survivor are so powerful and overwhelming that they could not have been anticipated before the loss and, because of this, they could not have been planned for. As a result, when a loved one dies, you may feel as if every part of your life—emotions, perceptions, actions, thoughts, and physical body—are in a state of disorder. Even the world itself may seem frighteningly unpredictable, unstable, and unmerciful.[5]

Ron Karnaugh was a member of the 1992 U.S. Olympic swim team. But during the opening ceremonies in Barcelona, Spain, his father, Peter, age sixty-one, collapsed and died from a heart attack.

"My dad was my best friend," Ron later told reporters. "We did a lot of things together throughout my life—outdoor things. We hunted and we did a lot of trout fishing. When he died, it was like a part of me died."

At 4 o'clock the next morning Ron was informed of his dad's death. At first he was speechless. He couldn't comprehend what had happened. "A few hours later, I went into the shower, and that's when it hit me," he says. "I just couldn't understand why this had happened to me. I was crying and really struggling."

Throughout his life Ron's dad had been his father, his coach, his cheerleader, and his friend. When at the 1988 Olympic Trials he missed making the team by seven tenths of a second, his dad came up after the race and said, "We still love you, and we're proud of you, and maybe this was for the best."

Ron recalled the night of the opening ceremonies. "I saw my dad in the stands, taking photos as I passed by in the procession. I looked over, and he had the biggest smile. I think he was having the thrill of this life."

He wanted to respond to the loss in a way that would please his dad. Peter Karnaugh had taught his son the value of hard work and perseverance. Never give up. Never quit. Ron had faced adversity before. But nothing like this. There was no question in his mind whether he would swim. But he found it difficult to concentrate. Just before the race Ron put on his father's old sweat-stained straw hat. "I felt with the hat a part of him was going to be with me," Ron said.

As soon as he hit the water he knew he was flat. He finished a disappointing sixth. At first he was devastated. However, like many people, especially men, he didn't understand the nature and process of grief. He hadn't taken into account the high emotional cost of his father's death. "A lot of people build up Olympians as superhumans," he said, "but when we are faced with adversity, we are humans."

When Ron returned to his hometown of Maplewood, New Jersey, he returned to a parade in his honor and fifty letters a day from people expressing their compassion, respect, and encouragement. "As much as I wanted to win the gold medal, this unique experience I had, with everyone reaching out to help me, especially in my hometown, is what sticks with me."[6]

STAGES OF GRIEF

If we have suffered a significant loss, we may carry the sense of loss over a lifetime. But grieving helps us to move through the loss and resume our normal experiences and activities. Perhaps a bit sadder but definitely wiser.

The most helpful way to understand the grief process is to take it apart and look at how it begins, progresses, and can eventually ease into a healthy and successful resolution of the loss. These phases, or stages, of grieving are flexible, fluid, and overlapping. There is no sequential set of clearly defined emotions, conditions, or responses. There is only a general progression. This progress can be best understood by what takes place in each phase.

1. Retreating—Early Grief Stage

Retreating, the earliest stage of grief, is the one part of the grieving process that is difficult to avoid. Even if you are able to anticipate a loss the reality can be much different than the anticipation.

The early grief phase is characterized by shock, a numbing effect, disbelief, and often denial. In this phase people can feel paralyzed mentally, emotionally, physically, and spiritually. It's common to hear such comments as "I feel like my world has stopped," "I can't believe this is happening," "I never dreamed I could ever hurt like this," and "I feel like I'm walking through a thick fog."

Losses invade our lives, damage our hopes, and destroy our dreams. The numbness can last from a few hours to several weeks. In this stage our thoughts are disorganized and we may wonder how we'll ever make it through it. Normal life activities may lose their importance. We can find ourselves flooded with a wide variety of conflicting and confusing emotions, including fear, guilt, anger at ourselves, at God, and at others. This is especially difficult for the many men who have grown up unaware and out of touch with their emotions.

People will often withdraw from normal activities. It seems like they are crawling into a shell. In a sense they are. Short-term withdrawal can provide some necessary self-protection and provide some time and space to regain our emotional balance.

2. Working Through—Acute Grief Stage

After the initial shock is over and the numbness begins to wear off, we are faced with a choice. We can either face our loss, experience our emotions, and grow through the crisis; or we can have a "flight from health" where through denial or spiritualizing we pretend that everything is fine and try to go on as if nothing happened.

What do people do who don't work through their emotions? One option is to suppress the emotions, keep them all inside. Suppression means a conscious inhibition of an impulse or feeling that you are aware of and consciously choose to keep the lid on. Others repress their emotions. In repression a person is not consciously aware of difficult, uncomfortable, or painful ideas, memories, and emotions. When we suppress our feelings long enough they can become repressed; they are denied and removed from our conscious awareness.

What happens to people who don't deal with their grief? For some their behavior becomes characterized by indecision; they can't seem to get started at anything. Others will do things that are detrimental to themselves, such as giving things away or selling their possessions for virtually nothing.

Still others may tend to blame and punish themselves, stay withdrawn, or avoid mourning by becoming hyperactive. Frequently those who haven't worked through a loss find it difficult being close to or spending much time with people associated with the loss. They may even appear to be insensitive to the loss.

What is it like to work through the emotions associated with the loss? What is it like to grieve? A dear friend of mine told me that it's somewhat like living on a roller coaster. It starts with a sudden drop, things are happening so quickly you can't keep track of what is going on. Then, as soon as you think it has leveled out there is another drop. You find yourself climbing up, you think you're making progress, and wham, another drop. "Roller coasters are fun to ride on, but they are horrible to live on."

In the working-through phase we ask ourselves many questions: "What could I have done differently? What did I miss? Why did I do what I did?" One of the most common questions is "What if?" We can replay scenes over and over again and each time change the scenario a bit.

Many people experience a kind of disorientation. They recognize the world around them, but at the same time it doesn't seem the same. One man who had just lost his job after spending twenty-three years with his company told me, "It was kinda like I was outside of myself watching myself go through life." That's not an uncommon response.

In this phase we're trying to make sense of and rebuild the present and set goals for the future, while holding on to parts of our past. Attempting to move three directions at once can be frustrating, confusing, and self-defeating.

Both our emotions and physical responses will vary. A man's feelings can range from emptiness and despair to guilt and anger. His body may react to the grief with insomnia, loss of appetite, exhaustion, headaches, and muscular pain, among other responses.

In order to move through this second phase you can't repress or suppress your memories or emotions. You need to think about your loss, talk about your loss, and weep over your loss. That's right, weep over your loss. One of the most damaging messages to men has been "real men don't cry." However, God created us with the ability to cry. David wept, Peter wept, and Jesus wept. Max Lucado describes our tears as "miniature messengers," and he describes the pain of some of those watching the crucifixion of Christ:

> Tears.
>
> Those tiny drops of humanity. Those round, wet balls of fluid that tumble from our eyes, creep down our cheeks, and splash on the floor of our hearts. They were there that day. They are always present at such times. They should be, that's their job. They are miniature messengers; on call twenty-four hours a day to substitute for crippled words. They drip, drop, and pour from the corner of our souls, carrying with them the deepest emotions we possess. They tumble down our faces with announcements that range from the most blissful joy to darkest despair. The principle is simple; when words are most empty, tears are most apt.
>
> A tearstain on a letter says much more than the sum of all its words. A tear falling on a casket says what a spoken farewell never could. . . . In sorrow, do you let your tears decompress that tight chest and untie that knot in your throat?
>
> Or do you reroute your tears and let them only fall on the inside?

Not many of us are good at showing our feelings, you know. Especially us fellows. Oh, we can yell and curse and smoke, yessir! But tears? "Save those for the weak-kneed and timid. I've got a world to conquer!"[7]

Herb Goldberg agrees that men need to cry, but says men fear their tears as badges of weakness:

There is something about a male in tears whether as a boy or as a man that offends, causes others to run away and to want to "do something," to stop it as soon as possible. . . . From a male, tears create discomfort at best and occasionally even mild disgust at his inability to "control himself." Manliness is still equated with poise and composure in the face of tragedy.[8]

If you want a bottom-line, here it is. Tears aren't the issue. It's what our tears represent. Our tears represent the heart and soul of the person. To stuff, repress, suppress, or ignore your emotions is to deny your humanity. Lucado does not overstate the issue when he writes, "To put a lock and key on your emotions is to bury part of your Christ-likeness!"[9] Someone once said that tears are love in liquid form. Where there is love there will be grief, and where there is grief, if you are lucky, there may be tears.

3. Resolving—Subsiding Grief Stage

Resolving is the final stage. It comes when we have accepted the reality of our situation. In this phase we turn the corner and start to reinvest our physical, mental, and emotional energy in a changed life. We begin to adjust to our environment with the sense of a changed identity.

People who successfully negotiate the grief process emerge changed. We see through different eyes. We hear with different ears. We feel with a different, a much more sensitive heart. We are aware of our wounds, and we become more aware of and sensitive to the wounds of others. And we begin to reorganize our lives. Our hopes and our dreams return, we begin to reestablish our daily routines. We are able to reinvest our energy in new plans and goals.

This doesn't mean that we feel great all of the time. In fact, from time-to-time we will experience what some have called

"The Dip-Ins." From time to time, we may "dip into" our grief when an old song, movie, place, or object triggers old memories and feelings. These "dip-ins" are an ongoing, normal response to a loss, and they do not mean we have not adjusted to a loss.

Several years ago the only son of one of my closest friends died. Several months after his death I called Harry just to chat and see how he was doing. I could tell by his voice that something was wrong.

I debated whether I should say something. Men do that a lot. If women think that a friend might be hurting, they are more likely to ask "What's wrong?" and to offer help. They show affection by noticing and by asking. Men are just the opposite. Most men believe that if something is wrong the other guy probably doesn't want to talk about it and so not asking is a male way of showing respect and affection. Besides that, the man wonders, *What if something really is wrong and I don't have the right thing to say? How awkward.*

I knew Harry was healthier than that, so after some small talk back and forth I decided to jump in. "How are you doing?" I asked. After a pause and a deep breath Harry said, "I'm really doing fine. I was riding my exercycle and some memories of Mark came to mind. I cried for about ten minutes and thanked God for the memory of my son and for His goodness to me."

That's how a real man deals with grief! He cries, he thanks God, and he's honest with his feelings. Harry went on to say, "That [crying] used to happen a lot for the first couple of months, and now it may happen only once a month. I know it's part of the process of letting go, grieving the loss, and moving on." No anesthetic, running, hiding, or denial. Harry was facing the loss with the help of God and his friends.

If you want to grow from grief, if you want to learn from your losses, if you want to successfully integrate the loss into your life, you can't stop at stage one. It is necessary to go through phases two and three.

GOOD GRIEF AND YOU: HOW TO GROW THROUGH GRIEF

As you go through those three basic stages of grief, there are several ways to endure the painful period. Here are six specific ways you can deal with grief as you walk through what feels like the valley of death or another loss:

1. Face the Loss

Acknowledging the loss may sound like an easy thing to do. Yet I've worked with hundreds of men who have spent enormous amounts of physical and emotional energy trying to deny the fact of or the importance of a loss. Sooner or later we all have to come to grips with the losses in our lives, and in every case the sooner the better.

2. Keep Your Eyes on Christ

In the midst of a loss it is easy to focus on the loss and become so consumed by what has happened that we forget God's love, promises, and provisions for our lives. At the end of this chapter I've included a list of verses I've encouraged men to write on 3x5 cards and carry with them. Read them several times a day.

At this stage your mental stability and energy will return much faster if you give your confusion, guilt, and agony to the Lord. You may feel alone, but remember the message of Hebrews 13:5: "For he hath said, I will never leave thee nor forsake thee." Don't ignore your feelings, but don't dwell on your feelings either.

3. Seek Out and Talk with a Trusted Friend

The inestimable value of a friend is reflected in the following account.

> I should say right here that Larry and I have been fishing together for most of our adult lives, which means we have sorted out the significance of our respective triumphs and failures, have seen each other through career crises, divorces, what have you. We have learned to read each other. So we know when enough distance has passed under the wheels, when the time is right, when it is safe to turn the radio down and do what we cannot do until we're going fishing. We talk.
>
> We ask indirectly, and in so many words: Why did our parents withhold praise from us while passing along favors to our siblings? Why do our wives and children forget we have feelings? Why is it always up to us to be calm and wise? Why does everyone make us feel so guilty? Why is it that we are misunderstood by the people we love? Why can't we escape our mothers? Why do sentimentality and melancholy and loneliness prevail over our natural inclination to be playful? Why, in the end, does it take us so long to learn that things are the way they are and always will be? . . .

Larry and I have bonded with each other, in fishing, in clowning around, in catastrophes and, occasionally, even in tears. We are bonded because we offer something to each other that most of the rest of our world does not, and that is safety.[10]

Verbalizing our pain often dilutes its power. Communicating our thoughts to a spouse or a friend is a great way to "take captive" those thoughts. A friend can help you clarify your thinking and just speak your feelings of loss. When you talk to your friend, just talk about your memories or what you are thinking. Talk about what you are feeling. Ask God to help you find words to communicate the pain you feel in your heart.

Sensitivity and compassion is a strength that comes out of a shared weakness. Grief helps us to recognize our humanity, our weaknesses, our mortality. As we discover acceptance in sharing our grief we realize with greater clarity that everyone is helpless and, at one time or another, will need and welcome love from us.

4. Consider the Need to Forgive

In dealing with your grief there may be a need to forgive. You may need to forgive the person who wronged you, the person you believe is responsible for the loss, yourself, or even God. Forgive the thoughtless people who were so sincere at the time of the loss but four weeks later seem to have forgotten about you. Forgive the shallow, superficially spiritual people who believe that if you were really spiritual you would be over it and moving on with your life.

5. Ask God to Bring Some Good Out of the Loss

The apostle Paul tells us that "God causes all things to work together for good, to those who love God, to those who are called according to His purpose" (Romans 8:28). If that is true, then God can make a way through the wilderness of your discouragement and despair to heal your heart and bring you hope.

One good is that in our grieving we learn how to later comfort others. In 2 Corinthians 1:3–4 Paul wrote, "Blessed be the God and Father of our Lord Jesus Christ, the Father of mercies and God of all comfort; who comforts us in all our affliction so that we may be able to comfort those who are in any affliction with the comfort with which we ourselves are comforted by God."

At the very least God can use our loss and pain to enable us to more effectively comfort and encourage those around us. Millions of people have been challenged and encouraged by the stories of people like Nazi prisoner Corrie Ten Boom, paraplegic Joni Earickson Tada, and baseball pitcher/cancer victim Dave Dravecky. As they've had the courage to share the struggle of working through their own losses, they've given the rest of us hope and courage.

6. *Find Some Way to Memorialize Your Loss*

The grief process is something that takes place inside of us, but it affects all of who we are and what we do. Many men have found it helpful to do something tangible with their sense of grief. One of the most helpful exercises is to keep a journal or write a letter, a song, or a poem. Writing allows us to confront, vent, explore, and memorialize our grief. It's an effective way to process our grief. If you're not sure what to write, ask yourself: *What am I feeling? What's getting me down? What am I dwelling on? Are some feelings more dominant than others? Which ones?* Those questions are guaranteed to get you started.

Other exercises that may be helpful include revisiting the site of the loss, going to a grave site, visiting the house you grew up in, going to the Vietnam Memorial. Make something. Take a trip. Get involved helping someone else. At the 1993 Grammy awards guitarist and songwriter Eric Clapton won six Grammys. Several of them were for the song "Tears in Heaven," written in memory of his son Connor, who had fallen from a 56th floor apartment to his death. At the awards he honored the memory of the short life of his precious little boy. Rather than turning to alcohol or drugs, Clapton chose to deal with his grief, in part, by creating a musical memorial that touched the hearts of millions.

7. *Feel Free to Ask the Question* Why? *But Don't Wait for an Answer*

This is a hard one. But it's also an important one. Whenever we experience a loss our almost immediate response is to ask "Why?" Unfortunately that question tends to be a dead-end street. First of all there are many experiences in life for which there is no answer to "why." We never do receive an explanation. We must trust that a good God will work for our good in spite of the tragedy.

Another problem with trying to know why is that usually several factors are involved in any particular situation. When there is an answer to why, it is rarely a single or a simple answer and sometimes it may take years for all of the pieces to come together.

Even if you are able to find out why, you still have to figure out what to do to get on with your life. Most of our why questions are only an exercise in spinning our mental wheels and in the process wasting our much needed energy.

HEALTHY GRIEVING

In Jeremiah 10:19 we read, "This is a grief, and I must bear it." With some things in life, all you can do with them is get through 'em. I'm convinced that it's a lot easier to read and write about grief than it is to go through it.

But don't ever forget that it's much easier to work through the grief and learn from it than it is to deny, repress, suppress, and ignore it. The only easy way to get through grief is to walk through it one day at a time.

At some point most people respond to grief in ways that block, delay, or distort the grieving process. Healthy grieving allows you to understand and resolve the loss, to learn from the loss, and to move on. Perhaps a sadder but definitely a wiser person.

You cannot restore what is lost, you cannot undo what was done, you can't bring a deceased loved one back to life. But you *can* recover from the loss. You can heal. You can accept the loss, learn from it, and move on. Eventually you can be happy again. You can learn to trust again. You can learn how to develop appropriate protective boundaries.

There is life after loss. In fact, if you learn how to successfully grieve, yours can be a much more mature and productive life.

TAKE ACTION

1. Read John 11:17–44 to observe how three people, two sisters and a good friend, dealt with the loss of Lazarus. When Lazarus died, Mary, Martha, and Jesus felt and expressed their grief in distinct ways. How did Mary and Martha express their grief? Why did Jesus cry?

2. Read John 11:17–44 a second time. Jesus offered comfort and a pattern for helping others deal with loss. Jot down how Jesus helped Mary and Martha through their grief. You should be able to recognize the following strategies used by Jesus:
   (1) Begin where they are
   (2) Listen
   (3) Help them feel comfortable in expressing their loss to you
   (4) Don't rush them
   (5) Empathize
   (6) Be sensitive and don't say too much
   (7) Don't use faulty reassurances

   In addition to these seven approaches, remember that when your friends are grieving, they need safe places, safe people, and safe situations. If you seek to be a help in these three areas, God will be able to use you in their lives.

3. Here are a couple dozen verses that address sorrow in our lives and remind us of our God and our resources in our Savior, Jesus. Place several on 3x5 cards and during the middle of the grieving process read them daily.

   Genesis 37:33–35
   Deuteronomy 33:27
   Joshua 1:9
   2 Samuel 18:33
   Job 1:18-21;
      4:16–18; 6:10; 7:9
   Psalms 5:1–3; 28:7;
      30:5; 34:18, 42–43;
      46:1–2, 7; 51:17,
      147:3–6
   Proverbs 10:2
   Isaiah 41:13; 43:1–2; 53:4

   Matthew 5:3–6; 11:28–29
   Luke 4:18
   John 11:25–26; 14:1–7,
      15–21; 16:22–23
   1 Corinthians 15:35–38,
      42–44, 53–54, 57
   2 Corinthians 1:3–5
   1 Thessalonians 4:13–18
   James 4:8
   Revelation 20:4; 21:4

14
JOY

One hundred twenty feet above the flat fields of Peoria, the pastor prepared to jump—straight down. And John had just *paid* for the privilege. His face wore a silly grin and just a bit of fear as the cage, now at its apex, steadied in the air. Then, release—and the minister plunged downward almost one hundred feet. Then the cage jerked upward, down again, up a little less, then down, up slightly, and to the ground, a wildly unraveling yo-yo over the Illinois plain.

Yes, John was a bungee jumper, and the elastic cord had done its job. Among the observers, theologian James Packer stared in disbelief—and admiration. Not that Packer would consider enjoying such recreation. But he admired John because his friend knew how to have fun in life.

"How grand a gift pleasure is!" Packer declared as he recalled the event for readers of *Christianity Today* magazine. Packer said his big joy would be listening to Wagner's Ring cycle, sixteen hours of opera spread over several days. Another personal delight, Packer confesses, would be to "flop in a hot tub."[1]

Some may wonder about this emotion, joy. To laugh, to delight in child's play—whether blowing bubbles with a nephew, playing touch football with friends, or sliding down the Slithering

Serpent at the water park—may seem foolish, not like anything real men do. But perhaps no emotion refreshes us more than joy and its frequent companion, laughter. The physical activity that often accompanies joy—play and recreation—even gives us strength for the tasks ahead.

Packer, author of the classic *Knowing God* and considered a senior Christian statesman (he's in his seventies), quickly answers the fears that fun is inappropriate for the Christian man. Some believe faith is somber, dealing with Christ's death, our sin, and the hope of heaven. But joy is a preview of heaven to come, Packer answers. "God intends our pleasures to act as a reminder of heaven, particularly our very intense pleasures. . . . Life's pulse-quickening pleasures remind us that heaven's delights are for real and are our proper goal."

Augustine chided those who enjoyed life's pleasures, but in the *Institutes* "Calvin caned Augustine for lacking a biblical appreciation of life's pleasures," notes Packer, "and the older I get the gladder I grow that Calvin did this." Packer concludes:

> To scoop out time for activities that are for your recreative pleasures (music, a hobby, reading, good conversation . . . tennis, trips away, evening with your spouse or whatever) is a proper and needful use of Christian liberty; without it, however you grow in Christian expertise and expression, you shrink as a person.[2]

A TIME TO LAUGH AND TO PLAY

Let's not shrink! As men, we need to laugh and to play. If grief leads to tears, if frustration and fear lead to anger, then joy leads to release and renewal. Joy gives us the power to face life's tough times with the comfort of a Savior at our side and the pleasures of His created world.

"A joyful heart is good medicine, but a broken spirit dries up the bones" (Proverbs 17:22) is a proverb we must take to heart. Norman Cousins, former editor of the *Saturday Review* and a college professor, is one of several researchers who have found therapeutic value in laughter. As he fought a serious collagen disease that caused great pain in his joints, medical specialists had little hope for his recovery. But Cousins believed a positive emotional state could only help him in the battle. He ordered a diet of funny TV shows, including episodes of Candid Camera and old Marx Brothers movies.

He reported that his inflammation was significantly reduced after each session of laughter; and one ten-minute period of laughter yielded two hours of sound sleep.³ Of course, laughter is no cure-all, but medical doctors have found that laughing elevates blood pressure, improves circulation, and helps us to breathe more fully and quickly, all aids to good health.

Joy comes when we can laugh at our own weaknesses and this sin-flawed world that's filled with people like you and me. We can laugh at our limited abilities, and, at times, vain actions and silly thoughts. "God has given us permission to enjoy incongruities, absurdities, and other normal experiences."⁴ The passing parade of life will soon be over; meanwhile we are to enjoy the funny moments, including our own mistakes and the unexpected scenarios of life. As Tom Mullen notes, "Humor is nothing short of the grace to see ourselves as we really are."⁵

Joy shows itself in the unexpected of life, a break from the routine of work and duty. That means leisure is as important as laughter. Charles Swindoll says we need to give "a place of dignity" to play, fun, rest and leisure.⁶ He should know. The pastor with the infectious smile and playful spirit usually releases at least one hearty laugh per sermon. His latest best-selling book is *Laugh Again*, a call to Christians to enjoy life on earth in preparation for life everlasting in heaven.

In the book, Swindoll, a former marine, reveals his passion for riding Harley-Davidson motorcycles. In fact, a famous poster shows this cool pastor on his Harley, dressed in leather jacket and dark sunglasses, ready to burn the road, free and easy. Is this how to enjoy life? It certainly is one way!

In the daily grind of making a living it's easy for men to forget how to relax. Whether its new knowledge and skills or simply the sense of accomplishment at tasks completed, we can often substitute such temporary satisfaction for the more substantial joys of family and friends and laughter that renew and invigorate us. As we look at this final emotion, joy, we must ask, "What gives *true* joy and fulfillment?"

Two conversations I had in the past make me want to answer that question. The first conversation took place in my office with a successful businessman; the second was a telephone call I received while speaking at a family camp in the Rocky Mountains.

A TALE OF TWO MEN

Ted, the businessman, was president of an international consulting firm. In his mid-sixties with a deep, distinguished sounding voice and wearing a well-tailored suit, Ted knew why he had come and what he wanted to talk about. After just a few minutes of small talk he said, "I've been a very successful man. I've lived a full life. But over the past several years I've lost a couple of longtime friends to cancer, and their deaths have made me think a lot more about my life. The older I get the more I find myself wondering whether or not my life has been a success. I've worked hard, I've been involved in my church, I've done a lot of good things; but at times I don't feel like my life has made much of a difference."

Much later I was speaking at a family camp in the Rocky Mountains. My family was with me, enjoying themselves as much as I was, when in the middle of the week I heard someone had called with an important message. I picked up the phone to learn that a man who had been my friend for more than ten years had been killed in a car accident while returning from a fishing trip. His younger son, Ryan, died with him. I couldn't believe it.

Jerry Schmidt was a committed Christian, a loving husband and father, active in the leadership of his church, a respected psychologist, and a good friend. In the past year we had been meeting together on a regular basis for fellowship and working on a writing project. This news of Jerry's death had a direct and immediate affect on me.

I had spoken with Jerry the day before Ryan and he left. Jerry loved his two sons and was very intentional about spending time with them. He did special things with each. This fishing trip would also be special, Jerry said. Ryan had wanted to go fly-fishing with his dad on the Madison River in Montana, one of the best fishing spots in the country. Jerry was excited and looking forward to some great fishing and some quality time with his son. I told him I would pray for him, and we made plans to get together for breakfast when he returned.

Jerry was only forty-four when he died. He was a gifted man and had a lot of good years left. It wasn't fair and didn't make any sense. But as I reflected on Jerry's life and his legacy, I realized that he understood what was most important in life and had true joy.

254

Unlike Ted, Jerry understood what true joy is. Real joy is not found in activity but in the process of relationship. Nor is joy an end result; it is a by-product. Joy does not occur by reaching a destination; it occurs while we are reaching in the right direction. Joy comes as we begin to change, and care for others.

SUCCESS AND JOY

Indeed, joy comes in serving people. As we help and serve others, we truly enjoy life. "There is joy in serving Jesus." the hymnwriter declares; there is also joy in serving God's created beings. As we enjoy family and friends, we enjoy life, for the essence of living is people.

In counseling and listening to people, I've learned a few things, including the ways we try to measure success. Some of us have bought the lie, yet we must remember the truth: At the end of life, a person's success is not measured by his finances or his fame. When all is said and done, a man can evaluate his life by looking at three areas: faith, family, and friends.

Many people spend much of their lives in the pursuit of possessions. They spend their time and energy acquiring things and getting ahead. In the early years of marriage many men are focused on climbing the ladder of success. In some cases the children are set aside and, in effect, are treated as peripheral to the really "important" tasks.

Such men do love their children, yet they are too involved with more immediate and demanding concerns to spend very much time with them. The children aren't the only ones who get the leftovers. Many couples have little time for each other. Typically, men who don't have time for their children or their wives are not spending much time with the Lord. If we don't make time for those we can see, it's highly unlikely that we're spending much time with someone we can't see.

After all is said and done, what's really important? At the end of life what really matters? Certainly it is important to have some financial security. There is nothing wrong with that. I think that is part of what it means to be a good steward.

But is that all you have? If so, you do not have true joy. Lasting joy comes through enjoying people, not possessions. I recently interviewed a man who is powerful, well-known, and worth millions; we'll call him Richard. He owns several companies. By many people's standards he is a success. He was having some stress-related problems and was hoping I could help.

As a part of my normal initial interview I asked about his wife and children. "What is your marriage like? Are you and your wife very close? How much time do the two of you spend together? Did you have a good relationship with your children? Do you see your grandchildren very often?" As Richard responded to my questions, tears began to well up in his eyes. At first he tried to hold them back, but after a few minutes he began to cry.

No, he wasn't very close to his wife or his children. His marriage was in shambles. He and his wife had become married singles. He didn't have a good relationship with his kids, and he didn't see his grandchildren that often.

Richard expressed deep sorrow and regret that while he had devoted most of his life toward being successful at business, now he realized that he had been a failure in the more important area of relationships. In his busyness he had become financially successful and relationally bankrupt.

"Gary, I spent my life climbing to the top of the corporate ladder, " Richard said. "I was so successful I bought the corporation and several others. Now at the end of my life I'm seeing that I climbed the wrong ladder."

As you look back on your life, have you been spending it on the pursuit of status, recognition, and possessions, or have you been investing it in spiritual growth and the development of relationships? In what specific ways have you been investing it? With what specific people have you invested it?

When you die will you be leaving behind the legacy of a listener, a friend, one who knew how to love, one who took the time to share, one whose life was a model of what he believed in? In what ways has your allocation of time reflected what is really important to you? To what degree have you made quality and quantity time for those you love?

Some men go through life always traveling but never arriving. They are planning and preparing for the future that never seems to come. There is always a new project or proposal or activity. There are new lists to make and more items to check off those lists. For many of us it is easy to fall prey to the "tyranny of the urgent" and allow the urgent things to crowd out the important things. In this day and age it is easy to spend our lives rather than invest them.

JOY THAT RUBS OFF

If we have proper priorities, our joy will be apparent to others as well. We can show them the appeal of the Christian life when, as Christians, we put God and people first. A friend of mine recently received a letter from a former boss who had moved out of town. His former boss was financially very successful. He wasn't a Christian. My friend had told him about his faith in Christ for many years with no response. Here's what the former boss wrote in the letter:

"I have decided that a close review of my own life might be in order. I have all the things you don't have. I have a terrific job that pays me far more than I am probably worth. I drive an expensive sports car. I belong to an expensive country club. But you are right. These things won't last forever. I am not happy, I am friendless, and I do not know God." He closed the letter by saying that after this review of his life and reading certain passages in the Bible he had asked Christ into his heart.

People who have invested their lives are different than those who have spent their lives. Successful men are men who have invested their lives in becoming whole men. They reflect the reality of the indwelling presence of Christ in their mind, their will, and, yes, in their emotions. Invested lives are characterized by a strong faith, a Christlike life, a solid marriage and family life, and some meaningful friendships. These men are considered by those who know them to have had successful lives.

I'm told that shortly before his death Jerry had breakfast with a good friend. They were discussing their families and the importance of the spiritual lives of their children. Jerry was excited that both of his boys knew the Lord and were walking with Him. Jerry turned to his friend and said, "In many ways, my most important life's work is done."

Jerry invested his life in serving the Lord, his wife, his sons, his church, his friends, and his patients. He sought to model the reality of the person of Christ in his life. He had a great mind, he made wise decisions, but most of all he had allowed God to help him develop a healthy heart. Jerry understood the value of, and was secure enough to express, his emotions.

He wasn't flashy, yet his life had a tremendous impact. His life was characterized by a compassionate heart, an active faith, a strong family, and many friends. Jerry didn't just spend his life. He invested his life. Jerry was a success.

Someone once said that we make a living by what we get and we make a life by what we give. Spenders live to get and investors live to give. As you look at your life are you spending or investing? Have you spent a major part of your adult life climbing the ladder, paying your dues, and trying to make your mark? Or have you invested your time in people—showing care, honesty, and giving of yourself?

FINDING THE SMILE

Among my patients and my friends, I've met few men who consider themselves to be having a joyful life. Many have lost the smile of a younger life. They are like Mitch, the sad central character in the movie *City Slickers*. Mitch (played by Billy Crystal) has a wonderful wife, two healthy children, a well paying job, and two close friends, Ed and Phil. He is also discouraged, depressed, and hopeless. The three men have traveled around the world trying to find something to give them meaning and purpose in life. In fact, the movie begins with the trio in Pamplona, Spain, for the running of the bulls. They had thought that being chased by bulls might do the trick.

Later, Mitch throws one more birthday party, but Phil is depressed. Afterward, Mitch's wife, Barbara, says, "I just know you're not happy here, you're not happy at work."

Mitch pauses. "I just feel lost," he says. Barbara tells him not to go with the family to visit her folks in Florida. She encourages him to join Ed and Phil on a two-week cattle drive. "Go and find your smile," she tells him.

"What if I can't?" he asks.

"We'll jump off that bridge when we come to it."

I've talked to hundreds of men who have lost their smiles. Some can't even remember the last time they had theirs. Oh, if they see a funny movie or hear a funny joke the corners of their mouths may turn up rather than down, and they will probably laugh. But it doesn't last long. Like Mitch in *City Slickers* they have lost their joy, their intensity, their reason for living.

For some men the older we are the better we understand what true joy is. Joy comes from serving people. As we enjoy family and friends, we enjoy life, for the essence of living is people. If success is viewed in terms of growth and becoming conformed to Christ, then every man can be a success.

Success and joy are closely related. Success starts with who we are and what we are becoming. Successful men are those who express and experience the deep joy that comes from knowing we are becoming the kind of men God created us to become. The first step to becoming this kind of man is for us to chose to come home to God and to make an intimate, growing, love relationship with Christ a priority.

A TIME FOR CHANGE

I've never met a man who in some way didn't want to be different. Do you have a "wish list"? I sure do. I wish I had more patience and more wisdom. I wish I didn't struggle with overcommitment. I wish I could practice 1 Corinthians 13 love with greater consistency. I wish I was a better husband and dad. And the list goes on.

Unfortunately for many, their wish list is just that. In five, ten, or twenty years they have made little headway. I was reminded why recently as I read again a chapter in *My Utmost for His Highest*, Oswald Chambers' classic devotional book: We don't act on our good intentions.

> Never allow a feeling that was awakened in you on the mountaintop to evaporate. Don't place yourself on the shelf by thinking, "How great that would be in such a wonderful state of mind." Act immediately—do something, even if your only reason to act is that you would rather not. If during a prayer meeting, God shows you something to do, don't say, "I'll do it"—just do it! Pick yourself up by the back of the neck and shake off your fleshly laziness. Laziness can always be seen in our cravings for a mountaintop experience; all we talk about is our planning for our time on the mountain. We must learn to live in the ordinary "gray" day according to what we saw on the mountain.[7]

Yes, the first step is "Just do it!" It's time to take action. If what you've read in this book has helped you understand better what it means to be a whole man, if you want to experience growth in your mind, will, and emotions, I encourage you to take the first step. Just do it. Begin with a prayer. Here's one I'd suggest:

> Lord, I want to make a commitment to become the kind of
> man You want me to be.
> I want to make a commitment to learn, to mature, to be a
> model;
> I want to reflect You in my mind, my will, and my emotions.
> I want to overcome my fear of feeling;
> I want to experience the joy that surpasses my ability to
> describe.
> I acknowledge that becoming a godly man is a process and
> takes time.
> I understand that maturity is not wind sprints, it's cross
> country.
> Lord, I want You to know that I'm in this for the long haul;
> With Your help I want to become a man that You and those I
> love can trust.
> I want to become a Hebrews 11:38 man.

Before you put this book down, write this simple prayer on a
3x5 card, and for the next thirty days begin and end each day
with it.

Christ said, "He who is faithful in little is faithful also in
much" (Luke 16:10). God doesn't expect you to change overnight. Just turn your eyes on Him and take a small step in His
direction. If you've lost your smile, you can find it again. If you've
lost your joy, you can begin to experience the only lasting joy
there is. It's the joy that comes from becoming the man that God
designed you to become. A man whose life is characterized by
godly thinking, godly behavior, and godly compassion. A man
who has the mind and the heart of God.

TAKE ACTION

1. How much do you relax? Sometimes even our weekends can fill up with work chores—repairing a car,
   mowing the lawn, shopping, projects from work, and
   so on. None of these is fundamentally wrong, but to
   devote all our weekends and spare time to chores is to
   ignore people and our own needs for recreation and
   renewal. On a sheet of paper, try to recount your activities the past four weekends (or other days off from

work). Then list what plans for play and fun and time with others that you have for this weekend. What's your conclusion—do you need to give more time to the joy of living?

2. What do you think of the definition of success found in this chapter? If you believe money is important for a certain amount of security for you, how much do you think you need? You (and if you're married, your wife) may wish to evaluate your budget and lifestyle to determine if everything you want is necessary, and whether you have a good savings plan. Read the following testimonials of two men who were wealthy and yet had no satisfaction, no lasting joy in their "successes." The first is James Couzens, a partner with Henry Ford in the Ford Motor Company, speaking in 1922.

> I left Ford when I was 43 because I got tired of making so much money. It became a burden. It was almost obnoxious, distasteful. I had no particular use for so many millions. So I stepped from under this avalanche of money —and I'm heartily glad I did.[8]

The second is Harry Helmsley, financier and hotelier who made millions in the 1980s:

> I remember a young woman interviewing Harry Helmsley. . . . At the time, he was certainly one of the richest men in New York. The reporter asked him why at his age (he was already well into his seventies) he continued to enter into deals and expand his real estate holdings. Surely it could not be simply to make money? He insisted that he was still very much interested in making money. She then inquired how much money he had; he demurred, according to the rules of the game, modestly suggesting that to state the amount would be boastful but that it was hefty indeed. She said, "I have a feeling that if you bought everything you personally wanted, there is no way you could possibly spend all of your money. Is that true?" He agreed that that was probably true. She then asked, "Then what in the world do you want to do with even more money?" His reply was: "You don't understand. In the game I play, money is the way you know you have won."[9]

Epilogue

AS A MAN THINKS

or
If You Find This Is
Harder Than You Thought,
Read This Chapter

I can't do it!" "I'll never get it right." "It's just too hard." "I've tried before and I blew it. Why should I try again? I'm not a glutton for discouragement." Have any of these or similar phrases ever passed your lips? Have any of these thoughts ever crossed your mind? They have mine.

I remember as a young Christian walking along a southern California beach feeling frustrated and discouraged. I had recently returned from a church camp and had once again recommitted my life to Christ. I promised God that I would have a "quiet time" every morning and that I would "flee youthful lusts." Well, I had missed several quiet times, and I had failed to "flee" as quickly as I should have and yielded to temptation. Once again I had blown it. Once again I had let God down. Once again I was a failure.

As you finish this book and think about the emotions we've discussed and the call to be a real man—a man with feelings—you probably have one of two responses. "This emphasis on emotions sounds good, but I just can't change that much. Like you said, Gary, we were raised from boyhood to hold it in, so we can't just unload our feelings and express them to other people." Or your response may be, "Well, I guess my mind and all my different thoughts are not so important after all. I should focus more on my feelings."

I agree partly with both responses. Yes, we can't change quickly, and, yes, we men must focus more on feelings. But, no, your ability to understand and express your emotions can change, and your mind does matter. What I'm describing is a balance between your mind and your feelings. Your emotions affect your thought life, but your thought life also affects your emotions. Therefore, let's conclude with some thoughts about using your thought life to become a mature man.

Your mind is important. Most men have a strong aptitude to analyze and evaluate situations. We can combine and process information and make recommendations based on our analysis. Our cognitive (thinking) abilities are significant and useful. God wants us to use our minds to make wise decisions, as we recognize His will for us (Ephesians 5:15–17). Yet often we feel confused and defeated in the Christian life.

A spiritual war is occurring in your life, and the battlefield is your mind. Let's explore how our thoughts can help us fully express our emotions. True thoughts about ourselves, based on how God sees us, will help us use our emotions positively. As we consider how our thoughts can be changed, we will learn the important balance between thoughts and feelings, and how Christ can renew our mind for a balanced life.

The major battleground for spiritual warfare is the mind. Part of being made in God's image means that we have a mind. Our mind is the seat of reflective consciousness and performs activities such as perceiving, thinking, problem-solving, remembering, learning, and choosing and experiencing thoughts and emotions. God has created our mind to receive sensations, interpret those sensations as meaningful information, determine what is important, access previously stored information from our short-term or long-term memories to help us make decisions, and then store this new information for future use.

The mind is the place that decisions are made for or against the truth. Satan's temptation of Eve started with the mind. Satan has had our mind since birth, but upon our spiritual salvation, God has established a beachhead in our thought life. Through the process of sanctification He wants to help our minds become more like the mind of Christ. We belong to Christ and are indwelt by the Holy Spirit; yet Satan can still influence our minds. That's why Peter exhorts us to "gird our minds for action" and to "be on the alert." Paul warns us that we don't wrestle against "flesh and blood" but against principalities and powers. That is why God instructs us to have a combat-ready mind.

Satan loves to defeat us men. His chief tactic is to throw us into discouragement when we fail. And it is a certainty that at times we will fail.

Most Christian men want to be strong and victorious. We desire to mature and become men to whom God can say, "Well done, thou good and faithful servant." We want our lives to be characterized by integrity. The only problem is that each of us has pockets of weakness, areas of vulnerability, and deeply entrenched habits that can sabotage our best intentions.

What hinders our change? What keeps us from being as successful on the inside as we are on the outside? Why is it easier to achieve success in what we do than in who we are? What detours our development? What sabotages our sincere intentions?

CONFRONTING SATAN'S BATTLE PLAN

It's the battle for our minds—a spiritual battle that caused the apostle Peter to warn us to be on the alert (1 Peter 5:8–9). To be a mature man, we must know who the enemy is (Satan), where he will attack (primarily our thought lives, or minds), and his method. Let's study Satan's three-phase method, as outlined by the apostle James. They we will look at how we can have victory in our thought lives.

James summarizes sin's approach and Satan's tactics in James 1:14–15: "But each one is tempted when he is carried away and enticed by his own lust. Then when lust has conceived, it gives birth to sin; and when sin is accomplished, it brings forth death."

Phase 1: Distraction

The first phase of Satan's plan is to draw us away from God. The evil one distracts, then he distorts and deceives, and that leads to discouragement, depression, and defeat. The distraction itself may not be sin. In fact, the most effective distractions are those that in themselves aren't bad. It may be something that on the surface seems small and insignificant.

I heard one speaker say that failure in the Christian life is rarely the result of a blowout. It's almost always the result of a slow leak. For some men it may start with the healthy desire to provide for our families and end by becoming men who are workaholics and driven by our insatiable appetite for more.

In *The Screwtape Letters* C. S. Lewis presents a conversation between a senior tempter and a junior tempter in which he describes the effectiveness of small distractions in defeating Christians.

> But do remember, the only thing that matters is the extent to which you separate the man from the Enemy. It does not matter how small the sins are provided that their cumulative effect is to edge the man away from the Light and out into the Nothing. Murder is no better than cards if cards can do the trick. Indeed, the safest road to Hell is the gradual one—the gentle slope, soft underfoot, without sudden turnings, without milestones, without signposts.[1]

Phase 2: Temptation

If we allow ourselves to become distracted it's much easier for us to fall for phase 2. We become tempted or enticed by sin. The word used for sin is the same word used for bait that lures a fish. Whenever I go fishing I always try to talk to someone who has recently fished at the particular place I want to fish. I check out what bait they have been taking. When I first learned how to fish, many times I wouldn't even get a bite while guys on my right and left were catching all kinds of fish. I found out that I was using the wrong bait. When I changed my bait I started catching fish.

In some ways we are a lot like those fish. Different people at different times of their lives are distracted and tempted by different things. There are some areas of our lives where we are strong, and Satan rarely attacks us here. There are other areas in which we are weak and thus more vulnerable to temptation. Satan knows exactly what those areas are and tosses us the appropriate bait.

We need to know those vulnerable areas too. Do you? Are there any areas of your life where you consistently struggle? Are there any particular sins you are consistently vulnerable to? During the past few months what has been the most effective "bait" that Satan has used in your life?

Temptation means to "put to the test." Remember that temptation is one of the main weapons in Satan's arsenal against us. But what Satan has designed for evil our God can use for good. He can reveal and remove sins and weaknesses in our lives. He can make us depend more on Him. He can develop virtue and godly character.

Be assured of this: being tempted does not mean you are a failure. In fact, as a Christian, you will be tempted. It isn't a sin to be tempted. Indeed, in some ways you should be encouraged by the fact that you experience temptation. John Vianney has stated, "The greatest of all evils is not to be tempted, because there are then grounds for believing that the devil looks upon us as his property."

We are all vulnerable to temptation because we still have some of the old patterns of thinking and acting that we had before we were saved. In many cases these patterns have become habits. Due to repetition many of these habits became strongholds. These become likely "target areas" for the adversary. After knowing Christ, Peter still struggled with self-control, James and John still had anger problems, and Paul still wrestled with doing what he didn't want to do and not doing what he wanted to do (Romans 7).

Phase 3: Sin

If we have allowed ourselves to become distracted and enticed, we have set ourselves up for the third step. Our lust gives birth to sin. Our desire notices, meets, and then embraces the evil. Thomas à Kempis stated, "First comes to mind a simple thought, then a strong imagination, afterwards delight, an evil moment and assent." It's that simple. It's that easy.

Obviously the most effective place to meet the enemy is *not* after we have become distracted and enticed. We need to act before we fall for the first step. If we don't let Satan distract us and draw us away from God we are much less likely to be enticed by sin. That's why the decision we make at the beginning of the day is so important.

SETTING THE STAGE FOR VICTORY

How can we take the offensive in the battle for the mind? How can we develop combat-ready minds? In Colossians 3:2 Paul instructs us to "Set you mind on the things above, not on the things that are on earth." As Curtis Vaughan explains, this means "that one's interests are centered in Christ, that one's attitudes, ambitions, and whole outlook on life are molded by Christ's relation to the believer, and that one's allegiance to Him takes precedence over all earthly allegiances."

In Philippians 4:8 Paul spells out for us how to set our minds on things above: "Finally, brethren, whatever is true, whatever is honorable, whatever is right, whatever is pure, whatever is lovely, whatever is of good repute, if there is any excellence and if anything worthy of praise, let your mind dwell on these things." What we choose to read, watch, think about, and contemplate will to a great degree determine whether we will be victims or victors, conquered or conquerors.

Most trains rolling through St. Louis pass through a large railroad switchyard. There is one particular switch that begins with just a thin piece of steel to direct a train away from one main track on to another. The trains that stay on one track will end up in San Francisco; those that switch to the other will eventually arrive in New York. The difference is the switching rail.

Our thought life is a lot like that switch. The small and simple choice of what we choose to set our minds on at the beginning of and throughout the day can determine the outcome of our spiritual warfare. Just a small deviation from God's standard can put us at risk and lead us far afield from our intended and desired destination.

TRANSFORMING OUR THOUGHTS

OK, if our thoughts can help us win or lose our spiritual battles, what can we do? If inaccurate thoughts about ourselves can hinder our emotions and make us unable to deal with such feelings as grief, anger, depression, and conflict, how should we respond? We must "renew our minds." Renewing the mind (Romans 12:2) means letting God's perspective on life control our thinking. Here are three keys to transforming our thought lives.

Key #1: Plant Good Seed

What do you think of when you hear someone talk about having a renewed mind? What does a "renewed mind" mean to you? The word *renew* means "to make like new; restore to freshness, vigor, or perfection; to make extensive changes in." Why is the mind so important?

In Proverbs 23:7 we read that "as [a man] thinks within himself, so he is." What we allow our minds to dwell on will to a great degree influence what we do. Someone once said, "We have never said or done an ungracious or un-Christlike word or action which was not first an ungracious and un-Christlike thought. . . . We have never wronged another person without first wronging them in our thoughts."

The first step to a renewed mind is planting good seed. Just as the farmer can't financially survive on last year's seed, we can't spiritually survive on last year's Bible study. As Christians this means spending consistent and quality time in the Word of God. The emphasis is on the word *consistent.* In this way, we plant God's truths and right directions into our thoughts.

This involves not merely getting into the Word but allowing the Holy Spirit to plant the truths of Scripture into our hearts and minds. This needs to be done on a regular basis. Only in this way can the seed grow and His truth flourish.

When I moved to rural Nebraska in 1976 I knew virtually nothing about farming. I still don't know very much about farming; but due to the patience of a couple of Nebraska farmers I have learned a few basic facts. There are several activities necessary to grow a good crop of corn. But it all starts with planting good seed in good soil. If you don't plant the seed, there's no way you'll have a crop.

Every spring the farmers have to plant new seed. It doesn't matter how many bushels of corn last year's seed produced. Now, it is true that every year a very small percentage of last year's seed that didn't take root may come to life and produce a stalk of corn. This is called "volunteer corn." But no farmer could ever survive on a crop of "volunteer corn."

Our minds are like plots of land. We must plant seed on a regular basis. You can either cultivate your "plot" and choose what you want to plant on it, or you can let it run wild, neither adding seed nor removing weeds. Either way the land will bring forth something—a healthy, productive crop, or weeds.

Most of us know that for the truth to flourish we must plant on a regular basis Scripture within our minds and hearts. We've known it for years. Yet many still struggle with this area of their

Christian walk. It's amazing that something so simple can for most Christians be so difficult. But it is.

The easiest way to do this is to schedule regular time with God. Make an appointment each day to spend time in the Word and in prayer. Most people try to squeeze God into their day rather than planning their day around their time with Him. If you are not used to spending regular time with God, don't make the mistake of trying to start with too much time. If you begin with only ten minutes a day, that's great. The first step, no matter how small, is the most important one.

Pick a time that you can be consistent with. I've found the best time to do this is in the morning before my boys awake. Keep in mind this is written by someone who is not a morning person. I used to humorously say that my life verse was Proverbs 27:14: "He who blesses his friend with a loud voice early in the morning, it will be reckoned a curse to him."

It's not easy for me to get up early. There are many times that I haven't had "blanket victory." The blanket can be a subtle adversary. It is soft, warm, and comforting. It can make you feel safe, secure, and comforted. And of course there is nothing wrong with sleeping in. But for this reluctant morning person, the best time is in the morning. You pick whatever time is best for you. But pick a time and stick with it.

Have a flexible plan. I usually start with a word of prayer, then turn to study, and close in prayer. On some mornings I spend only ten minutes and other mornings I'll spend over thirty minutes. You can't gauge the quality of your time by the quantity of your time. I think the most important part is doing it.

As you open the Bible don't just read for the sake of covering so many chapters each day. Read for nourishment, read for growth, read for life. With each passage ask yourself, "What principles can I with God's help apply today in my life?" "What does this mean, for me, today?" Approach the Bible in new ways to help you gain fresh insights. Read from different translations, such as the King James, *New American Standard*, Phillips, and the *New International Version*. Utilize a paraphrase such as *The Living Bible*.

Indeed God's Word is a lamp unto our feet, a light unto our path, a compass by which we stay on the straight and narrow path, a straight-edged ruler by which we measure the crookedness around us. That is why Paul exhorts to "set your mind on the things above, not on the things that are on earth" (Colossians 3:2). We can "set our minds on things above" by starting each day focused on truth. The truth of who we are because of Christ's completed work for us on the cross. The truth of who are are becoming. The truth of who we will be when we see Him face to face.

Key #2: Let the Seed Sprout

With the help of the Holy Spirit we have "set" our minds in the right direction. We have planted good seed by daily time with God. Now we must cultivate that seed and let it sprout. Those true thoughts, those good thoughts from Scripture should lead to appropriate behavior. If we are steeped in the truth we are more likely to recognize error. We will choose certain actions and reject others as wrong.

When Joshua prepared the Israelites to enter and conquer the promised land, he reminded them of what God has revealed to them and His promises (Joshua 1:2–6). He exhorted them to focus on what they know to be true and "do not turn from it to the right or to the left" (verse 7). Why? "So that you may have success wherever you go."

Just to make sure they got the point, he repeated his exhortation to focus and meditate on God's Word day and night. And he added: "Be careful to do all that is written in it" (verse 8). Why? Because if there is healthy thinking it is much more likely there will be healthy behavior. And if you combine healthy thinking with healthy behavior, "then you will make your way prosperous, and then you will have success."

We find a similar principle in Jeremiah 31:21: "Set for yourself roadmarks, place for yourself guideposts; direct your mind to the highway." Warren Wiersbe once said, "Wrong thinking leads to wrong feeling, and before long the heart and mind are pulled apart. . . . We must realize that thoughts are real and powerful, even though they cannot be seen, weighed, or measured."

Key #3: Recognize and Yank the Weeds (Unhealthy Thoughts)

In any given day thousands of different thoughts cross our minds. Some are good, some are neutral, and some are bad. Do you ever have thoughts enter your mind and you wonder where they came from? Have you ever been in prayer and suddenly been aware of a bitter, angry, selfish, or lustful thought? You're not alone. In fact, I've yet to meet a man who didn't answer "yes" to those questions.

When that happens, many of us get discouraged and frustrated. Or, even worse, we let that thought stay in our minds. We allow ourselves to get distracted by it and dwell on it. In 2 Corinthians, Paul gives us a hot gardening tip: "We are destroying speculations and every lofty thing raised up against the knowledge of God, and we are taking every thought captive to the obedience of Christ" (10:5).

How do we do that? The first step is to identify the thought. What kinds of thoughts in the past have increased your vulnerability to sin? What kinds of thoughts have taken your eyes off of Christ and caused you to become more discouraged? Remember that the initial thought itself may not involve sin. Initially King David saw Bathsheba and observed that she was beautiful (2 Samuel 11:2). So far no problem. The fact that David noticed Bathsheba's beauty was not in itself sin. Unfortunately David didn't stop there.

Step two is to weigh that thought and the consequences of pursuing the direction of that thought in light of what we know to be true. What do I mean by true? Well, of course I mean the truth, God's Word. But God can also reveal His truth to us through the wise counsel of godly friends. Also consider what God has shown you to be true in the light of your past experience. Sometimes truth will come in the form of common sense.

Let's go back to David. Although his initial thought was not sin, his continuing to focus and dwell on that thought led to sin. Certainly David was smart enough to know that with every second he was increasing his vulnerability. Surely the still small voice within him was telling him this was wrong. But he didn't listen. He didn't take the initiative to do the right thing. He refused to submit his thought life to what he knew to be true.

Step three is to choose *not* to dwell on that thought; instead, we capture the thought and give it to God and immediately replace it with healthy thinking. We are told to resist the devil and he will flee from us (James 4:7). David not only didn't resist, he sent his messengers to find out who Bathsheba was, and, when he found out she was a married woman he still had her brought to him. He allowed himself to get distracted and forgot how powerful temptation can be. David Swartz has written,

Temptation is the striptease of sin. In seducing our hearts, it promises satisfaction and fulfillment that never genuinely materializes in the way originally anticipated. One thing is promised, another is delivered. Temptation may be alluring, but sin always exacts a price for that shallow come-on.[2]

That's the way temptation works. To overcome temptation we must immediately identify the thoughts and take those thoughts captive to what we know to be true. Then we need to immediately replace the wrong thinking with right thinking. Otherwise we become so weak that we don't care what we do—that is, we don't care until after we have sinned and begin to experience the consequences.

The price of not immediately "taking every thought captive to the obedience of Christ" is a price that is too high for any of us to pay.

WHEN WE FAIL

From time to time we don't take our thoughts captive. We allow ourselves to become distracted. We don't plant and cultivate the good seed. And we end up in sin. Whenever we sin there are basically two options. The first is to choose not to acknowledge and deal with our sin. Some respond as did David and try to cover it up and hide it. Others try to repress, suppress, deny, or ignore it. The main problem with this approach is that it doesn't work.

The second option is the one that, in time, all of us must come to. Here we acknowledge what we have done and admit that it was sin. Then we confess our sin knowing that "He is faithful and just to forgive us our sin and to cleanse us from all unrighteousness" (1 John 1:9). We pray to God to "create in me a clean heart, O God, and renew a steadfast spirit within me. Restore to me the joy of Thy salvation, and sustain me with a willing spirit" (Psalm 51:10, 12).

Unfortunately many believers stop here. We've acknowledged and confessed our sin. We have asked God to forgive us and renew us. What more do we need to do? Remember, forgiveness is just the starting point. We can learn lessons from the temptation and from our failure that can help us in the future.

Although David learned the hard way, often the hard way can be the best way to make sure you never forget. Sin that's been confessed, wrestled with, and overcome is one of the finest teachers we can have. Our struggles and defeats can increase our spiritual growth just as much as our victories—if we learn from them.[3]

To learn from our sin we need to ask ourselves several important questions. We come to God alone. Meet Him with your Bible, a pen and some paper, and a desire to truly learn. Ask the Holy Spirit to bring to your remembrance whatever He knows is necessary for you to learn from your sin. Ask yourself the following questions and write down whatever comes to mind. (No matter how minor or insignificant it may appear to be, write it down.)

Ask yourself: What first distracted me? What enticed me? What lured me into complacency? What was Satan able to use to take my mind off of Christ? What were the specific first thoughts that set me up and increased my vulnerability? Were there any warning signs that I ignored? What were the first actions that moved me closer, that distorted my perspective, that made it harder for me to flee?

Take a few minutes to look over your list. Do you notice any areas in which you seem to be consistently vulnerable? What are the similarities between how you responded in this situation and previous ones? Do you see any pattern?

I have yet to meet a Christian who didn't have at least one area of weakness. Most of us have more than one. When Satan attacks he tends to strike at our weakest point. What are some of your areas of weaknesses? How consistently is Satan exploiting certain "blind spots" in your life? God can use our failures to help us recognize these blind spots, identify ongoing patterns of sin, and develop specific steps we can take to help us become overcomers.

Now ask yourself these questions: How many times in the past have I fallen for the same temptation? How many of the conditions in my past failures were similar to my most recent one? At what points could I have resisted? What specific thoughts did I need to "take captive?" What could I have replaced those thoughts with? What are some of the warning signs I can be aware of in the future? What specifically did or didn't I learn from those past experiences? What specifically can I learn this time?

As you make this final list, keep your Bible open. Identify two or three warning signs you can be aware of in the future. Then ask God to give you two or three specific principles you can utilize and specific promises you can claim when you see one of those warning signs. Put them on a 3x5 card and keep it in your wallet. Pull it out periodically to refresh your memory.

It's never too late to learn. We don't have to go through life reinventing the wheel. What Satan has designed for evil God can use for good. There are powerful lessons God can teach us through our failures. Thus whatever happens to me or whatever I make happen, whether it is good or bad, God can use it in a constructive way for my growth. He can cause "all things to work together for good," especially our failures, our mistakes, our sins.

God is "able and just to forgive us our sins," but He wants to go beyond forgiveness. He wants us to learn, He wants us to grow, He wants to help us become mature, Christlike men. He wants us to become real men.

NOTES

Introduction: A Cardboard Goliath

1. "When I Grow Up to Be a Man," lyrics and music by Brian Wilson. © 1964, renewed 1992, Irving Music Co. All rights reserved. Used by permission.
2. Herb Goldberg, *The New Male* (New York: Signet, 1980), 13.
3. Joyce Brothers, *What Every Woman Should Know About Men* (New York: Ballantine, 1987).
4. Aaron Kipnis, *Knights Without Armor* (Los Angeles: Tarcher, 1992), 20.
5. Ibid., 24
6. Ibid., 21.
7. Ibid.
8. Ibid., 29.
9. Goldberg, *The New Male*, 32.
10. Ibid., 49.
11. Ibid., 157. For these and other statistics about male and female differences, see also Daniel Weiss, *The Great Divide* (New York: Poseidon, 1991).

Chapter 1: The Myths of Masculinity

1. Frank Pittman, "The Masculine Mystique," *Networker*, May/June 1990, 42.
2. J. H. Gagnon, "Physical Strength, Once of Significance," in D. S. David and R. Brannon, eds., *The Forty-Nine Percent Majority: The Male Sex Role*, (Reading, Mass.: Addison-Wesley, 1976), n.p.
3. Frank Butler's memoirs cited in Bonnie Kreps, *Subversive Thoughts, Authentic Passions* (San Francisco: Harper & Row, 1990), 78.

4. Carol Zisowitz Stearns and Peter N. Stearns, *Anger: The Struggle For Emotional Control in America's History* (Chicago: Univ. of Chicago, 1986), 50.

5. Katharine Hoyenga and Kermit Hoyenga, *The Question of Sex Differences: Psychological, Cultural, and Biological Issues* (Boston: Little, Brown, 1979), 358; as quoted in Aaron Kipnis, *Knights Without Armor* (Los Angeles: Tarcher, 1991), 254.

6. Ashley Montagu, *The Natural Superiority of Women*, rev. ed. (New York: Collier, 1974), 181–83.

7. As cited in Kipnis, *Knights Without Armor*, 79.

8. Willard Gaylin, *The Male Ego* (New York: Viking, 1992), 8–9.

9. Carol Tavris, *The Mismeasure of Woman*, (New York: Simon & Schuster, 1992), 296.

10. John Williams and Deborah Best, *Sex and Psyche* (Newbury Park, Calif.: Sage, 1990), 183.

11. Gaylin, *The Male Ego*, 33.

12. Kaye Cook and Lance Lee, *Man & Woman: Alone & Together* (Wheaton, Ill.: BridgePoint, 1992), 129.

Chapter 2: Becoming a Real Man

1. David Mains, *Healing The Dysfunctional Church Family* (Wheaton, Ill.: Victor, 1992), 123.

2. C. S. Lewis, *The Great Divorce* (New York: Macmillan, 1978), 92–93.

3. C. S. Lewis, *The World's Last Night and Other Essays*, (New York: Harcourt, Brace, Jovanovich, 1973), 109.

4. Miriam Neff, *Women and Their Emotions* (Chicago: Moody, 1983), 13–14.

5. William Kirwan, *Biblical Concepts for Christian Counseling* (Grand Rapids: Baker, 1984), 46–53.

6. Barbara Ehrenreich, "Cauldron of Anger," *Life*, January 1992, 65.

7. "When Did I Become a Man?" is an unpublished poem by James Ryle. Used by permission.

Chapter 3: Real Men Have Feelings Too

1. Samuel Osherson, *Wrestling With Love* (New York: Fawcett Columbine, 1992), 17.

2. *Los Angeles Times*, 9 September 1976.

3. Dorothy C. Finkelhor, *How to Make Your Emotions Work for You* (New York: Berkley Medallion Books, 1973), 23–24.

4. R. W. Osborne, "Men and Intimacy: An Emprical review," in symposium conducted at the annual meeting of the American Psychological Association, San Francisco, 1991; as cited in Ronald Levant, "Toward the Reconstruction of Masculinity," *Journal of Family Psychology*, 5 (3 & 4): 388 (March/June 1992).

5. D. Dosser, "Male Inexpressiveness," in K. Solomon and N. Levy, eds. *Men in Transition* (New York; Plenum, 1982); R. Levant and G. Doyle, "An Evaluation of a Parent-Education Program for Fathers of School-Aged Children," *Family Relations*, 32 (1983): 29–32; and D. Moore and B. Haver-

kamp, "Measured Increases in Male Emotional Expressiveness," *Journal of Counseling and Development*, 67 (1989): 513–17; all as cited in Levant, "Toward the Reconstruction of Masculinity," *Journal of Family Psychology* 5: 388.

6. H. Krystal, "Alexithymia and the Effectiveness of psychoanalytic treatment," *International Journal of Psychoanalytic Pychotherapy*, 9 (1982): 353–78; as cited in Levant, "Toward the Reconstruction of Masculinity," *Journal of Family Psychology* 5: 388.

7. Levant, "Toward the Reconstruction of Masculinity," *Journal of Family Psychology* 5: 388–89.

8. Dan Jones, *Words for Our Feelings* (Austin: Mandala, 1992), 22–23.

9. As adapted in Henry Dreher, "Do You Have A Type-C (Cancer-Prone) Personality?" *Redbook*, May 1988, 108–109, 158, 160.

10. Adapted from Martha R. Bireda, *Love Addiction: Developing Emotional Independence* (Alexandria, Va.: AACD, 1991), 3–4.

11. A. J. Hostetler, "Feeling Happy, Thinking Clearly," *APA Monitor* 19 (4): 6–7 (April 1988)

Chapter 4: Fear

1. Gaylin, *The Male Ego*, 104.

2. Ibid., 248–249.

3. Norman Vincent Peale, *Dynamic Imaging* (Old Tappan, N.J.: Revell, 1982), 186–87.

4. Sam Keen, *Fire in the Belly* (New York: Bantam, 1991), 138.

Chapter 5: Anger

1. Harriet Lerner, *The Dance of Anger* (New York: Harper & Row, 1985), 1.

2. Carol Tavris, *Anger: The Misunderstood Emotion* (New York: Simon & Schuster, 1982), 23.

3. For more information on individuation, see M. Karpel, "Individuation: From fusion to dialogue," *Family Process*, 15:1 (1976): 65–68.

4. Barbara Ehrenreich, "Cauldron of Anger," *Life*, January 1992, 62–68.

5. Susan Jeffers, *Opening Our Hearts to Men* (New York: Fawcett Columbine, 1989), 35.

6. Gary J. Oliver and H. Norman Wright, *When Anger Hits Home* (Chicago: Moody, 1992), 78–79.

7. Ibid., 46.

8. Ibid., 46–47.

9. Nancy Marx Better, *Self*, June 1992.

10. Leo Madow, *Anger: How To Recognize and Cope With It* (New York: Charles Scribners Sons, 1972), 85.

11. Diane Eicher, "Violent Emotions Left to Fester May Be Hazardous to Life," *Denver Post*, 28 December 1987, 1D.

12. Ibid., 7D.

13. Here are some of the questions about anger that other men have asked:
    What is the emotion of anger?
    Why did God create it?
    Do men have a more difficult time with anger than women?
    How can anything good come from anger?
    Where does my anger come from?
    Why is anger such a difficult emotion to deal with?
    Why are my anger responses so hard to change?
    How can I make my anger work for me rather than against me?

14. The five responses to anger and the Irritability Indicator are from Devon Weber, *Angry? Do You Mind If I Scream*. Reprinted with permission of the publisher, Health Communications, Deerfield Beach, Fla. Copyright 1991.

Chapter 6: Where Does My Anger Come From?

1. For a greater understanding of your parents' influence on your adult years, read *Making Peace With Your Past*, by H. Norman Wright, and *The Blessing*, by Gary Smalley and John Trent.

2. Dick's story is adapted from Oliver and Wright, *When Anger Hits Home*, 98–99.

3. David Stoop and Stephen Arterburn, *The Angry Man* (Dallas: Word, 1991), 58–59.

4. Oliver and Wright, *When Anger Hits Home*, 97–98.

5. Willard Gaylin, "Violence And Anger In Modern Life," *Physician & Patient*, May 1985, 10–13.

6. John Bradshaw, *Healing the Shame That Binds You* (Deerfield Beach, Fla.: Health Communications, 1988), 137.

7. David Seamonds, *Healing Grace* (Wheaton, Ill.: Victor, 1989), 168.

8. This story first appeared in Oliver and Wright, *When Anger Hits Home*, 102.

9. Carol Staudacher, *Men and Grief* (Oakland, Calif.: New Harbinger, 1991), 29.

10. Paul A. Hauck, *Overcoming Frustration and Anger* (Philadelphia: Westminster, 1974), 65.

11. Adapted from Oliver and Wright, *When Anger Hits Home*, 248–249. Copyright 1992 and used by permission.

Chapter 7: Answers to Anger

1. Gary J. Oliver and H. Norman Wright, *Pressure Points* (Chicago, Moody, 1993), 268.

2. Ibid., 262.

3. The three questions and discussion that follow are closely adapted from Oliver and Wright, *Pressure Points*, 263–65.

4. This section is based on and quotes largely from pages 269–76 of *Pressure Points*, Gary J. Oliver and H. Norman Wright. Used by permission. Copyright 1993 by the authors and Moody Press.

5. See H. C. Leupold, *Exposition of Ecclesiastes*, (Grand Rapids: Baker, 1978), 154–155; and Franz Delitzsch, *Commentary on the Song of Songs and Ecclesiastes* (Grand Rapids: Eerdmans, 1970), 318–19.

6. Janet L. Kobobel, "But Can She Type?" (Downers Grove, Ill.: InterVarsity, 1986), 93–94.

7. This section is based on and quotes largely from pages 276–77 of *Pressure Points*, Gary J. Oliver and H. Norman Wright. Used by permission. Copyright 1993 by the authors and Moody Press.

Chapter 8: Loneliness

1. Ken Olson, *Hey Man! Open Up and Live* (New York: Fawcett, 1978), 147–48.

2. Samuel Osherson, *Wrestling With Love* (New York: Fawcett Columbine, 1992), 14.

3. Adapted from Michael Segell, "The American Man in Transition," *American Health*, January/February 1989, 60.

4. Cited in Jeff Meer, "Loneliness," *Psychology Today*, July 1985, 30.

5. Ibid.

6. Albert Mehrabian, cited in H. Norman Wright, *More Communication Keys for Your Marriage* (Ventura, Calif.: Regal, 1983), 91–92.

7. H. Norman Wright, *Communication: Key to Your Marriage* (Glendale, Calif.: Regal, 1979), 55.

8. John Powell, *Why Am I Afraid to Tell You Who I Am?* (Allen, Texas: Tabor, 1969), 65–78.

9. Herb Goldberg, *The Hazards of Being Male* (New York: Signet, 1976), 127.

10. C. S. Lewis, *The Four Loves* (New York: Harcourt, Brace & Jovanovich, 1960), 96–97.

Chapter 9: Love

1. Ronald F. Levant, "Toward the Reconstruction of Masculinity," *Journal of Family Psychology*, 5 (3 & 4): 389 (March/June 1992).

2. "My Dad" was written in 1991 by Daniel Richards, Ph.D., 202 U.S. Route 1, Box 353, Falmouth, Maine 04105. Used by permission.

3. Arnold Kipnis, *Knights Without Armor*, 192–93.

4. Mary Gergin, "Life Stories: Pieces of a Dream," In G. Rosenwald & R. Ochberg, eds., *Storied Lives* (New Haven, Conn.: Yale Univ., 1992); as quoted in Carol Tavris, *The Mismeasure of Woman* (New York: S. & S. Trade, 1992), 303.

5. As quoted in Carol Tavris, *The Mismeasure of Woman*, 303–4.

6. Barbara J. Risman, "Intimate Relationships from a Microstructural Perspective: Men who Mother," *Gender and Society* 1 (1987): 6–32.

7. Leonard W. Kaye and Jeffrey S. Applegate, "Men as Elder Caregivers," *American Journal of Orthopsychiatry* 60 (1990): 86–95.

8. Judith Viorst, *Love & Guilt & the Meaning of Love* (New York: Simon & Schuster, 1984).

9. C. S. Lewis, *Mere Christianity* (New York: Macmillian, 1952), . 84–86.

10. Tavris, *The Mismeasure of Woman*, 252.

11. "Harper's Index," *Harper's*, February 1991, 19. The index cited Hallmark Cards.

12. "Dear Abby," *Los Angeles Times*, 14 March 1990, E3.
13. Jack Balswick, *Why I Can't Say I Love You* (Waco, Tex.: Word, 1978), 96–98.
14. Ibid., 98.

Chapter 10: Worry

1. C. Barr Taylor and Bruce Arnow, *The Nature and Treatment of Anxiety Disorders* (New York: The Free Press, 1988), 1.
2. A. J. Lewis, "The Ambiguous Word 'Anxiety,'" *International Journal of Psychiatry*, 9:62–79.
3. Cecil Osborne, *The Art of Understanding Yourself* (Grand Rapids: Zondervan, 1972), as quoted in H. Norman Wright, *Christian Use of Emotional Power* (Old Tappan, N.J.: Revell, 1974), 52.
4. O. Quentin Hyder, *The Christian's Handbook of Psychiatry* (Old Tappan, N. J.: Revell, 1971), 104.
5. Many of the research studies are described in E. E. Levitt, *The Psychology of Anxiety* (Indianapolis: Bobbs-Merrill, 1967), vii, 1.
6. This study is reported in Irving Janis, *Stress and Frustration* (New York: Harcourt, Brace & Jovanovich), 1971.
7. John E. Haggai, *How to Win Over Worry* (Grand Rapids: Zondervan, 1967), n.p.
8. C. S. Lewis, *The Screwtape Letters and Screwtape Proposes a Toast* (New York: Macmillan, 1961), 34.

Chapter 11: Depression

1. D. Martyn Lloyd-Jones, *Spiritual Depression: Its Causes and Cure* (Grand Rapids: Eerdmans, 1966), 10–11.
2. David D. Burns, *Feeling Good*, (New York: William Morrow, 1980), 21.
3. Ibid., 205–25.
4. John White, *The Masks of Melancholy* (Downers Grove, Ill.: InterVarsity, 1982), 17.
5. Willard Gaylin, *The Male Ego*, 237.
6. Emil Kraepelin as quoted in Max Hamilton, ed., *Abnormal Psychology* (New York: Penguin, 1967), 66–69.
7. Tina Adler, "Depression Stalks Young; Rate Drops for Elderly," *APA Monitor*, July 1989, 20: 7, 10.
8. Ibid.
9. Gaylin, *The Male Ego*, 37.
10. Chart is adapted from H. Norman Wright, *Now I Know Why I'm Depressed* (Eugene, Ore.: Harvest, 1984), 38.
11. H. Norman Wright, *Beating The Blues*, ed. Ed Stewart (Glendale, Calif.: Regal, 1988), 44–45.
12. Theodore Rubin, "Psychiatrist's Notebook," *Ladies Home Journal*, May 1976, 26.
13. Archibald Hart, *Depression: Coping and Caring* (Arcadia, Calif.: Cope, 1978), 11.
14. Ibid., 22.

Chapter 12: Conflict

1. Mark Twain, *Diaries of Adam & Eve* (Lawrence, Kan.: Coronado, 1971).
2. Gaylin, *The Male Ego*, 251.
3. Deborah Tannen, *You Just Don't Understand* (New York: William Morrow, 1990), 3.
4. Richard L. Meth and Robert S. Pasick, *Men in Therapy: The Challenge of Change* (New York: The Guilford Press 1990), 198.
5. Adapted from Math and Pasick, *Men in Therapy*, 198.
6. James G. T. Fairfield, *When You Don't Agree* (Scottdale, Penn.: Herald Press, 1977). The five conflict styles are presented on pages 15-52, and this discussion is adapted from those pages.
7. Harriet Goldhor Lerner, *The Dance of Anger*, (New York: Harper and Row, 1985), 199–201.

Chapter 13: Growing Through Grief

1. Carol Staudacher, *Men & Grief: A Guide for Men Surviving the Death of a Loved One* (Oakland, Calif.: New Harbinger, 1991), 8.
2. Frank G. Boldon, Jr.; Larry A. Morris; and Ann E. MacEachron, *Males At Risk: The Other Side of Child Sexual Abuse* (Newbury Park, Calif.: Sage, 1989), 106.
3. Gaylin, *The Male Ego*, 239.
4. John Bowlby, *Attachment and Loss*, vol. 2 (Tavistock, England: The Tavistock Institute of Human Relations, n.d.), 18.
5. Carol Staudacher, *Men & Grief*, 4.
6. Adapted from William Plummer, "Bittersweet Journey," *People*, 14 September 1992, 47–48.
7. Max Lucado, *No Wonder They Call Him the Savior*, (Portland, Ore.: Multnomah, 1986), 106–7.
8. Herb Goldberg, *The Hazards of Being Male* (New York: Signet, 1976), 50.
9. Lucado, *No Wonder They Call Him the Savior*, 107.
10. Patrick Dillon, "The Healing Place," *West* magazine, *San Jose Mercury News*, 26 January 1985.

Chapter 14: Joy

1. J. I. Packer, "Bungee Jumping, Anyone?" *Christianity Today*, 5 October 1992, 17.
2. Ibid.
3. As cited in Tom Mullen, *Laughing Out Loud and Other Religious Experiences* (Waco, Texas: Word, 1983), 97–98. For a fuller description of laughter for dealing with stress and pain, as well as Cousins' laughter therapy, see Norman Cousins, *Anatomy of an Illness as Perceived by the Patient* (New York: Norton, 1979).
4. Mullen, *Laughing Out Loud*, 19.
5. Ibid., 50.

6. Charles Swindoll, *Leisure* (Portland, Ore.: Multnomah, 1981), 15.

7. Oswald Chambers, James Reimann, ed., *My Utmost for His Highest: An Updated Edition in Today's Language* (Grand Rapids: Discovery, 1992), April 16.

8. As quoted in *Forbes*, 21 December 1992, 347.

9. Gaylin, *The Male Ego*, 188.

Epilogue: As a Man Thinks

1. C. S. Lewis, *The Screwtape Letters* (New York: Macmillian, 1961), 64–65.

2. David Swartz, *Dancing With Broken Bones* (Colorado Springs: NavPress, 1987), 59.

3. Ibid., 67.

Real Men Have Feelings Too launches a new series of titles on men's issues for Moody Press. Called "Men of Integrity," this series wrestles with the core challenges and very essence of what it means to be a man in contemporary society. *Bonds of Iron: Forging Lasting Male Relationships* by James Osterhaus, Ph.D., will be the next title.